The Romantic and Notorious History of
Brown's Park

By
Diana Allen Kouris

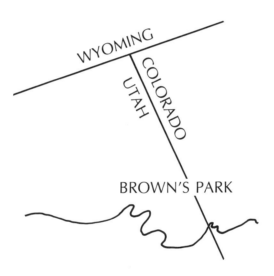

WYOMING

COLORADO

UTAH

BROWN'S PARK

Wolverine Gallery:
Basin

Cover from **"Brown's Park,"** an original oil painting by Pat Allen.

LCCN: 88-50456
ISBN: 0-941875-03-2

Printed in the United States of America

4 5 6 7 8 9 10

Published by Wolverine Gallery
P.O. Box 24
Basin, Wyoming 82410

Printed by Pioneer Printing
P.O. Box 466
Cheyenne, Wyoming 82003-0466

To

The memory of my mother
Marie Taylor Allen

whose enthusiasm for life was an inspiration to all who
knew her, and whose deep love for Brown's Park formed the
roots of this book,

and

my father
William E. Allen

whose honesty and strength of character heartily endure.

QUARTER
CIRCLE A

SEVENTY TWO

T BAR

MA

LAZY YE

Y UP Y DOWN

CIRCLE E

THREE QUARTER
BOX TWO BARS

F R BAR

D BAR K

FOUR QUARTER
CIRCLES

DIAMOND K

FLYING BOX

Contents

PREFACE

From the time I was a little girl, happily growing up in the old Charlie Crouse log house at our ranch in Brown's Park, I was very aware of the unique history surrounding me. I often drank from the icy spring where the outlaws had drank, near the cabin at the mouth of Crouse Canyon, where they once hid. When I was still so small that I had to find a boulder or a fence to climb on so I could get my foot in the saddle stirrup, I was entranced by the stories my mother told about the valley I cherished.

In the very kitchen where we ate our supper each night, outlaw Butch Cassidy had many times eaten his. In that same warm kitchen so many years ago, a young cowboy had been killed by a knife during a poker game. My sister, brother, and I sometimes visited his grave on the hill nearby. Although I listened with great interest to the stories about the valley, I listened and promptly forgot the details. I left it to my mother to tuck them in a corner of her mind or write them in her journals for safe keeping. After I grew up, I still depended on her to take care of the history preserving, which she ardently worked to do. Then, suddenly, she was gone.

In time I began to feel nudgings to gather together my mother's notes and stacks of research. They were soft nudgings at first. But as I began to read through her collection of books, journals, interviews, unpublished manuscripts, and her handwritten notes in tablets, spiral notebooks, on the backs of envelopes, and on napkins, the urge to continue her work grew strong. She stood next to me, and her dream to write a book about the history of Brown's Park became mine.

During my own search for Brown's Park's history, I journeyed into the world of the pioneers, outlaws, cowboys, and wolves. Through the vivid memory of my Uncle Jesse, I traveled with him and my grandparents to Brown's Park in a covered wagon and lived with them there. As I continued on, I met my parents as youngsters, shared their lives, and watched them grow. It was a lovely journey.

This is their story, and the story of the valley which held them so close.

vii

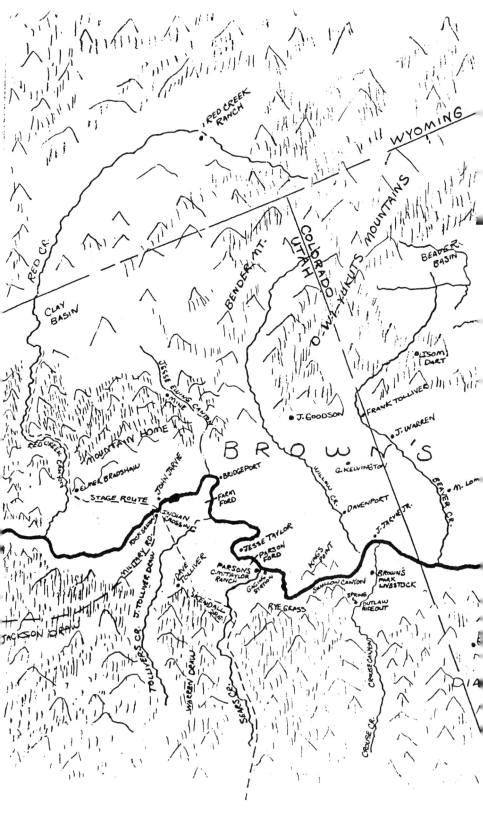

A BAR

CROSS TURKEY TRACK

QUARTER CIRCLE EIGHT

QUARTER CIRCLE SIXTEEN

M L BAR

TWO BAR

W D SLASH

PIPE

TRIANGLE BAR TRIANGLE

S LAZY S

T FOUR

GR

DOUBLE CROSS

ACKNOWLEDGEMENTS

I wholeheartedly thank the many people who entrusted their memories and family histories to me. And to all of those who have given me so much time, help, and support, I am deeply thankful. My sincere gratitude to my father William E. Allen; my uncle, the late Jesse G. Taylor; E. W. "Wilson" Garrison; my sister, Lucille Fleming, for her love of books; Hazel Overy; Bertha Simkin; my aunt Zora Gurr; the late Stanley Crouse, Jr.; Allen and Francis Taylor; Harry and Marybeth Carr; Clyde and Velma Thompson; Georgia Kadlecek; my teacher Lavinia Dobler; Sandy Barton and the Erickson family; Georgia Raftopoulos; John Raftopoulos; and Pat Allen for her beautiful artistry for the cover.

I wish to express a very special thanks to my "best friends" for their constant encouragement and confidence. They include my husband Mike and son Nick, along with Nonie David and Bob Allen, my sister and brother.

My deepest thank you goes to my dear mother, Marie Taylor Allen, who started it all. Also, I am indebted to those who were so much help to her in her research. A few of them include Jesse Taylor, Pete Parker, Kerry Ross Boren, Bruce and Marian MacLeod, Queen Steele, and Minnie Crouse Rasmussen.

This special valley is where spring wedded to summer seems to have chosen this sequestered spot for her fixed habitation, where when dying autumn woos the sere frost and snow of winter, she may withdraw to her flower-garnished retreat and smile and bloom forever.

Chapter I

THE DAWNING

She may, at first glance, appear to be a placid and ordinary valley. However, Brown's Park is neither - she never was.

In ancient times, fracturing in the earth's crust, along with gnawing water and wind worked to give birth to a certain canyon in the Uinta range of the Rocky Mountains. Water trapped there broke free and as it drained away, land fill of sand, gravel, and clay was ever so gradually left behind. This accumulation spread across the floor of the young gorge and filled her like a sugar bowl to the tops of her surrounding mountains.

Eventually, as water downcutting started and the land fill was washed away, bluish green, deep red, and beige mountain peaks rose against her skyline. Sometimes the drainage was interrupted and lakes were formed adorning the canyon, and resembled diamond-like broaches as they reflected the blue of the sky. Minute algae plants and small fresh water crustacean thrived in the standing water. Not wanting these small living things to be forgotten, the widening canyon retained evidence of their existence as fossils in her thick lake-bottom muds.

Volcanos often erupted in fiery explosions filling the sky with tons of torched embers. As the ash settled, the canyon swished her dusty skirts in the wind and welcomed the cleansing rains. The run-off from the rainstorms and melting snows carried the brilliant white ash off the ridges and walls and deposited it in huge, hilly heaps on her floor.

Not yet satisfied with the canyon's appearance, forces continued to cleave, dimple, forge, and scrub her contours. Again and again, misty sunrises faded into evening dusks and seconds melted away into centuries. Eventually, the long canyon softened to become an expansive and attractive valley and had grown to approximately thirty miles in length and averaged four miles across.

The valley sprouted an abundance of greenery, forage, and animals. Numerous brushy creeks flowed from her mountains and into her heart, the meandering river below. She was virgin and unsophisticated and watched over the wolf as tenderly as the pinion jay. She never allowed the weather to be as severe there as it was around her. Because of that, she became a favored wintering home for animals and, later, Indians.

In time centuries of stone chips were left by skilled reddish-brown fingers. The shiny chips, along with burned spots from campsites, were scattered across the valley's formations. Stirring chants and drums and the smell of pine and cedar smoke floated on the breezes. Tribes of the Shoshone, Ute, and Crow came to the valley. Navajo and Bannocks visited occasionally to gamble and dance with the Kohogue or Green River Shoshones.

The valley enjoyed the dark-eyed, short-legged people, with their belief in self-magic and that all should exist in harmony. They named the valley O-Wi-U-Kuts "Big Canyon" and called her river Seeds-Kee-Dee "Prairie Hen," later to be known as Green River. The children ran naked and learned that a cactus was prickly and a flame hot by touching and feeling the pain for themselves. If there was a cranky baby who cried too much, a bit of water was poured into its mouth and it soon learned to be still. Lessons were quickly learned and seldom forgotten.

Hunting was the responsibility of the men, while their squaws worked long, full days. The women prepared the food and gathered poles for lodges and wood for fires. They butchered and skinned the slain animals, then treated and softened the hides and fashioned garments, moccasins, pouches, and lodge coverings from them.

Though survival was sometimes difficult, it was a life of freedom. It was good.

One late winter in the early 1800's, the beaver families once again waddled out of hibernation with their pelts shiny and thick. It was then that the valley first saw the light-skinned mountain men and fur trappers come out of her passes and cross her river and creeks. She saw some of the men climb from their dugout canoes made from hollowed-out trunks of cottonwoods or other large trees. Others were on horseback, and some were walking. They were a crafty, skillful bunch usually dressed in wool shirts and pants and sometimes buckskins. In the cold weather, they stayed warm in long, wool-lined buckskin coats. They stood an average height of five and one-half feet, with a few reaching six feet. Beards were not in style then, but mustaches and shoulder-length hair were common. The mountain men usually had a powder horn slung over one shoulder, and a tobacco pouch, butcher knife, and muzzle-loader handy. Each commonly carried a leather bag containing five-pound beaver traps and had a horn bottle around his neck. This bottle contained castor, a liquid bait taken from the body of a beaver. The mountain men brought beads, blankets, and trinkets, which smoothed the way for them with the Indians. They brought with them a love for the mountainous frontier, which smoothed the way for them with the valley.

One of them, his identity a mystery shrouded by time, named the valley Brown's Hole. Many believe that man was a French Canadian trapper, Baptiste Brown. It is a possibility that he built a cabin and lived in the valley with his Blackfoot squaw and was one of Henry Fraeb's men who battled Indians east of there on the Little Snake River. Some think Baptiste Brown was an alias for Jean-Baptiste Chalifoux. Chalifoux did visit the area in 1835, where he carved his name on a cliff side. It is doubtful, though, that such a visible character could or would have lived two identities. Chalifoux is known to have been the leader of a group of horse thieves who was in California in the 1830's. He later operated a trading post in New Mexico and in 1869 built the first house in Trinidad, Colorado.

Others may be correct when they say the name of Brown's Hole came from "Bible Back" Brown, who is said to have recommended the valley as a good place to "hole up" in the winter months. Other possibilities include "Old Cut Rocks" Brown and Charles Brown. Both men did some trapping in the area.

William Henry Ashley and his small party of men were the first recorded white men to look across the then unnamed Brown's Hole. One of Ashley's men was named Henry "Bo'sun" Brown; he makes still another possibility as being the namesake of the valley.

The Ashley party was a branch of a larger expedition exploring new territories west of the Missouri. In a time when beaver was in fashion and plentiful, Ashley and his party floated the Green River in two bullboats. These boats looked like big baskets and were made by stretching green buffalo hides tightly over a frame of willow branches and cottonwood. On the spring morning of May 5, 1825, Ashley looked from his bullboat as "the mountains gradually recede from the water's edge, and the river expands to the width of two hundred fifty yards, leaving the bottoms on each side from one to three hundred yards wide, interspersed with clusters of small willows."[1] The party made camp there, near the valley's edge. On the 7th of May the men floated ten miles into the valley. There they set up camp "on a spot of ground where several thousand Indians had wintered. Many of their lodges remained as perfect as when occupied. They were made of poles two or three inches in diameter, set up in circular form, and covered with cedar bark."[2]

When the Ashley party left the quiet waters of the valley the next day, they were inhaled by the huge red-cliffed mouth of a canyon. Suddenly the expedition took on a different mood. Ashley wrote: "As we passed along between these massy walls, which in a great degree excluded from us the rays of heaven and presented a surface as impassable as their body was impregnable, I was forcibly struck with the gloom which spread over the countenances of my men. They seemed to anticipate a dreadful termination of our voyage, and I must confess that I

3

partook in some degree of what I supposed to be their feelings, for things around us had truly an awful appearance. We soon came to a dangerous rapid which we passed over with a slight injury to our boats. A mile lower down, the channel became so obstructed by the intervention of large rocks over and between which the water dashed with such violence as to render our passage in safety impracticable. The cargoes of our boats were therefore a second time taken out and carried about two hundred yards, to which place, after much labor, our boats were descended by means of cords."3

With much courage the party made it through the canyon and traveled onward. After they had floated the Green for three weeks, they abandoned their boats and made their way back where they were to meet up with the other three branches of the main party at the rendezvous site at the mouth of Henry's Fork.

The trappers and mountain men made Brown's Hole an important fur trading center between 1826 and the early 1840's. Included among this special breed were: Former teamster on the Santa Fe Trail and employer of the American Fur Company, Uncle Jack Robinson (or Robertson); Joseph "Joe" LaFayette Meek; Joe's lifelong friend Robert "Doc" Newell; and Christopher Houston "Kit" Carson. Kit Carson, the most famous of these men, first arrived in Brown's Hole in 1829, while trapping with Uncle Jack Robinson.

Kit Carson was born to Lindsey and Rebecca Robinson Carson in Kentucky the day before Christmas, 1809. The towheaded boy moved with his family to Missouri when he was a year old. Eight years later his father was killed by a falling tree limb while he was burning timber.

Kit never received any formal education, but at the age of fourteen he reluctantly began learning the leather trade. Describing this time in his life Kit Carson said:

> For fifteen years I lived in Missouri, and during that time I dwelt in Howard County. I was apprenticed by David Workman to learn the saddler's trade, and remained with him two years. The business did not suit me and, having heard so many tales of life in the mountains of the West, I concluded to leave him. He was a good man, and I often recall the kind treatment I received at his hands. But taking into consideration that if I remained with him and served my apprenticeship, I would have to pass my life in labor that was distasteful to me, and being anxious to travel for the purpose of

seeing different countries, I concluded to join the first party that started for the Rocky Mountains.[4]

After Kit ran away, the following appeared in the **Missouri Intelligencer:**

Notice is hereby given to all persons,

That Christopher Carson, a boy about 16 years old, small of his age, but thick-set; light hair, ran away from the subscriber, living in Franklin, Howard County, Missouri, to whom he had been bound to learn the saddler's trade, on or about the first of September last. He is supposed to have made his way to the upper part of the state. All persons are notified not to harbor, support, or assist said boy under the penalty of the law. One cent reward will be given to any person who will bring back the said boy.

Franklin, Oct. 6, 1826. DAVID WORKMAN[5]

Charles Bent, who probably never saw the notice, took the teenager in. He gave Kit the job as "cavvy" boy with the Bent's Santa Fe Caravan. Thus, Charles Bent helped a young man who was to become a cook, interpreter, team driver, Indian fighter, trapper, guide, buffalo hunter, and legend, with his first important step to his adventure-filled life.

In 1838 trapper Kit Carson attended the rendezvous in the Wind River Mountains on the Popo Agie River. He wrote:

In twenty days the rendezvous broke up, and I and seven men went to Brown's Hole, a trading post, where I joined Thompson and Sinclair's party on a trading expedition to the Navajo Indians. We procured thirty mules from them and returned to Brown's Hole. After our arrival Thompson took the mules to the South Fork of the Platte, where he disposed of them to Sublette and Vasquez and returned with goods suitable for trading with the Indians. I was now employed as hunter for the fort and I continued in this service during the winter, having to keep twenty men supplied with meat. In the spring of 1838 I joined Bridger.[6]

The fort mentioned is Fort Davey Crockett built by William Craig, Phillip Thompson, and St. Clair sometime in the 1830's. It was named after the famed frontiersman who had been killed at the Alamo. It was not built as a fortress but was the main center of the fur trade in the area.

In August, 1839, a tired and hungry Thomas Jefferson Farnham arrived at the fort. He was the leader of a venturous group called the Oregon Dragoons. They were traveling from Peoria, Illinois to Oregon with hopes of ending the British fur monopoly and establishing a settlement there. However, most of the Dragoons ended up deserting along the way. Brown's Hole was a welcome sight to Farnham and he left a portraiture of the period when he told of the way Fort Davey Crockett greeted him:

> The dark mountains rose around it sublimely, and the green fields swept away into the deep precipitous gorges more beautifully than I can describe.
>
> The Fort is a hollow square of one-story log cabins, with roofs and floors of mud, constructed in the same manner as those of Fort William (William Bent's fort on the Arkansas). Around these we found the conical skin lodges of the squaws of the white trappers, who were away on their 'fall hunt', and also the lodges of a few Snake Indians, who had preceded their tribe to this, their winter haunt.
>
> Here also were the lodges of Mr. Robinson, a trader, who usually stations himself here to traffic with the Indians and white trappers. His skin lodge was his warehouse; and buffalo robes were spread upon the ground and counter, on which he displayed his butcher knives, hatchets, powder, lead, fish hooks, and whiskey. In exchange for these articles, he receives beaver skins from trappers, money from travelers, and horses from the Indians. Thus, as one would believe, Mr. Robinson drives a very snug little business. And indeed, when all the 'independent trappers' are driven by approaching winter into this delightful retreat, and the whole Snake village, two or three thousand strong, impelled by the same necessity, pitch their lodges around the Fort, and the dances and merry makings of a long winter are

6

thoroughly commenced, there is no want for customers . . .

There is in this valley a fruit called bulberry . . . of these berries I obtained a small quantity, had a dog butchered, took a pound or two of dried buffalo meat which Mr. St. Clair kindly gave, and on the morning left the hospitality of Fort David Crockett.[7]

Dr. F. A. Wislizenus, a man who would become U.S. Minister to Turkey in 1854, arrived at Fort Crockett less than a week after Farnham. He saw the fort in a much different way:

The fort itself is the worst thing of the kind that we have seen on our journey. It is a low one-story building, constructed of wood and clay, with three connecting wings, and no enclosure. Instead of cows, the fort had only some goats. In short, the whole establishment appeared somewhat poverty-stricken, for which reason it is also known to the trappers as Fort Misery.[8]

The high-top beaver hats which came into style among the rich in England and spread to America back in 1780, had through the years remained the popular fashion. When suddenly silk became popular the beaver trade floundered. One of the last rendezvous Brown's Hole saw was in November, 1842. It was reported by William T. Hamilton and appears to have been a success despite the dwindling demand for beaver pelts. It reads:

Several traders had come from the states with supplies, and there was quite a rivalry among them for our furs. Bovey and Company were the most liberal buyers, and we sold them the entire lot.

Besides the trappers, there were at the rendezvous many Indians - Shoshones, Utes, and a few lodges of Navajos - who came to exchange their pelts for whatever they stood in need of. Take all in all, it was just such a crowd as would delight the student were he studying the characteristics of the mountaineer and the Indian. The days were given to horse racing, foot racing, shooting matches; and in the evening were heard the music of voice and drum and the sound of dancing. There was also an abundance of reading matter for those inclined in that direction.[9]

The years of the mountain men, fur traders, and their rendezvous passed quickly. It was hard on the men who had relished that life and who were getting "long in the tooth," to admit the end was near. It hurt to see their reputations being blackened by newcomers who were dishonest and thieving. Regardless, their time came and went and it was necessary to move on. These are the stirring words of fur trapper Doc Newell to his old friend Joe Meek:

> We are done with this life in the mountains - done with wading in beaver dams and freezing or starving alternately - done with Indian trading and Indian fighting. The fur trade is dead in the Rocky Mountains and it is no place for us now . . . What do you say, Meek? Shall we turn American settlers?[10]

More than likely Joe Meek agreed with his friend because in 1839 he told of sixty trappers wintering in the Hole with a tribe of Indians. He said that little trapping was done as there was little pleasure or profit in it. Much of that long winter, he said, was spent drinking the rum supply.

The valley saw fewer and fewer of her mountaineers. Fort Davey Crockett was abandoned and left to crumble into history. When Doc Newell died, Joe Meek wrote the following words to summate his deep feelings for the death of his friend, and the end of their way of life:

> I feel like one who treads alone
> Some banquet hall deserted:
> Whose lights are gone whose spirits flown
> And all but me departed.[11]

The passing of the trappers left a silence in the valley. She missed the clanking together of their traps and the rambunctious merrymaking of their rendezvous. However, the Hererra brothers and the cattle herds were on their way. New adventures were beginning.

8

Chapter II

THE LONGHORNS AND THE COWBOYS

Once they began riding in behind the cattle herds, slapping coiled ropes against leather chaps and stepping out of their stirrups to knock the dust from their hats, Brown's Hole was never the same. The valley was soon caught up in a bitter-sweet romance with these men and their way of life.

The cowboys would have had to look a far distance over their shoulders to see their beginning, as far back as 1521. It was then that the Spaniards introduced large numbers of Spanish Longhorns into Mexico and the southwest range country. The cattle that eventually became known as "Mexican Cattle" were made up of soft creams, whites, brown-flecked brockle-faces, brindles, blue-gray roans, reds, and chocolates. A separate breed became known as Black Cattle. These waspy, shorter-horned, brownish-gray duns and sleek blacks were bred for the bullring. They were the pride of the Spaniards. A combination of these dust-lifting herds and the heavy-boned cattle from the American east, laid the foundation for the Texas Longhorn and the eventual American cattle industry.1

In the late 1760's, when the Franciscan missionaries arrived in California, they brought with them small herds of cattle for dairy and breeding purposes. The domestic cattle flourished, easily finding all they wished to eat in the warm grasslands. Eventually, Yankee ships sailing into California ports began trading with the twenty-one religious missions. They bought the beef by-products which were in such demand by the candle, soap, and leather goods manufacturers in the New England states. The padres immediately enjoyed substantial profits and their herds steadily grew.

Many of the California padres were sons of Spanish nobility and were groomed since childhood to be excellent horsemen. This greatly benefitted their handling of the cattle. However, as the herds increased, so did the work, creating the need for more trained horsemen to tend the spreading cattle. Although it went against old Spanish custom, the padres began, out of necessity, to share their expert knowledge with the Indian converts. It proved to be a wise decision. As the skill of the cattle tenders increased, so did the profits.

The riders made their way through the clawing chapparal thickets with legs protected by leather leggins called **chaparreras**, later to be known as chaps. They modified the old Spanish War saddle, making it more comfortable and practical to a rangehand. They learned to catch and hold a steer by throwing a loop of braided rawhide rope called **la reata** or lariat, then to take swift turns around the saddle horn to hold the steer tight. This was called making a **dar la vuelta** or dally. The horsemen gained fine and well-earned reputations and became known as vacqueros.

In 1821 Mexico struggled from beneath Spanish rule and within a short twelve years had taken the rangelands away from the Spanish missions. The first cattle barons began to emerge as the expansive, rich rangeland became divided into privately owned **ranchos**. There was a continued need for the vacqueros and they took their place on the **ranchos** as skilled, respected, and well-paid rangehands.

The vacquero had evolved into an extremely talented, if flashy, spectacle. He wore fancy, tight-fitting clothing and large rowled spurs that jingled with the gait of his horse. The richness of silver adorned his saddle and bridle. The roundup was called a **rodeo** and when it occurred each year, it brought together thousands of milling cattle on the open range. The "decked out" vacqueros displayed their talents in cutting out, working and branding their employer's cattle. Sometimes two vacqueros worked together to catch the cattle they wished to brand. One roped the head, then as the hooves skidded and stomped, the other roped the hind feet. When working alone, the vacquero would maneuver his horse behind a running steer. Then he would reach down, grab the animal's tail, and flip the several hunderd pound beef, end over end, into a daze in the flying dust.

After the roundup there were the **matanzas** or mass slaughters, also done on horseback. Cow after cow was brought down by a single thrust of a long-bladed knife pulled from the vacquero's boot scabbard.[2]

Things changed suddenly for the vacquero when war erupted between the United States and Mexico in 1846. Retreating Mexican troops were forced below the Rio Grande and the **ranchos** were left unprotected. Dust and smoke of yellow and gray clouded the sky. Both Indian and white marauders, called **Californios**, raided and plundered the vulnerable ranches.[3] They stole, scattered, and slaughtered thousands of cattle. Not even the breeding stock was spared. A drought settled over the country at the same time. It left the straw-colored countryside moistureless and the cattle dying of thirst. Lastly, most of what was left of the herds was driven to San Francisco where the discovery of gold had caused a large influx of hopeful, and very hungry, miners.

The time of the Spanish vaquero was over. Yet he would live on in the equipment, techniques, and "lingo" which he left to the range.

Juan Jose Hererra was familiar with the vaquero methods which had seeped out of California and drifted to the Texas and New Mexico territories. This good looking young man was dark-eyed but of lighter complexion than the Mexicans who surrounded him. He could dress and act the part of a gentleman. It was of burning importance to him that everyone knew that the blood of Spanish aristocracy flowed through his veins.

Juan had a fiery personality and had gotten tangled up in the war between the United States and Mexico. A year after the war started he became involved in the deaths of three prominent men, including a militia officer in the New Mexico territory. He knew he had to leave the area and encouraged some of his Mexican friends to go with him. He told of having a map from an early expedition of his ancestors, that held the promise of gold.

"Come with me to the valley of the Green, we will find the gold and we will build a **rancho**!" The words convinced his large-built brother Pablo and a group of young Mexicans to follow him north.

The journey took the group across endless miles of open range and through some small herds of domestic livestock. When Brown's Hole opened before them, they saw her grin from over the backs and horns of a nice bunch of cattle that had either been purchased or "picked up" along the way. So in 1847 when Juan Jose Hererra and his followers stopped at a spring at the base of the O-Wi-U-Kuts Mountain, they had a new home and Brown's Hole had her first permanent cattle herd.4

The Hererra bunch was not alone in the valley. Besides the Indians, and a few lingering fur trappers, there were more and more travelers passing through. Juan became known to them as both "Spanish" and "Mexican" Joe. It was eventually "Mexican Joe" that stuck with him for the rest of his life.

In 1848 Brown's Hole was included in the land ceded to the United States by Mexico. The year before, when Mexican Joe was riding to Brown's Hole, the Mormons following Brigham Young were traveling north of there, heading for the Salt Lake Basin. For just one year, 1849, the valley became by decree part of the independent Mormon State of Deseret. Years later Brown's Hole would be divided almost equally by Utah and Colorado, with her northern edge a mere whisper away from the Wyoming border.

Though the Mormon Trail did not bring those pioneers into Brown's Hole on their trip west, another famous group of emigrants, with a herd of cattle, spent the winter of 1849-1850. Appealing stories of the California gold rush, with descriptions of the place itself, reached a tribe of Cherokee Indians. They were a well-educated, far-sighted tribe, but after being pushed from their native Carolinas and Georgia to west of the Mississippi, they had become dissatisfied. They applied for and received permission from the United States government to emigrate to California. The group of Indians, including some who were doctors and lawyers, headed west with high hopes of greater happiness and opportunity.

Having had their roots imbedded deeply in the warm, humid south must have made the opposite in terrain and climate feel strange and frightening. But the Indians, their cattle, horses, and mules survived their winter spent beside the silvery, ice-covered Green River. When the days got longer and warmer the following spring, the valley turned green and watched the group drive their cattle away, through Red Creek Canyon. Unfortunately, the warmth of the sun on the snowdrifts in the high country brought on the spring runoff. When the Cherokees reached the fording place between Currant and Sage Creeks, the river was fierce and swollen. When it was over, getting across the river had cost the lives of three men and several head of livestock.

The Indians went on, making their way up Black's Fork, across the knolls and ridges, and on toward their destination. Their tracks and footsteps would be traced time and time again throughout the years as many travelers counted on the "Cherokee Trail" to lead them west.

In 1852, two frontiersmen rode into the valley over the O-Wi-U-Kuts Plateau. In the lead was Kit Carson's son-in-law, Luther "Louie" Simmons. Louie was not a stranger to the valley. He had trapped her streams as early as 1831. Riding behind Louie was a former government scout on the Overland Trail, named Samuel Clark Bassett. The two had apparently met when Louie was exiting from, and Sam was heading to, the California gold fields. Louie had allegedy fought with and killed his wife Adeline's lover.

History has been fortunate that men such as these often kept journals. Sam Bassett was one who put a descriptive pen to the pages of his diary. About his first meeting with the valley he wrote:

Brown's Hole. November, the month of Thanksgiving, 1852. Louie and I down in. Packs off. Mules in lush meadows. Spanish Joe's trail for travel could not be likened to an "up state" high lane, suitable for coach and four.
Mountains to the right of us, not in formation but highly mineralized. To the south a range of

12

uncontested beauty of contour, its great stone mouth drinking a river.

Called on our neighbors, lest we jeopardize our social standing, "Chief Catump" and his tribe of Utes. "Male and female created He them" and Solomon in all his glory was not arrayed so fine. Heads, bones, quills and feathers of artistic design. Buckskin tanned in exquisite coloring of amazing hues, resembling velvet of finest texture. Bows and arrows. "Let there be no strife between thee and me."

Samuel Clark Bassett5

In time Louie Simmons traveled on, wearing his buckskins and being trailed by his pack mule and greyhound dogs. Sam Bassett, however, was drawn to the valley and stayed to make his home with her. Though he was not a cattleman, in the years to come the Bassett name would be strongly linked to the valley's cattle history.

In Texas, the cattle herds were steadily increasing. Long-horns that had escaped or been abandoned years before by their Mexican owners, had survived and multiplied. They were as wild and quick as any game animal, with horns which could stretch eight to nine feet from tip to tip. They numbered in the thousands in 1845 when Texas was admitted to the Union. Many Texas cattlemen got their start by claiming a piece of open range, hiring a few hands, and directing them to round up and brand the wild cattle. As tastes began to turn from pork to beef, a few small trail drives began trickling toward the eastern markets.

By the early 1850's, the depleted Spanish cattle herds of California were not sufficient to feed the ever-increasing population surrounding the California gold fields. The large demand for beef caused a few Texas cattlemen to turn their thoughts and eyes westward. Soon beef was on its way to California! Some of the first cattlemen to make the grueling trip were W.H. Snyder and the men he hired to help him.

Men who tended cattle were called drovers or herders. The term "cowboy" referred to Texas bandits who stole cattle from, and sometimes murdered, Mexican herders. In Revolutionary times, it had labeled a Torrie who tricked patriot farmers into an ambush by jingling a cowbell in the same way the farmer's wandering cows would sound.

Therefore, it was W.H. Snyder's "drovers" who prodded and pushed the herd of "through" cattle up the Rio Grande, over the Continental Divide in southern Colorado, across the White and Yampa Rivers, and finally into Brown's Hole. The valley

13

enjoyed the cattle and gave freely of the nutritious, sun-cured grasses along her river bottoms, creek banks, and foothills. There the herd rested and waited out the winter. In the spring, after the green grass had taken hold along the trails, the drovers urged the cattle out of the valley. They headed to Fort Bridger, then on to California. Though the trip took two summers and a winter, Snyder ended up making a profit.

Another cattleman, W.A. Peril, later followed the same route. He told of buying eleven hundred head of cattle in Texas for ten dollars each, coming out of the winter in Brown's Hole with his herd "fat and sassy," then selling the cattle for a profitable thirty dollars a head in California.

Although the American cattle industry had seen a modest beginning, it was nothing compared to the enormous business it would soon become. Ironically, a forced pause of four years served to enhance its progression. In 1861 ranchers and their sons saddled up and rode away to fight in the Civil War. During their absence, the wild and untended Texas longhorns burgeoned to an immense five million head!

When the war was over, many young men were homeless and jobless. There was little money left in the south and carpetbaggers were everywhere with their hands "stuck out." The cattle were next to worthless. However, in the north, east, and west, the beef market was opening wide.

Men began gathering and burning brands on any loose longhorn they could run out of the mesquite thickets or off the bed grounds at night. Sam Maverick was one rancher who didn't feel it was necessary to brand the stock he was running on his rich spread along the San Antonio River. He barely got turned around when he found himself rustled right out of the cattle business. Because of his unfortunate experience, any unbranded calf, from then on, carried his last name.

Beside branding "mavericks," there were some men who weren't above re-branding a neighbor's longhorn. Especially if it carried a brand which could be easily altered. While some gained nothing but a hangman's noose for their trouble, others stepped from behind crooked branding irons as successful ranchers.

From these men, came the cattle barons who ruled over vast amounts of range and cattle. Following their orders, men including a good share of youngsters who had been "jerked" to manhood by the Civil War, began the great trail drives north.

Though there were good times and laughter, driving cattle for weeks on end was a dusty, demanding, and sometimes dangerous life. Some of the drovers wrote in diaries about the challenges and hardships. Their words told of Indian fights, stampedes, drownings, tormenting flies, and of having to deal

14

with worn-out horses and exhausted men. They wrote about storms with scads of thunder and lightning and of being drenched in the downpours. They told of hauling cattle out of mud bogs with ropes, with the help of the oxen and saddle horses. They told of the misery of blistered backs, cracked lips, boils, ague, sick headaches, and the blues. Nevertheless, most of them endured it all and reached the end of the drive with a deep feeling of pride.

For twenty years, thousands of such drives trampled trails across the country. They reached the stockyards and railroads and sent beef to the world, and brood cattle to the northern plains.

The one man most depended on by the entire crew was the cook. He was the first to climb from his bedroll in the morning and usually stayed the busiest all day. He tended wounds, coughs, broken bones, and hard feelings. His grub supplies usually included pinto beans, salt pork, onions, potatoes, sugar, flour, dried apples, coffee beans, and sometimes fresh beef. He usually managed to serve three hearty meals a day from these basics.

Many of the drovers were Mexicans and just as many more were Negroes who had learned roping and riding skills as slaves on Texas ranches. Though, without a doubt, they all had a lot of "salt," many were barely more than self-conscious kids averaging twenty-four years of age.

A drover stored his bedroll in the chuck wagon and tied about everything else he needed, including canteen and slicker, on his saddle. He usually wore long johns, a plain cotton or flannel shirt, and sometimes woolen pants reinforced with buckskin sewn over the seat and inner thighs. Suspenders and belts were irritating and could gall, so they were seldom used. Tooled leather cuffs or gauntlets were sometimes worn for show and to prevent rope burns. Deep-pocketed vests held tobacco, a packet of cigarette papers, matches, and maybe a tally book. His boots were modified from the Civil War, flat-heeled, round-toed style, to one with a higher heel and reinforced shank or arch. It had a more pointed toe to make the boot fit the stirrup more safely and comfortably. His climb-in "shotgun" or wide wraparound "batwing" chaps protected his legs from brush, trees, rope burns, and weather.

The herder was never without his broad-brimmed hat. A source of pride, it kept hail, rain, branches, and wind off his head and face. The bandanna or scarf he wore knotted around his neck was pulled over his nose and mouth when the trail dust got too thick. The drover could ease the heat, bearing down from the sun, by wadding the bandanna and stuffing it inside the crown of his hat.

Each young man learned ways of finding water. He followed game trails, or watched from what direction a swallow flew when it had mud in its beak to daub on its nest. He learned to stave off thirst by sucking on a small rock or a bullet, and to calm his gnawing hunger by chewing or smoking tobacco.

Chewing tobacco came pressed in a twist, or a chunk called a plug. It was cased with a secret formula of licorice, molasses, sugar, fruit juices, and syrups. There were many brands to choose from including Winesap, Daniel Webster, Star of Virginia, Henry Clay, and Rock Candy. The most common smoking tobacco for men on the cattle drives was packaged in a little muslin sack with a drawstring and was called Bull Durham.

Sometimes during the night, songs, including "Billy Vanero," "Red Wing," and "Little Joe the Wrangler" followed the rhythm of the horse's walk and drifted softly across the herd. The cowhand could tell when his shift riding night herd was over by the position of the Big Dipper in its twenty-four hour journey around the North Star.

Most important, the drover learned to work cattle. He learned to "read" their actions and could prevent trouble by keeping a steer from cutting back or a straggler from getting spooked.

One of these hard-riding young men who Brown's Hole would later claim as her own, was Hiram "Hi" Bernard. The pock marked youngster was only fifteen when he followed his first herd north. Two years later, Texas Panhandle cattleman and designer of the chuck wagon, Charles Goodnight, made him trail boss of eight thousand head of longhorns. The young man proved his ability by taking the herd safely through, selling half in Ogallala, Nebraska, and the other half at the Canadian border.6

Hi Bernard, along with every man since the Spanish vaquero, who had known the constant gait of a horse beneath him, the smell of new territory drenched in rain, and the low rumble of hooves on the move, rode out of the trail dust a hero. He became a legend, known as the American Cowboy.

Chapter III
MEXICAN JOE

Juan Jose Herrera "Mexican Joe" did establish a ranch in Brown's Hole as he had promised. But it surely was not a wealthy **rancho.**

Headquarters for the ranch was merely a cabin on the river bottom, with a dirt floor. The place did manage to support Joe, his brother, and the eight or ten Mexicans who were usually around. Mexican Joe worked his followers as much as he could. He provided the "peons" with room and board. In return they grubbed the tough-rooted sage and greasewood. After the ground was cleared, they worked to build a dam across Vermillion Creek in an effort to irrigate the cleared ground. The group of Mexicans maintained a respectable-sized cattle herd by raising calves and scouring the hills for strays from the big drives. Occasionally, they received one or two head of stock as payment for helping tend, or round up, Texas cattle after their winter stay in the valley. In spite of Joe's map, Brown's Hole offered no Spanish gold mine to Mexican Joe and his men.

Joe had heard the rumors of gold finds being reported as early as 1842 up north in the territory of Wyoming. However, the locations were deep in hostile Indian country and therefore not strongly pursued. Then word sailed into Brown's Hole, in the summer of 1867, that in Wyoming territory a party of Mormon prospectors had spent the winter on Willow Creek, a tributary of the Sweetwater River. They had returned to Fort Bridger with fifteen thousand dollars in gold from the Carissa Lode. This had caused a rush of two hundred Gentiles and Mormons to South Pass.[1]

The following year, in 1868, the treaty of Fort Bridger gave a large chunk of land in mid-Wyoming to the Shoshone Indians for a reservation. (This took the Shoshone people out of Brown's Hole and left the Utes the dominant tribe.) Under the leadership of Chief Washakie, friendly relations between the Shoshone and the white men were established. That same year, at the southern tip of the Wind River Mountains, the three South Pass mining towns of South Pass City, Atlantic City, and Hamilton City (Miner's Delight), were swamped by a few thousand people of all types. Mexican Joe was one of them. It wasn't long until Joe had acquired two pair of sturdy oxen and a wagon. With a bullwhip in his hand, he began bullwhacking (hauling) freight from the newly constructed Union Pacific Railroad to South Pass. Unlike the miners, his profits were steady and assured.

Joe indulged in the night life in saloons run by William H. Bright, John Morris, and other saloon keepers in the area. He especially enjoyed the banking game of faro where players bet on cards drawn from a dealing box. One evening Joe met an interesting character named "Judge" Asbury Conaway (or Conway), a down-on-his-luck attorney from Iowa.

Asbury Conaway was born October 13, 1837, on a farm in McLean County, Illinois. Education was important to Asbury's father, and after moving his family to Mt. Pleasant, Iowa, he saw to it that his children attended private schools. Asbury was intelligent and completed the four-year liberal arts program at Wesleyan University in three years. He received his LLB degree from the University Law School in 1860. Asbury was soon elected Mt. Pleasant justice of the peace where he acquired the lingering title of "Judge." When he moved with his parents to Chariton, Iowa, he briefly became a school teacher. Then, as for so many, his life took a swift turn when the fighting of the Civil War commenced. Asbury signed up, and quickly rose from army private to captain. By the conclusion of the war his service had been so admirable he was given the honor of being breveted a major for "meritorious conduct." He returned to civilian life a practicing attorney and soon held an elected seat in the Iowa State Legislature.[2]

Judge Asbury Conaway was the picture of a man destined for success. Yet, shortly thereafter, the large, good-looking bachelor was living alone, clear out in Wyoming territory. He was without funds, having little luck as a prospector, and even less luck staying sober. The circumstances surrounding his puzzling change of direction remain a mystery. However, Mexican Joe and Judge Conaway soon became good, although somewhat unlikely, friends.

All the money and activity of a boom area, like South Pass, inevitably breeds the con man. Joe had no trouble dealing with their sort. His alert manner (not to mention his double-edged "Arkansas Toothpick" knife) chilled any thoughts a bunco artist might get about him. Except for a certain pretty saloon girl. When she sidled up to Joe, she melted every bit of common sense he ever had. He fell hard for her and for her line. Before Joe·had a chance to figure her out, she had stripped him of about everything he owned, including his freight wagon and oxen. When the reality of her scheming became clear to Joe, she had already sold his belongings and bid him and South Pass City farewell.

Joe's large ego was crushed! He began to gamble and drink in excess. To retain some self pride, he became insolent and overbearing. He was a lot like a rattlesnake in August - touchy and dangerous. A group of the "gentler" citizens could not abide his

18

threatening manner. They were afraid of him and wanted him gone - one way or another.

The tough-acting black man the group hired to get rid of Mexican Joe never had a chance. In a rough situation, it was Joe's way to psychologically play with his opponent's nerves. When the Negro began to make his move against Joe one evening in a saloon, the Mexican's eyes, cold and threatening, never left the black man's face. Joe appeared calm as he sat at his table, running his knife slowly back and forth across his whetstone. The sound of the steel sliding across the rough stone made a spine-pinching, grating sound. Then Joe, in a low guttural voice, began to belittle his adversary. The Negro began to sweat. He was unsure what his next move ought to be. Joe never let up and got steadily louder and more abusive. The black man whirled to run. He flinched when he heard the explosion behind him and was suddenly knocked to the floor by a bullet painfully imbedded in the heel of his foot.

Though Joe's bullet wasn't meant to kill, blood poisoning developed in the wound and it was fatal. As he had twenty-one years earlier in the New Mexico territory, Joe knew it was time to hurry for Brown's Hole.

There hadn't been much gold found at South Pass anyway and many of the miners who had seen enough of "Sweetwater gold fever" were pulling out, also.

When James Chisholm, a reporter for the **Chicago Times,** arrived in the area, he found many deserted cabins and little activity. Few of the dwindling mining population were making more than meager wages. Chisholm reported the people "would have done better (and they know it) to remain where they came from."[3] It's a cinch the black man who went up against Mexican Joe would have done better!

As Joe headed for his home in Brown's Hole, instead of a group of Mexican followers, he rode in the smiling company of his new friend, Judge Asbury Conaway. Their journey to Brown's Hole probably took them through the new coal mining town of Rock Springs. Perhaps they stopped there for a toddy or two before setting out on the remaining miles of their journey.

When the two arrived in the valley, Brown's Hole made friends with Judge Conaway. She heard him quickly pick up the Spanish language from Joe, Joe's brother Pablo, and the other Mexicans. She sighed with the drifting loveliness of the violin melodies Judge Conaway learned to play by ear. She echoed the Indian chant-like chords he reproduced after listening to the neighboring Utes. The rhythm often caused visiting Indian children to move up, down, and about as they danced with free expression.

Though he was a likable and intelligent fellow, when Judge Conaway watched the sun set behind the mountain peaks, his bleary eyes continued to mirror his alcoholic addiction. Then his occasional jaunts with the Tip Gault Gang revealed yet another puzzling contradiction with his past.

"The Sagebrush King of Bitter Creek," Tip Gault, was generous with his friends, including Mexican Joe. He was witty, jovial, and a notorious outlaw. Tip Gault, his Mexican lieutenant Terresa, and the rest of his gang headquartered at a large meadow called Charcoal Bottom. It was not a far distance from the town of Green River City, south of the muddy waters of Bitter Creek. The gang scouted both the Oregon and Overland Trails from there. They watched for easy "pickin's" from the westward-moving wagon trains and the horse herds being driven east from California.

Sometimes after running off some stock in the night, a couple of members of the gang would "happen on" the search party the next day and offer assistance. Of course they would urge the stock owners in the wrong direction. They knew the searchers couldn't spend too much time looking for the stock. The gang members would "generously" offer to buy the animals for a small sum, saying they would continue the search. The travelers would usually agree that a little money was better than none. With or without a legitimate bill of sale, the gang members would drive the horses and cattle into Brown's Hole and fatten them up. They would then sell them to the Indians, to the next group of travelers going through, or even to Mormon settlers in Utah.

Tip Gault worked the Overland Trail halfway across Wyoming. If the animals were stolen toward the east, the gang would sometimes gather the stock at the meadow at Antelope Spring. They would then push the animals to Pine Butte, over what is now Kinney Rim, trail them to Jack Knife Spring, up Rife's Rim, across to Red Creek, then down to Brown's Hole.

Perhaps it was the idea of being a free spirit that attracted Judge Conaway to ride with Tip Gault. Or maybe it was just one more way for him to rebel against the life from which he had turned.

Chapter IV
THE EXPEDITION OF
JOHN WESLEY POWELL

While Mexican Joe was having his fling in South Pass City, Brown's Hole was busy taking part in a historical river expedition led by scientist-soldier-explorer Major John Wesley Powell. Powell stated that geographic boundaries are often "clearly drawn by nature." He was the first to attempt to divide the country into regions based on physical features.

John Wesley Powell was born in New York in 1843. As he grew up in Ohio and Wisconsin, he became a self-educated student of naturalism. In 1861 he joined the fighting of the Civil War, serving as a captain in the Union Army. In the aftermath of the battle of Shilo, Powell was left with a badly wounded arm, an injury so severe he was forced to have his arm amputated. Powell never let the absence of an arm deter him in his ambition as a naturalist. Nor did the bushy sideburned man let the lack of financing and public interest dissuade him in his desire to explore the wild and unknown rivers.

On May 24, 1869, Powell's party, consisting of the major and nine men, loaded their four wooden boats with enough gear and supplies to last ten months. Finally the four boats, the **Emma Dean,** the **Kitty Clyde's Sister,** the **No Name**, and the **Maid of the Canyon,** were pushed away from the banks of what is now called Expedition Island just below the town of Green River, Wyoming.1

They were all excited to go, but under orders from their leader they took their time. It was the group's intention to behold, geologize, and name sites along the Green and Colorado Rivers. They were surely not very experienced in handling their specially-built boats. Only about a mile into the journey, the men riding in the **Kitty Clyde's Sister** had a battle with her. One of the men described it in his diary:

> She ran on a sand bar in the middle of the river, got off of that, she ran ashore on the east side, near the mouth of Bitter Creek, but finally off and came down to the rest of the fleet in gallant style, her crew swearing she would not "gee" or "haw" a "cuss."2

Four days later the expedition party drifted into a "brilliant red gorge." They named this fiery-colored cleft in the earth, Flaming Gorge.

21

Soon they traveled into Red Canyon where a swift current, a rocky channel, and a battle with moderate rapids gave the men some valuable lessons in handling themselves and their boats.

> June 1, 1869 - Today we have an exciting ride, and make almost railroad speed. Here and there the water rushes into a narrow gorge; rocks roll it into great waves, and the boats go leaping and bounding like things of life.
>
> An old Indian named Pariats told me about one of his tribe attempting to run this canyon. "The rocks heap high; the water go hoo-woogh; water pony heap buck. Water catch 'em; no see 'em Injun any more! No see 'em squaw any more! No see 'em papoose any more!"[3]

A couple of miles after Red Creek had helped stir up those rapids as it dumped into the river, Red Canyon ended. It was then that the valley of Brown's Hole first saw the curious group as they bobbed along on the back of her river. It had taken Powell about a week to reach Brown's Hole.

Since the term "hole" had for many years been the connotation of any large, sheltered valley, it fit Brown's Hole just fine up to then. However, someone, most likely Major Powell, decided the sweeter term of "park," meaning an open meadow or a level valley between mountain ranges, was more befitting. The valley accepted the new sound of Brown's Park, but never fully let go of her first name and came to be called by both.

Whether it was really Powell's idea or not, he was using her new name when he wrote about his arrival there.

> June, 1869 - Brown's Park is a valley, bounded on either side by a mountain range, really an expansion of the canyon.[4]

As the Powell Expedition drifted onward through the valley, Major Powell wrote about naming one of her canyons.

> June 4, 1869 - A spur of red mountain stretches across the river, which cuts a canyon through it. A vast number of swallows have built houses on the cliffs.
>
> The swallows are swift and noisy, sweeping by in curved paths or chattering from the rocks. The young stretch naked necks through the doorways of their mud houses, clamoring for

22

food. They are a noisy people.
We call this Swallow Canyon.[5]

Two days passed.

June 6, 1869 - At daybreak I am awakened by
a chorus of warblers, flickers, meadow larks and
geese. Our cook, a "bullwacker," breaks in:
"roll out! Bulls in the corral! Chain up the gaps!
Roll out!" This is our breakfast bell.[6]

The next day the Powell expedition stood at the bottom edge
of Brown's Park. They watched and listened to the Green River
rush headlong into the maroon opening of a high canyon. It was
"the stone mouth drinking a river" which Samuel Bassett had
written of in his journal.

During the bright warmth of the day, the doorway out of
Brown's Park made a promise of the beauty hidden within.

June 7, 1869 - When I came down at noon,
the sun shone in splendor on its vermillion
walls shaded into green and gray when the
rocks are lichened over. The river fills the
channel from wall to wall. The canyon opened
like a beautiful portal to a region of glory . . .[7]

One of the boaters, Andrew Hall, remembered the last line of
a poem by Robert Southey, . . . and this way the water comes
down at Lodore. As Andrew Hall wished, the canyon was
named Lodore.

Later, as the sun lay down behind the western peaks and the
butterscotch light darkened, the giant walls of the Gates of
Lodore became a threatening place of hidden secrets.

Now, as I write, the sun is going down, and
the shadows are settling in the canyon. The
vermillion gleams and the rosy hues, the green
and gray tints, are changing to sombre brown
above, and black shadows below. Now 'tis a
dark portal to a region of gloom.
And that is the gateway through which we
enter our voyage of exploration tomorrow - and
what shall we find?[8]

The first day into Lodore Canyon, the major wrote:

June 8, 1869 - Waves in a river differ from
waves of the sea. Water of an ocean wave

merely rises and falls; the form passes on. But here the water passes on, while the form remains. A boat leaps and plunges along with great velocity.[9]

The next day the group got a fierce introduction to the power held by Lodore Canyon. Suddenly, the sound within the canyon walls became deafening with the pounding, echoing roar of the river throwing a fit. As the rapids multiplied and swelled, the boats humped and pitched. The water twisted, buckled, rudely splashed the men, and threw everything forward. Amid the turmoil rose the screams of men and the cracking of boat timbers.

> I see the boat strike a rock, careen and fill with water. The men lose their oars; she strikes another rock with great force, is broken in two, and the men are thrown into the river.
> We are as glad to shake hands with them as though they had been around the world and wrecked on a distant coast.[10]

Powell named this place Disaster Falls. One of the crew, an English adventurer named Frank Goodman, shook his head and vowed to go no further. He left the party there and was thankful to make his way back to the peaceful security of Brown's Park. He made his home with her and left his name to Goodman Gulch.

Major Powell carried on despite many nerve-twitching close calls and the dissatisfied grumbling of his men who felt their leader was often "too cautious, slow and fooled around too much." Plus, it seemed to them, he had a definite knack for picking damp and bug-infested campsites. Three more men would desert at the head of a massive stretch of rapids. They stayed safe from the clawing hands of the river, only to perish in the wilderness.

By the end of August, 1869, Powell and the five remaining men walked away from the canyon country of the Colorado River and into instant fame!

Two years later, Brown's Park saw the one-armed major again as he led a highly supported second expedition onto her waters. Although they were taking in the scenery the valley offered them, they probably barely noticed when they drifted beside a steep and rocky hillside. All eyes were drawn to the flat on the opposite bank. There, camped beneath the deep green shade of some cottonwoods, were the chuck wagons, horses, and cowhands of a Texas cattle drive. The Powell men wrote of meeting "Texas gentlemen" named Harrell and Bacon, "and a dozen or so Mexican herders." The herd of twenty-two hundred head of cattle had wintered in the valley on its way from Texas to California.

Later, in enjoyment of the valley's content waters, Powell had the boats tied together so they would drift as one. He then proudly made his seat on a camp chair lashed to his boat's stern. He entertained the valley and his men when he tilted his head back and loudly recited the rhythmic flow of "The Lay of the Last Minstrel."

Brown's Park said goodbye at the Gates of Lodore once more and Powell went on to successfully complete the trip. He later accomplished many things, including becoming the director of the United States Geological Survey and the head of documenting Native American culture for the Smithsonian Institute.

A frosty morning on the Green River in Brown's Hole

Chapter V
MAGGIE'S NIPPLE

A trail boss named George Baggs pushed his nine hundred head of Texas cattle into Brown's Park in late fall, 1871. He got the herd on good grass, then settled in with his common-law wife, Maggie, to wait out the winter.

Although it was well into November, throughout the west it still had not turned very cold. When it began to storm on the 15th, the snowflakes were heavy with water and soon melted into rain. The moisture was welcomed by the cattlemen who expected it would soften the coarse blades of grass upon which their stock was grazing. It would also help bring on a good stand of grass the next spring.

That evening a sharp wind began to whisper through the bare branches of trees, bushes, and through the evergreen boughs. Before long the wind had gathered strength and was howling, becoming more bitter with each passing hour. The drizzle froze; the sky was filled with stinging chips of ice that pelted and clung to the cedars, brush, and wet cattle hides. The bottom dropped out of the thermometer. The ground and grass froze solid. The wind let up, then blew again. All the while the snow tumbled from the sky, to a depth averaging eighteen inches. From California to the Mississippi River, cattle stood bawling on solid drifts of snow, or waded through the crust to their knees. By the thousands they starved - by the thousands they froze.₁

Brown's Park had braced herself within the mountains and used all her natural defenses to fight the winter storms. George Baggs sat tight and watched his nine hundred head of steers. Day after day they contentedly fed along the valley's snow-bare ridges and river bottoms. When spring finally came, George Baggs was one of the few cattlemen who had his entire herd alive. However, his relationship with Maggie had not fared the winter so well!

Pretty Maggie was tiny and as high-strung as a yearling heifer. The young woman liked men, and usually showed it. The cowhands would blush and fall all over themselves if she paid any attention to them. But because of her suggestive actions, the men sometimes made Maggie the subject of snickering comments.

One cowboy made the mistake of referring to a nearby hill as "Maggie's Nipple." Maggie heard the remark and instantly grabbed her whip. She liked feeling that she had control of the men and this impertinence made her furious. The air hissed with the sound of her horse quirt. Again and again Maggie slapped the whip across the stunned man. The others, sitting on their horses nearby, could only clench their jaws and hide their faces behind lowered hat brims.

Mexican Joe's brother, Pablo, was another matter to Maggie. She was attracted to the dark-skinned man and the way he touched her with his eyes, letting them slide across her.

When spring came, Maggie left Brown's Park with George to deliver the cattle to Crawford and Thompson Company in Evanston, Wyoming. However, George should have picked a different route home to Texas. When he and Maggie passed back through the valley on their way south, Maggie's desires, and Pablo's invitation, caused her to desert George and move in with the Mexicans. Maggie soon persuaded Pablo to leave the crowded cabin in Brown's Park and take her to his home in New Mexico.

The flame didn't burn very long. It either didn't take long for Maggie to get her fill of Pablo, or for him to tire of her. While Pablo stayed in New Mexico for a while, Maggie hurried north and was soon "honeying" up to George. Because he had a weakness for her, George took her back. It was then he began to work building a ranch on the Little Snake River. Later the small town of Baggs (Wyoming), named after him, was established nearby.

Maggie really did try. After she and George talked it over she went to New York City to adopt a family of three half-grown children. Things were rather good, for a while. But Maggie still had a strong attraction to other men, and she couldn't seem to ignore her desires. In the evenings when the cowhands stripped off to swim in a nearby pond, Maggie watched from a hidden place and chose her next lover.

As was probably inevitable, one day George Baggs got enough. He sold his outfit to the Swan Cattle Company and kicked Maggie out without a cent. Maggie protested to the law and was awarded a share of George's money. She took off for California with Mike Sweet. Mike was a cowboy described as having "raw eyelids and kinky red hair." It was told that he lasted only as long as Maggie's money. Eventually, Maggie found her place in life, running a rooming house in Galveston, Texas.

Just north of Brown's Park there is still a reminder of peppery little Maggie. Below Middle Mountain, in the bottom of 4-J Basin near Johnson Canyon, a little round hill still holds the name for which the cowboy took such a beating. It is known as Maggie's Nipple.[2]

Chapter VI

J.S. HOY

Jesse S. "J.S." Hoy was a twenty-five year old man who had left his well-to-do family in Pennsylvania and made his way west driving freight wagons. He had spent the summer of 1872 haying near Evanston, Wyoming along the Bear River, for William Crawford of the Crawford-Thompson Company. He had been employed by Crawford just before George Baggs arrived with the cattle from Brown's Hole. The young man heard stories about that valley. He heard about her worsening reputation for being a shelter for outlaws and fierce "blood-drinking" Utes. He wanted to stay away from that country. He wasn't very interested in the mild winter George Baggs had just spent there. J.S. grew more leery about the valley after listening to a fellow hay hand by the name of Joe Lemmon. Joe told J.S. he had abandoned the trail of five missing team horses because "the trail led into Brown's Hole, and it is worth a man's life to go there."[1]

Now there was talk of taking the Crawford-Thompson herd back to Brown's Hole for the winter. Just as J.S. feared, his boss asked him to accompany the cattle on the drive and remain in Brown's Hole with them through the winter months. J.S. "acceded to his request with about the same zeal of a man challenged to a duel with rifles at ten paces."[2]

In October, while making preparations for the cattle drive from Evanston to Brown's Hole, J.S. was still reluctant to go. He did feel fortunate that he would be accompanied by a cowboy who had originally gone north with the herd and had stayed on to tend the cattle. J.S. respected his knowledge even though the cowboy was a bit homely. J.S. described him as "a runt of a man wearing clothes big enough for a man twice his size."

It turned out to be a good thing the Texan was along on the drive. He had to get the boss and his assistant out of trouble more than once. One night he helped stop a near stampede caused by Crawford and J.S. The two men sheepishly realized they had used poor judgment because of their lack of knowledge about trailing cattle. J.S. decided that "trailing could be learned only by experience, it being entirely different from looking after stock on the range."

When the cattle drive reached the fording place on the Green River a couple of days from Brown's Hole, Crawford left his herd to J.S. as planned, and headed back to Evanston. Though chilly, it was calm and sunny the morning he left. The drovers were busy working and prodding the cattle through the brush and willows and into the Green River. The cattle were extra contrary and the cowboys could manage to cross only a few at a time. The riders whistled and hollered. They rammed their horses back and forth, and cussed while they beat on the balking cattle. The men hardly had time to care that the sky was steadily growing grayer and the air colder.

When the rest of the riders and cattle were safely across, J.S.'s horse finally climbed up the river bank, dripping and beginning to shiver. The cold had become so intense that soon the horse's "wet tail was frozen in icicles that rattled like a chain as he trotted along." Throughout the afternoon and evening, the storm steadily built around them.

When the wind and snow hit in the night it was terrible. It was so cold that "the cowboys crawled from their beds and the men on herd abandoned their charge." Their mounts were miserable as well. The "saddle horses, with saddles still on their sore backs, had had little time to graze for a week and nothing to eat for the last twenty-four hours, stood with bowed backs to the wind, their noses nearly touching their knees, their four feet so close together they could stand in a bushel measure." All the while the cattle drifted with the blizzard.

By dawn the next morning the storm had passed, leaving behind a biting breeze and eight or so inches of wind-blown snow. The half-frozen drovers climbed on their gaunt horses. They figured they would be gathering scattered cattle for a week. They could hardly believe their luck when they found most of the cattle in one big bunch near the entrance to Brown's Hole at the head of Red Creek Canyon. It wasn't luck, though, that drove the cattle. The animals had been driven over the trail once before and were ready to return to the protection of the low-lying valley.

In a while J.S. Hoy, the cowboys, and their herd came out of the mouth of the gravelly canyon and waded across muddy Red Creek one final time. Upon seeing Brown's Hole open wide before him, J.S. Hoy grew less fearful of the valley and observed:

> While winter storms raged on the mountains around about, and snow fell deep and lay until warm spring rains and summer came, down in Brown's Hole all was calm with bright sunshine, although cold enough to freeze Green River over except where it ran rapidly. When we emerged into the Hole the ground was bare of snow, while the mountains all around showed white except where the ground was hidden by cedars and pinions. This difference was one of

the mysteries of this unknown, wonderful and dread country. Nothing here was like things elsewhere.

The herd was pushed about four miles to the edge of a sage-covered, cedar-speckled bench. When the cowboys trailed the cattle off the hillside to a narrow river bottom, they found a grave. J.S. rode to the mound and read the name "H.M. Hook" on the wooden headboard.

The herd continued moving slowly. The drovers were busy keeping their oxen-pulled chuck wagon from pitching over sideways and tumbling off into the river from a steep and narrow portion of the trail. They fastened their lariats to the axles and threw the ropes over the top of the wagon. Then walking on the upper slope, the men held tight to the ropes to support the load as the oxen moved down the trail. Suddenly their eyes shot upward to a commotion at the top of the hill. J.S. and the others were startled as sixteen young Ute braves kicked their horses in the sides and plunged down the hillside toward them, waving blankets and screeching war-whoops. In the last instant, to keep from running over the cowboys, "they had to rein their horses so suddenly as to set them back upon their haunches." Then there was silence.

The cowboys, unarmed and helpless, waited for the Indians to do something. The cowboys stood on syrupy legs and remained quiet. Finally: "The tension was broken and the silence ended when their leader, glaring fiercely, asked, 'Where you come from? My grass. Injin grass.' waving his arms so as to take in all of Colorado, Wyoming, and Utah." Then pointing at the herd the spokesman said, "Injin hungry; heap hungry; give um meat."

As it turned out the Indians were not looking for a fight, but for food. J.S. Hoy breathed deeply for the first time in several minutes and said, "All right, Injin white man's good friend; you take-um meat, heap meat, all meat Injin wants." Seconds later the Indians had a steer cut from the herd and were driving it away on a gallop.

The cowboys took the rest of the herd about a mile further. There they stopped and let the cattle spread and feed as they wished. J.S. was disappointed to see that the grass wasn't as good as he figured it would be. The reason was because Brown's Park was getting tired. The Crawford-Thompson herd was not alone in the valley. Asa and Hugh Adair had driven in twenty-three hundred head of through cattle in September and shortly after that the Keiser-Gibson herd with another thirteen hundred head had arrived. Over four thousand hungry mouths ripped and pulled at every stem of grass and edible brush.

With little else to do, the drovers spent the winter keeping an eye on the cattle, lying low so as not to stir up any Indian trouble, and braiding rawhide ropes. Although the Mexicans didn't often go to the white men's camp, J.S. got acquainted with Judge Conaway, Mexican Joe, and the other ten Mexicans or "greasers," as the white cowhands called them. J.S. saw that things could get mighty rambunctious when the Indians visited the Mexican camp to wrestle, race horses, and gamble.

Two men, Pardon Dodds and Murray Evans, credited with being among the first settlers in Ashley Valley, Utah, passed through during the latter part of the winter. During their stay, Dodds purchased one hundred head of cattle from the Adair herd. Evans was so impressed with the way the Mexicans used horse mane and tail to make belts, hackamores, quirts, and bridles that he bought a multicolored, braided bridle for seventy-five dollars.

All the while the hungry cattle ate and searched for more. Brown's Park gave all she had. As hard as she tried, by the time the meadowlarks and robins returned, five hundred head of cattle, dead from starvation, were scattered across her fed-out floor.

When the warmth of the season settled over the valley, the Adair cattle went west to California and Keiser went south to start the "K" Ranch near the present town of Jensen, Utah. J.S. Hoy trailed his herd back to Evanston. With most of the cattle gone, the valley began to heal. Her cropped grasses began to sprout, thicken, and spread. The scars of the overgrazing soon began to disappear.

J.S. got a good, or perhaps bitter, taste of what life was like in Mexican Joe's dwelling when he returned to Brown's Hole looking for straggler cattle.

J.S. wasn't fond of the Mexicans, but he was afraid of the Indians and he didn't want to camp alone. Moving in with Mexican Joe and his bunch, however, didn't prove to be very good for his health either. **Natilla de leche,** corn meal mush and milk, was about all the Mexicans were eating. The milk was fresh enough, but no one bothered to strain the cow hair, manure clumps, bugs, or dirt specks from it. Often, dogs or cats lapped their fill from the bucket before it was taken to the house. Not surprisingly, J.S. begn to feel a bit puny. Soon his illness worsened and he developed a high fever. For four days he moaned in and out of consciousness while lying in his "shakedown" bed on the dirt floor. Once he woke up long enough to hear that four white men were in the valley, and were five miles away. They were staying in the cabin where J.S. had spent the previous winter.

His head was in a fog when he asked the Mexicans to get his

horse and help him into the saddle. Clinging to the saddle horn and hardly able to keep his eyes open, J.S. slumped forward and rode for the Jack Gunn camp. He made it there and found the food and care he needed.

As J.S. Hoy became acquainted with the four men, he learned that George W. Richards, Jack Gunn, a man named Smith, and a bear-killing trapper dressed in buckskin and called "Old Wes" had wintered some cattle just up the river from Brown's Hole. It was in a pretty spot known as "Little Brown's Hole." It had been rough weather and they hoped their cattle would do better in the larger valley.

A few days after J.S. arrived at the Jack Gunn camp, he was back on his feet. One afternoon he and Jack were alone in the cabin when they heard Jack's little dog let out several frightened barks as he ran toward the doorsteps of the house. Before J.S. or Jack could get the door open, a gray wolf ran from the trees, grabbed the yelping dog in its jaws, and disappeared into the underbrush.

Later, George and Mary Richards started a ranch and left their name to both Richards' Peak and to a gap on Red Creek just across the Wyoming line where they built a two-story house. Jack Gunn also did well in the cattle business. He made his headquarters in the large mountainous meadow of Beaver Basin on Cold Spring Mountain.

J.S. Hoy discovered that he was partial to this "unknown, wonderful and dread country" and decided he wouldn't mind sharing her with the Mexicans, outlaws, Indians, or even the wolves.

Chapter VII
THE BIG GRAY

He was wild and shy, and the valley tried her best to keep him well hidden among her cedars and ledges. From the rear he looked a little comical with his narrow flanks, long, knock-kneed hind legs, and oversized feet. However, the wolf's build was anything but funny. It was intricate and precise and created to stalk and bring down prey much larger than he.

With his front and hind legs swinging in the same line, he was wonderfully suited to trotting. Along with his pack he could cover forty or fifty miles in a day and still be able to hunt and make a kill. He was an adept swimmer, even in Brown's Park's icy winter waters, and the hardships of deep snow on her high mountain slopes were easily overcome.

When he turned his large head to look over the territory which he claimed, he was nothing less than magnificent. From beneath his ears, brushed tufts of hair extended downward and outward framing his handsome face. His captivating, light eyes, with the dark pupils standing out distinctly in the center, were outlined in black.

From the side he showed the muscular, sinewy power of his huge body, which could reach a height of three feet at the shoulder. The white, black, gray, and brown hairs of his coat intermingled to a predominate shade of gray. Usually the underside of his legs, ears, and muzzle were a soft tawny color. When the wind rippled across his coat of many colors, it folded the thick fur back and forth. The breezes stirred up little circular spots showing a buried, lighter silkiness of underfur.

He courted his female and she responded with mutual terms of endearment. The two gently rubbed their heads together, snuffled one another about the face, nipped at each other's noses and bunted them together. When it came time for his lifemate to give birth to her pups in a hillside den, the gray stayed behind with his female and took seriously his responsibility as a father. But if the pack members left, even for a short time, he felt great happiness when they returned. He rushed among them and they all wagged their tails crazily. They bounded about, put forepaws on each other's necks, and greeted one another with licks, whines, and special soft utterings.

As was almost always so, his pack was his family. There was a great deal of affection displayed among the pack members, and his new pups were cared for by all the adults. Strong attachments developed early. There were no orphans in a wolf pack.

Hours of play taught the pups stamina and courage. By the time they were seven months old, they were ready to travel from the den with the pack and join in the hunt. The first hunt was crucial. Deer, elk, and mountain sheep fought with sharp horns and hooves. The slower pups often sustained fatal injuries while their stronger, more intelligent littermates learned quickly and became skilled hunters.

For the big gray to retain his position within the pack, he often exhibited his authority. Sometimes he trotted up to a wolf of lower rank and stood in a proud, lordly manner over him. The other wolf showed his respect and a plea for friendliness by tucking his tail between his legs, crouching, then rolling over on his back exposing his belly. The submission was usually gracefully accepted with a few gentle sniffs and licks from his superior.

When the wolf's temper was tested, his hackles or thick mane extending along the center of his back and neck and behind his front shoulders, stood on end. As he was joined by his family, a low, throaty growl would threaten and warn through bared fangs. Yet, if the intruder was an aggressive animal, such as a bear or wolverine, the wolf usually retreated, even from a fresh kill. The protection of the den was an exception. The pups were defended to the death.

When Brown's Hole saw her wolves, she usually also saw some black, shiny-feathered ravens. They often followed along in sight of the pack, or flew directly over a trail, tracking the wolves ahead. During the excitement of the hunt, the coarse-voiced cousins of the crow swirled around, squawked, and cawed from the safety of tree branches. Later, they dined on any tasty pieces of meat or droplets of blood left behind. During leisure times of the day, they picked apart wolf droppings and sometimes played light-hearted "catch-me-if-you-can" games with the wolves.

The big gray seldom liked to sing in the wind. But when the air in the valley was calm, at any time of the day or night, he would begin to whine and wag his tail. Then he would pull his lips forward, lift his nose to the sky, and howl. The rest of the scattered pack, eyes growing bright with excitement, were hardly able to wait. They ran to join him, uttering little sounds as they hurried. Soon the pack was assembled, all blending in the chorus with low, mournful howls. Brown's Hole could detect the female voices for they were always a bit more delicate and higher pitched. Each howl lasted anywhere from one-half to eleven seconds. For miles within the valley the sound glided, filled the air, and stirred emotions in many living things. After about a minute and a half, the howling was over and the gentler sounds of the valley became noticeable again.

All the mammals, reptiles, birds, water, soil, formations, and vegetation of the valley had a complex relationship. Along with the lizards, eagles, and the flower-covered cactus, the wolf was in touch with his environment. It was nearly always the sick, the old, the very young, or the lame that fell prey to his cunning and his clamping bite. Even then, it was only in about one in ten tries that his major hunts were successful. Occasionally he would feed on small rodents, rabbits, or birds.

It had been the wolf's destiny to live out his normal life span in the secure company of his pack. He survived by following the rules which nature dictated. However, with the coming of man and his livestock, the rules began to change. The sickening picture of a ham-strung colt, mangled calf, or mother cow with her throat, entrails, and flanks eaten away made the wolf the stockman's enemy. Although he was wise, the family-oriented wolf usually stayed in a group which made him a large target.[1]

During the 1873-74 winter, J.S. Hoy came upon an old horse that had gone off by himself to die. The old saddle horse had chosen a shaded place in the brush beneath some cottonwoods about two hundred yards from the Hoy cabin. J.S. saw the paw prints all around what was left of the carcass and realized a wolf pack had been coming in under the cloak of darkness to feed on the dead animal. He decided it would be hard to find any better opportunity to be rid of the entire lot. From experience, J.S. knew the senses of the wolf were extremely keen, and he would have to be very cautious if his plan was going to work. On horseback, the man rode beside the old gelding's body. Leaning out of the saddle, he sprinkled the killing grains of strychnine over the raw flesh of the freshly-eaten places. J.S. then rode on, never touching human hand nor foot near the poisoned area. J.S. didn't go back to the site for a while. But when he did, he found the wolves had not returned at all!

During that same winter, J.S. noticed the huge prints of a single wolf moving along the river bank on the trail tromped flat by his cattle. When it became obvious that the wolf was making a habit of using the trail, J.S. prepared to get rid of him. With a two-inch auger, he drilled a half-inch hole in a flat block of wood. He melted down some beef tallow, then poured the hot fat into the hole. Before the fat cooled and hardened, he sprinkled it with poison. J.S. then placed the wood block in a well chosen spot on the trail. The man figured the wolf, after being attracted to the offer of tallow, would soon be lying lifeless among the winter-grayed sagebrush. J.S. Hoy tells what happened next:

> The following morning, early, I mounted my horse and visited the bait. I did not find a wolf, dead or alive. But what he did was so human, so characteristic of man, that I was not only surprised but shocked at the boldness and insolence of the beast. What he did was as plain to be seen as if I had caught him in the act -there being two or three inches of snow on the ground, he raised one leg and discharged his urine all over the bait, the yellow fluid plain to be seen - then he let fly both hind feet backward, scratched dirt loose and threw it behind him in the way peculiar to a dog.
>
> I set the same kind of fresh bait on three successive nights and he repeated the same performance. He did not do this accidentally, without design. It was an act both humorous, sarcastic, sneering. Human beings express the same thoughts and feeling by putting their thumbs on their noses and wiggling their fingers.2

Though the wolf may have gained a certain admiration and respect from the early stockmen, the intelligent, sensitive creature would be no match for man's fear of him and his determination to be rid of him. Throughout the country and the world, steel traps, edge traps, box traps, deadfalls, corrals, pits, piercers, fishhooks, snares, ring hunts, set guns, ropings, den-pup slaughterings, professional hunting, bountying, and poisonings with strychnine, cyanide, fluoroacetate of barium, and sodium fluoroacetate took their toll.

Brown's Hole would hear the calls of her wolf families for several years after J.S. Hoy encountered them. Nevertheless, the valley's threads of security had begun to unravel and she was helpless to prevent it. It was the beginning of an ending.

Chapter VIII
THE SCUFFLES

J.S. Hoy was pleased that he had made friends with the Indians camped nearby. Although he was still cautious, his admiration for them had grown. He especially enjoyed the excitement when they were preparing for their big fall hunt.

One brave, watching the clouds gather over the mountains, said to J.S., "Purty soon snow, heap buckskin."

Snows in the upper country meant the wildlife would be making its way downward to warmer days and better feed. When it was time, the Utes packed up and split into groups of six or so "wickeups." The wickeups, used mostly in the summer, were shelters built from small poles covered with hides, brush, bark, or whatever was available to insulate and shed moisture.

The happy bands of braves, squaws, kids, horses, and dogs left for their own special hunting areas. The deer were so thick that fall that "every hunter came to camp at the close of each day with all the game his horse would carry; on top of which the warrior-hunter sat."[1] Soon they returned to the river bottom and busily went about pitching their lodges.

The next fall after his stay with the Mexicans, J.S. was still employed by Crawford and Thompson. He received another thirteen hundred head of cattle to tend through the winter. He had heard from his brother Valentine that Valentine and his partners, Sam and George Spicer, were having a hard time making a go of their cattle operation near Greeley, Colorado. Valentine didn't figure they could hold on much longer since they were continually butting heads with the sprawling Iliff cattle outfit. Through the encouragement of J.S., Valentine and the Spicers came to Brown's Hole, pushing three hundred head of cattle. Valentine moved in with J.S. and the Spicers moved to a cabin not far away on the same grassy bottom.

Though there were unfriendly renegades around, J.S., his brother, and the Spicers got along and traded with the two nearby tribes. The two chiefs were called "Judge" and "Dana," and up to now had remained friendly with each other.

On the night of December 25th, Brown's Hole was silent and crisp. In the words of J.S. Hoy, "The night was not cold for a winter night; the moon shown brightly and serenely in a cloudless sky; not a hoot of owl nor yelp of coyote nor howl of wolf to disturb the universal stillness of this glorious Christmas night. The universal lull was ominous - the calm before the storm."[2]

The storm was not of wind, clouds, or snow, but one of too much whiskey! Just after dark, J.S. went for a walk and saw the bottles that a group of twelve or so watery-eyed Utes tried to conceal. He was afraid of what kind of night it was likely to be and hurried back to his cabin.

The ruckus disturbed the quiet just after midnight. Drunken Indians began to fight; squaws screamed; dogs barked, yelped, and howled. By then both the chiefs, Dana and Judge, were very drunk. Dana decided Judge was being a nuisance and it would be a good idea to throw him down and hog-tie him. Of course, Judge resisted that idea and the two chiefs began to argue and scuffle.

In the middle of the struggle, Dana bopped Judge on the head with an empty whiskey bottle, sending him sprawling and leaving him unconscious. Dana, feeling victorious over the easy defeat of Judge, decided he needed to brag a little to the whites. Leading the way, Dana and his drunken followers went to the Hoy cabin and forced their way through the cottonwood slab door. The unruly mob pushed and crowded each other inside the small cabin. Chief Dana was worked up and cocky. J.S., dressed only in trousers he had quickly jerked on, tried to calm him. He reached out his hand and laid it on Dana's shoulder.

Speaking in the form of English the Utes used (being unable to prounce th or f, according to J.S. Hoy), J. S. said, "Dana pretty good man, my bruller."3

The drunken chief's arm flung outward, knocking J.S. against the log wall. Then from beneath his blanket, the chief pulled out a sheath knife.

Flashing the knife he boasted, "Yes, me heap good Injin, big chief, me pight, me no lie, me no steal."4

The chief's tirade continued on. Meanwhile, some other braves were going in and out of the cabin with arm loads of wood to pile in the already blazing fireplace. J.S. cautiously moved among them, not wishing to push his luck with Dana any further. Finally, with great relief, the Hoy brothers watched the staggering, pushing group leave their cabin and make their way back to their own camp.

Later on, smarting from the blow to his skull, Judge appeared in the Hoy doorway. He was very timid. The six-inch gash on his head was caked with clotted blood and dirt.

He appealed softly, "Make medicine, head heap sick."5

The Hoys doctored him with soap and water, bacon grease, and "Perry Davis Pain Killer."

As soon as he felt like getting around the next morning, Judge got busy rounding up his people telling them to make ready to return to the White River Agency in Colorado. He was very upset and feeling sorry for himself over the way Dana had treated him. Just before Judge left Brown's Hole he went to J.S. and asked him to write a letter to White River Indian Agent Littlefield.

Hoping to gain some sympathy he said, "You tell 'im Dana kill Judge. Yes, you tell 'im."[6]

Hiding a smile, J.S. wrote the note. He didn't mention the fight but simply said that all was okay with the Indians.

Before long Dana moved his tribe, but only a few miles down river to Mexican Joe's.

Of all the children, it was Dana's little four-year-old boy who loved Judge Conaway's violin music the most. Indians, Mexicans, and whites laughed and nodded as they watched the little boy dance. Dressed in a dirty pink shirt, he would twist his body and hop around, stomping his tiny moccasin-covered feet.

Later that winter the boy got sick with a cold. As the days passed his fever rose and his cough worsened. In spite of everything done for him, the chief's son got weaker. Dana stood over his son's hot body, with worried eyes and slumped shoulders. The squaws began to wail and weep. After a three-week fight, the boy died.

His body was sewn inside a blanket along with all his special belongings. His pony was shot, so that the boy would have him for his journey. Then Brown's Hole took him from his father's trembling hands, down through a hole cut in the ice, and into the cradling river current.

Although they joined their Indian friends in their sorrow, Mexican Joe and J.S. Hoy were fast becoming enemies. They had not gotten along for some time and had argued, among other things, over supplies, hay, and unpaid debts.

The following spring J.S. and one of his hired hands rode into Mexican Joe's headquarters. J.S. got off his horse and started to look through the cowhides which were thrown over the corral fence and scattered around on the ground. He was searching for the hide of a steer he had been missing. Joe was insulted.

A group of Mexicans surrounded J.S. and jabbered in Spanish. Joe yelled, "You t'ink me steal, eh? Examine de hides! Look more! Here is annoder one."[7]

When J.S. ignored the Mexican leader, Joe grabbed for his double-edged knife. There is little doubt he would have used it on J.S., if not for the interceding of Judge Conaway. The Mexicans reluctantly stepped aside and let J.S. ride away, unharmed.

J.S., traveling with his brother Valentine, left Brown's Hole without seeing Mexican Joe again. The men, with some help from some drovers, trailed thirteen hundred head of Crawford-

Thompson cattle up the Fort Bridger-Brown's Hole road - a military road established in 1863 by Major Noyes Baldwin - and on to Evanston. When they arrived there, J.S. quit his job tending cattle and he and Valentine went to search along the Bear River for a permanent location to start a ranch. They put up hay on the river that summer so they could winter the sixty head of cattle they had accumulated. However, the mosquitoes, gnats, and horse and deer flies were unbearable. They decided not to remain in that country. Later that fall, Valentine stayed to look after their interests on Bear River and J.S. took some of the cattle back to Brown's Hole.

When J.S. rode back into the valley, his friend Jack Gunn warned him about Mexican Joe. Through his tobacco-stained mustache Jack said, "Old Joe's not forgot your quarrel. He's out to get you, boy."

J.S. was spooked. Without letting anyone know he was leaving, he saddled his horse and fled Brown's Hole for the safety of Bear River and his brother. Upon hearing J.S.'s story, Valentine immediately left for the valley to take his brother's place. He was not going there with his eyes closed. He knew what Mexican Joe was capable of, having met him in South Pass in 1868.

It was bound to happen, the confrontation between Mexican Joe and Valentine Hoy. It happened when the two men met at Jimmy Goodson's place on Willow Creek. Valentine didn't back down when Joe began to goad him.

Instead, he instigated an agrument about some missing Hoy cattle. As he had done so many times in the past, Joe began his game. He took his knife from its scabbard and, with the words starting low in his throat, began making fun of the other man. The tension was strong.

Suddenly, yelling out that J.S. was "a lying son-of-a-bitch," Joe lunged with the purpose of slitting Valentine Hoy wide open. Unexpectedly, Valentine jumped up to meet Joe. With his fist moving in a blur he slammed Joe between the eyes, knocking him halfway across the cabin. As Joe landed head first in the corner, Valentine "drew his sheath knife from his boot top and aimed with one blow or slash to rip the Mexican from end to end. As the blow was descending, two or three other men who were in the cabin at the time, caught his arm so that the stroke only split one of Joe's buttocks half in two."[8]

The injury Joe received was so painful that standing was the only position in which he found comfort for over a month. He had never been put down before. He was miserable. His ego ached worse than the wound. It was the common belief among the cowhands that one would kill the other when Valentine Hoy and Mexican Joe met again.

That meeting occurred amid a large group of cowhands at the head of Willow Creek. However, everyone was surprised when "Joe was the quietest and most peacefully inclined. All he wanted was to make a treaty with his late antagonist."[9]

Knuckling under to the white man was not easy for Joe, who had never stopped believing that because of his ancestry, he deserved some prominence in life. He was bound to try to regain some of his lost esteem, which was unfortunate for a young Brown's Hole cowboy named Charlie Harper. That confrontation, too, took place in the Goodson cabin. However, the outcome was far different.

When Joe rushed Charlie with his knife, the man panicked and fumbled for his gun. Before the revolver cleared the holster, Joe had Charlie in his grip.

"Help! Somebody help me!" Charlie screamed.

Two cowboys hurried to Charlie's aid, but not in time to save him from being badly cut. As soon as Charlie Harper could ride, Brown's Hole never saw him again.

The valley did eventually see J.S. Hoy. He bought the James Widdop ranch near Evanston and served in the Wyoming Territorial Legislature in 1876. After he learned that his other brothers, Benjamin and Adea, had settled in Brown's Hole and that Valentine had put Mexican Joe in his place, J.S. returned. (The Spicers broke their ties with the Hoys and eventually left the valley to go into the sheep business.) Using family money, the Hoys took control of the Brown's Hole river bottoms on the north side of the river to start five ranches. They also gained a reputation. The newly-arriving Brown's Hole settlers considered them to be "a grabby bunch."

Mexican Joe's manner mellowed with age and less was heard about him as time went on. Exactly how his days in the valley ended is not known. Some say he returned to New Mexico; others say he was stopped by a bullet in the chest; still others say he died of old age, while working for room and board as a Brown's Park ranch hand.

Chapter IX

THE WOMEN

A sprinkling of fair-skinned women had begun arriving in Brown's Hole by the mid-1870's. Their presence added a spice to the valley which had not existed before. These women, often the backbone of their families, were no strangers to hard work. Each day was filled with it. With stinging eyes and noses, they stirred boiling pots of lye and tallow or left-over kitchen grease and wood ashes, to make soap. Then with the hardened, parsnip-colored bars, they scrubbed grubby clothes and dirty kids in a creek, or if they had one, a washtub. They cooked beans and biscuits in camp kettles and dutch ovens in open fireplaces, and rocked sick babies beside the fire's amber warmth. Some of the women had the convenience of wood-burning stoves. From their ovens the smell of corn bread filled the house. On the flat iron surface above, potatoes and onions popped and fried beside simmering stew, or fresh deer steaks.

A few of these Brown's Hole women were good cowhands. Some were accused of rustling and even murder. Some were romanced by outlaws. Still others were content to mother their own brood, as well as anyone else who needed it. Some of their lives were rich and highly colorful, while others frayed and wore out early. Nevertheless, each had her place in the patchwork of lives which spread across the valley.

Before Brown's Hole had seen "Snapping Annie," her first white woman, she had heard her. Across a dew-scented morning in 1854, there had come the echoing crack of a bullwhip. Then, a little closer, rose a throaty "Whoa, Turk! Gee, Lion!" Moving slowly into sight, a wagon lurched and bumped across the roadless sagebrush. Loretta Ann Parsons sat upon the hard wooden seat with her husband, Warren P. Parsons, at her side, and easily handled the oxen lines.

When Annie and her husband moved into the cabin near the mouth of Lodore Canyon, it gave the bachelors of the valley something to think about. Taking in an Indian squaw for companionship, to cook and do chores, as well as for sexual pleasures, had been the common way of the early mountaineers. White women were rare and highly respected.

Samuel Clark Bassett, the California forty-niner and confirmed bachelor who had arrived with Louie Simmons two years earlier, couldn't help but admire the "female bullwhacker." With mixed emotions, he wrote in his diary:

Brown's Hole, June 22, 1854. Warren P. Parsons and his wife Annie, have arrived. Our first white squaw, "Snapping Annie," is expertly driving her slick oxen, Turk and Lion . . . Houri tells me that man's freedom in this paradise is doomed.

Annie and Warren Parsons had originally traveled from Quincy, Illinois, and made their home at Clear Creek (later known as Denver), before finding their way to Brown's Hole. How long the two stayed with the valley before returning to Denver is not known. Apparently Annie never did go back to Brown's Hole. However, her husband returned to their place on Dummie Bottom in 1876 and became the valley's first white man to die of natural causes when he passed away in 1879.

A brief visit with some of the other earliest female pioneers who came to the valley after Snapping Annie, would lead us to the doors of a medley of women.

Madame Forrestal was a flashy redhead who once worked in a circus side show as a contortionist. Prospector Jesse Ewing picked her up in Green River City and took her to his cabin in Brown's Hole in Jesse Ewing Canyon. Madame Forrrestal would be Jesse Ewing's worst mistake.

Molly Sears came from Denver in 1875 with her husband Charles B. Sears. The couple located on the south side of the river and would leave their last name to the nearby canyon and its clear running creek. Molly later helped her husband with his sheep business.

Mary Jane "Molly" Goodson married good-natured, trapper-prospector Jimmy. She went to live with him in the cabin where Mexican Joe fought with Valentine Hoy. Along with her husband, she raised a few vegetables, some kids, and a lot of hogs. Hog Lake got its name from wild descendants of the Goodson pigs.

Jennie Jaynes was kind-hearted and married to hardworking Henry Whitcomb Jaynes. Henry was a "working fool" with a shovel. He built a flume in Sears Canyon and spent time digging two long ditches. While living in a dugout, Jennie served as the valley's first schoolteacher.

Mrs. William Blair lived with her husband at the bottom edge of Brown's Hole in a deep, narrow canyon called Bull Canyon, where the Hoys wintered their bulls. She taught school after Jennie Jaynes, in a log school house built on Beaver Creek. She was upstairs in her son-in-law's Red Creek ranch house when a teenage boy was shot in the back. This event would touch off the end of the outlaw era in Brown's Hole.

Julia Blair Hoy was the daughter of William Blair and married the dashing Valentine Hoy. Along with her mother, she taught school at Beaver Creek. She donated the land for the Brown's Hole cemetery. The repercussions of the shooting of the teenage boy at Red Creek would tragically touch her.

Mrs. G.W. "Griff" Edwards was married to a big Welshman who had prospected, then ran stores in Evanston and Rock Springs before taking up the cattle business with W.G. "Billy" Tittsworth. He stood his ground in Brown's Hole when "asked" to leave by the Hoys. She stood by Griff when he became a sheep rancher.

Elizabeth Goodman was married to the heavy-bearded oarsman who had quit Major John Powell at Disaster Falls. She was persuaded by her husband to return with him to the valley in 1876.

The Law sisters, Elizabeth, Jean, and Mary, traveled the Overland Trail in 1868, along with their mother, father (who was a Scot and a Mormon convert), and five other children. Although Deseret, Utah, had been their destination, when they reached Rock Springs their father decided to follow a hunch. He built his family a dugout in a hillside and eventually opened the first coal mine in the area. All three sisters were pretty girls. Billy Tittsworth met and fell in love with Jean. At age fourteen, she was the first of the girls to marry. She moved with her new husband to his ranch on Gap Creek. When George Law moved his family on, to the Mormon community of Paradise, he allowed Elizabeth and Mary to visit their married sister at the Tittsworth Gap Ranch. Before a year had passed, cheerful Lizzie had married proper acting Charles Allen. They located on the Green River meadows (Allen Bottom) and Charles became a justice of the peace in Brown's Hole.

Seventeen-year-old Mary, with her long hair and kind disposition, married a good friend of Billy Tittsworth's on May 15, 1879. Life with Charlie Crouse was not dull, but neither was it easy. Mary's husband was destined to be one of Brown's Hole's most salty and memorable characters.

Nellie Barr Jarvie emigrated from the British Isles with her family. They had settled for a while in Pennsylvania, but were on their way to Ogden, Utah, when Nellie met John Jarvie, a Scottish emigrant and a saloon operator in Rock Springs. Her husband would become one of Brown's Hole's most loved and respected friends.

Alice Davenport married a Welsh coal miner from Rock Springs by the name of Tom Davenport. She then made her home with him for some time at their Willow Creek Ranch. Alice was a large, billowy woman with a cozy disposition and a love for neighbors and friends. She, like several other Brown's Hole women, had to put up with her man's fondness for the whiskey bottle.

Elizabeth Cooper Erickson was a pretty daughter of early western pioneers. She married John Erickson, a young man from Nodra Lulea, Sweden, who had been ranching in Wyoming at Mud Springs with his brother, Oscar. After their marriage, John and Elizabeth were familiar faces in Brown's Hole. They homesteaded just north of there in Wyoming, on the edge of a lush meadow which they named Meadow Gulch. When John died, Elizabeth married Henry Kent and helped with the running of what became the successful Erickson-Kent Sheep Company. Elizabeth's husband, Henry Kent, along with Charlie Sparks, would later escort hired killer Tom Horn to Cheyenne to be tried for murder.

Catherine Warren was a tall, dark-eyed waitress in Rock Springs when she met and married the huge, bushy-faced Jim Warren. He had once studied for the ministry but had given it up to become a rancher and part-time cattle rustler on Diamond Mountain. Catherine was a good influence on Jim and bore him five children. After they sold out on Diamond, they lived for a while on Beaver Creek.

Armida "Auntie" Thompson had served as an army nurse during the war between the states. She married "Longhorn" Thompson and moved with him to a homestead just a little east of Brown's Hole. Tough, yet kind, she became an important influence to a Brown's Hole family of motherless children.

Daphne Dunster Parsons married Snapping Annie's son, Dr. John D. Parsons, on Sept. 19, 1849, in Illinois. She gave birth to a son, Warren D., and a daughter, Helena. She followed her dynamic husband to Denver where he was a physician, dairy farmer, and businessman. In financial ruin, they started anew in Brown's Hole in 1875. Daphne's husband would be the valley's only medical doctor and first postmaster.

Helena Parsons was born on May 17, 1861, in Leadville, Utah. She came to the valley with her parents at the age of fourteen. She married Lewis Allen on August 11, 1879, in her father's home. It was the first white wedding ceremony in the valley. Her oldest daughter died when only eleven months old and was buried in the meadow at the Parsons place.

Mary Eliza Chamberlain Bassett, a slender blonde, was born to a well-to-do family on a southern plantation on August 28, 1857. Elizabeth, as she was called, was orphaned early. She and her sister, Hanna, moved to Norfolk, Virginia, to live with their mother's parents, Grandmother and Grandfather Crawford.

At the young age of fourteen, she married Amos Herbert Bassett, a soft-spoken, educated, and gentle-natured man of thirty-seven. Her husband was an "indoor" man and was never very strong. In contrast, Elizabeth was exceptionally capable. Her classic breeding and strength of character remained with her always. Elizabeth had grit, as well as grace, and would pass both of these qualities on to her Brown's Hole reared daughters. One daughter would be whispered a murderess, the other would be called "Queen of the Cattle Rustlers."[1]

Dr. John Parsons

Chapter X
THE FAMILIES

The families came to Brown's Hole packing their belongings and their dreams. Snapping Annie's son, John D. Parsons, came to Brown's Hole in about 1874. He had been born February 26, 1818, in Illinois. He and his wife, Daphne, and their children, Warren and Helena, later moved to Denver. There John was a practicing physician, dairy farmer, and businessman. John established a mint where $2.50 and $5 gold coins were made. He helped write the by-laws of the newly organized Colorado Stock Growers Association and served as its president in 1868. In 1870 he started the Denver Woolen Mills. Unfortunately, on top of his land-mining-smelter obligations, he invested very heavily in a Denver irrigation project. Shortly after that, the bottom dropped out of things.

When Dr. John Parsons, his wife, Daphne, and daughter, Helena, reached Brown's Hole, they were nearly broke. Nevertheless, at fifty-six years of age, being a man of much determination and energy, the doctor started building.

Before long a solid, three-room cabin sat near a creek, closely protected from behind and on the right by hills with plenty of cedars looking off the ridges. The front view was of the Green River with the mountain border beyond. Dr. Parsons later built a smelter across the river on Bake Oven Flat where he worked at mining and smelting ore. He and Daphne had a new home and Brown's Hole had her first family and medical doctor.₁

Samuel Bassett and Dr. Parsons discovered they had common interests, so they visited often and became good friends.

Samuel had a brother, three years his senior, living and working as a judge in Arkansas. For some time Samuel had been urging Herbert to come to Brown's Hole, feeling certain the dry climate would relieve his older brother's bouts with asthma. Word finally came that Herbert had agreed and, along with his wife and two children, would soon be arriving at the Green River City train station.

Amos Herbert Bassett had been born on July 31, 1834, in New York. He graduated from college and became a school teacher in Illinois. As with so many, the Civil War changed his life. In 1861 when President Abraham Lincoln called for three hundred thousand more men, one of the volunteers was Herbert. A player of many instruments, he served as the company bandleader. After the war, he worked for a while as a revenue collector in Norfolk, Virginia. It was there that the tall man of thirty-seven captured the heart and won the hand of Mary Elizabeth Chamberlain.

When Herbert, Elizabeth, four-year-old Josephine "Josie," and little Sam stepped from the train, Samuel and Dr. Parsons were waiting. Each had driven a wagon in order to haul all the family's belongings in one trip. Samuel's wagon was pulled by two huge oxen. Although Josie watched the big steers suspiciously, she liked Uncle Samuel and rode all the way of the several day trip to Brown's Hole in his wagon. The fact that the wagon was hitched to the lumbering oxen etched the bumpy trip forever in Josie's mind.

When Elizabeth saw Brown's Hole and smelled the fragrant blend of sage, greasewood, river moisture, cedar, wild flowers, and cottonwood leaves, she sighed. The woman felt the valley's warm welcome and declared that the place should never be called a "hole."

The wagons reached Willow Creek, turned left, and followed the stream to a cabin in a grove of cottonwoods. It sat in a meadow which fanned out and sloped gently toward the river.

Josie gave the building the once over and said, "This is a funny little cabin, isn't it, Mother?"

Elizabeth answered, "Well, I suppose the men who built it had no real use for windows or a floor. It served them fine as a shelter and that's what we need right now, too."

Before long the abandoned cabin was clean and made cozy. It had feather beds, shelves lined with supplies, and the smells of a family settling in.

Uncle Samuel introduced his brother's family to the Indians and their ways. The Utes were camped all around and became an everyday sight to the family from the east. Two kind-hearted old cattlemen, Hank Ford and Frank Orr, who lived across the river, came to visit occasionally. Hank Ford only had one eye, the other being nothing more than a hull. Josie and her little brother, Sam, loved the two old fellows and were thrilled with the river rides they were given in the men's skiff.

The Bassetts also met Mexican Joe, Judge Conaway, and their friend and sometimes partner, John "Jack" Rife.

Occasionally Herbert engaged in enjoyable and educated conversations with Judge Conaway. Mexican Joe was very friendly to the family. He told them of a fine home site he thought they should consider that was down his way, at either Joe Springs or Pablo Springs.

Jack Rife had come to Brown's Park about 1869 and was a jovial mountaineer with a big dangling watch fob and lots of rings on his fingers. He knew and understood the way of the

Indians and smoothly spoke the Ute language. He had a deep fondness for, and a special way with animals. With the permission of Ute Chief Douglas, he attempted to establish a wildlife preserve on the north side of Douglas Mountain just east of Brown's Park. Shaggy-haired Sampson and Delilah were his two pet buffalo and the reason he came to be called "Buffalo Jack." He became a good friend to the Bassetts.

One evening in May, 1874, when Brown's Park was busy dealing with a late spring snowstorm, Elizabeth was busy dealing with childbirth. As the storm grew worse, so did the pain. Finally, with the gentle coaxing of Dr. Parsons, Elizabeth gave birth to a daughter. The valley's first white baby sucked gulps of air and cried. She was healthy but hungry. The birth had been a difficult one for Elizabeth and her body refused to give the warm nourishment tiny Anna needed. It was Buffalo Jack who gathered the squalling infant and carried her out into the snowstorm. In a Ute camp not far away, another newborn slept soundly; his belly was full. After a few signs were made and a few words spoken, the little Indian boy's mother, See-a-baka, willingly put the white child to her breast. See-a-baka continued to be wet nurse for little Anna until the day Judge Conaway came into sight, heading toward the Bassett door. Moving along slowly in front of him, her head bobbing gently with each step, walked a milk cow.

Within the next year, Brown's Park made room for Buffalo Jack's brother, Edward, and his wife, Genevieve, as well as Charles B. and Molly Sears. The Rifes settled on Diamond Mountain near Pot Creek and the Sears' made a home up the creek from the Parsons place.

In an attempt to fit into the ways of the valley, Herbert bought twenty head of heifers. Neither he nor Elizabeth had ever branded a cow before. However, with the help of friends, the smell of singed cow hair soon curled into the air. Later as the little Bassett herd spread to feed in the meadow, branded on the ribs of each heifer was a fresh U with a P connected. Elizabeth watched the stock, proud of her and Herbert's start in the cattle business.

Then in September, 1879, word came that there may be trouble. For quite a while things had been tense at the White River Agency in Colorado, southeast of Brown's Park. Nathan C. Meeker, agent in charge of the Yampatica Ute Reservation, had pushed and bullied the Indians to live the way he dictated to them. He was adamant, even though it went against their nature, that the Indians settle into routine home lives as farmers. Meeker wouldn't let them move around in the summer, and also tried to put a stop to their enthusiasm over horse racing by plowing up their race track and their best pony pasture.

53

Finally, in his obsession to subdue the Indians, he held back their rations with threats of "You'll work or you'll starve!"

Though rumblings from the reservation were heard in the surrounding areas, they were ignored. One day an angry sub-chief assaulted Meeker while other braves set fire to the haystacks. The white agent realized he had lost control and summoned help. Troops were immediately dispatched from Ft. Steele in Wyoming. However, Major Thornburgh and his 190 men never reached the reservation. On the Milk Creek branch of the Yampa River, the company rode into an Indian ambush. During the battle, Joe Rankin slipped past the Indian lines and rode hard for Rawlins. His ride was incredibly swift, 170 miles in 28 hours. Nevertheless, by the time Colonel Merrett and his five hundred men from Ft. Russell arrived, Major Thornburgh and thirteen of his men had been killed. The surviving soldiers had defended themselves in hand-dug trenches.

While some Indians had held the Ft. Steele company down, a group of the enraged Utes rode back to the reservation and killed Meeker and some other white men. They kidnapped Meeker's wife and daughter, along with several other white women and children.

Fear swept across the country like a fast-moving storm, leaving people hurrying to gather belongings and heading for various settlements in the area. Chief Marcisco told the Bassetts no one in Brown's Park would be bothered. Elizabeth wasn't afraid and would just as soon have stayed in her little home overlooking the Green River. However, the Parsons' went to Ashley (later called Vernal), Utah, and the Bassetts and Charles and Molly Sears moved to the protection of Green River City in Wyoming.[2]

Before long the military troops put an end to the uprising. The northern Colorado Utes were relocated further west, to the Whiterocks Agency in Utah. In 1881 Ft. Thornburgh was established near there in order to insure against anything like the Meeker Massacre happening again.

The Bassetts returned to their place on Willow Creek, anxious to find their cows and see how they had fared. They were dumbfounded when they discovered that in their absence, a man by the name of Metcalf had altered their brand to look like his by simply putting a 7 in front of their UP brand.

Herbert walked back and forth across the room and said to Elizabeth, "Well, I guess we're just stranded, that's all. Just stranded!"

"Oh, no we are not!" Elizabeth answered. "I know some of those cows and I'm taking them!"

After she and Metcalf stood toe to toe, he went on his way and she did just as she said she would, she took her cows.

Elizabeth helped re-brand the cows using her new D-K brand. She continued to use the D-K brand from then on.3

In a short while the Bassetts packed and moved to the eastern edge of Brown's Park. At Joe Springs they found the spring water cold, sweet, and plentiful, and the shade of the tall cottonwoods enjoyable. Before long a row of small poplar trees stood beside a new two-room cabin of pine and spruce logs. Directly behind the cabin folded some foothills and beyond the foothills stood a mountain, nearly black with cedars and pines. Strewn among those trees were large red sandstone cliffs with orange lichen-splotched ledges. Across the valley towered the Gates of Lodore. The cabin was hugged on the right by a rocky, sage-covered hill. Behind the hill each evening, the sun painted an ever-changing sky with golds, lavenders, and pinks.

Although the Bassetts hauled in some fine pieces of bedroom furniture and an organ, Herbert made most of their furniture from birch and rawhide. Stitched buckskin cushions were stuffed with milkweed floss. Sturdy shelves soon held Herbert's many books.

Curtains for the windows were made from velvety-tanned buckskin bought with ten pounds of sugar from a friendly squaw named Indian Mary. They were hung from birch rods on curtan rings sawed from deer leg bones.4

Herbert soon went to work organizing a school district. The first school was held in Henry and Jennie Jaynes' dugout. Teacher Jennie had four students, including her own two children and Josie and Sam Bassett. School was held for three winter months, with the Bassett children boarding with the Jaynes family during the week. By the time Ann was old enough for school, a nice log building had been built on a nearby hill.

Judge Asbury Conaway started drinking less whiskey. He enjoyed his visits with the Bassett family and brought several books to add to Herbert's library. One day, with a sparkle in his eyes, he took young Sam and little Ann on an adventure to Pablo Springs. The children were intrigued when he showed them what looked like tiny moccasin tracks chipped along the large boulders. They followed the footprints and were led to a big, gnarled cedar tree. As their eyes lifted upward, they saw a little burial scaffold of willow and sinew in the top branches. Cradled in it were the remains of a little papoose, wrapped in a woven blanket of cedar bark threads and gray rabbit fur. The two white children stood in silence. No place on earth would ever seem more special, no secret more sacred.

Not long after that, Judge Conaway left his friend Mexican Joe and Brown's Park. He moved to Green River City to practice law, the occupation he had been educated for and had run away from so long ago.

Although he was a sight, dressed in his shrunken buckskin trousers, worn Prince Albert coat, and top hat, A.B. Conaway became an influential Wyoming legal figure. Starting as a practicing lawyer, he became the Sweetwater County Attorney. Eventually his legal brilliance took him to the high office of Justice on the Wyoming Supreme Court. In spite of his success, he didn't lose his fondness for Brown's Park. He occasionally visited to do some prospecting and to see the Bassetts and his other friends.

The Bassett family had grown to four children, with the birth of Elbert "Eb" on June 21, 1880, in Green River. (Elizabeth later gave birth to her fifth and final child, George, on March 29, 1884.) Their home, being near the east entrance of Brown's Park, became the common place for travelers to stop. Elizabeth and Herbert opened their home to anyone needing a hot meal or a night's sleep.

By 1880 Brown's Park began to hear voices and music at social gatherings and dances. Several new families had come to share their lives with her. Many ranches, including the Bassett Ranch, were forming in and around the valley. By then the Hoys had squatted on a good share of Brown's Park and planned to have much more.

In 1884 when the survey of Brown's Park and surrounding country was completed, Herbert Bassett went to Hahn's Peak on September 22, to have his place at Joe Springs properly recorded. Some other Brown's Park people put off going, only to discover later that the Hoys had beaten them to the land office and gained control of a lot of their ground. Herbert was shocked to learn that Valentine Hoy, who had gained inside information while cooking for the survey crew, had tried to swindle Joe Springs away. Many, including Herbert, never forgave the Hoys for their underhanded actions.

After his return to Brown's Park, even though he married, J.S. Hoy didn't get along very well with anyone. He often found fault with the men and was stand-offish, even with his family. He occasionally swore out warrants on a Hoy family member or some neighbor for encroaching on his property and stealing his stock. Through the years he often hurt Brown's Park and damaged her reputation by writing letters to the surrounding newspapers. In them he said, "Brown's Park is a den of unclean beasts, and a roost for unclean birds." Then he would go on to tell of rampant rustling and thievery among the valley's residents. One day, when a group of Brown's Park women were visiting, someone mentioned, "That Jesse Hoy is getting more ornery every day." Another agreed and said she had made a deal with him for some hay because he would have nothing to do with her husband.

"Well, he's a different sort all right," Mrs. Adea Hoy said. "But, it's a rather sad tale that's back of the way he acts. My husband, Adea, told me that when J.S. was a baby he took sick. He said that for some reason, in order to save the boy's life, the doctors had to remove his testicles. I think it works on him and he's jealous of other men."

It then came to Elizabeth and the others why they had occasionally heard J.S. referred to as "the Old Steer."

The Bassetts were lucky the day a tall, black, Texas cowboy named Isom Dart left Clay's Middlesex Land and Cattle Company where he was wrangling horses, and went to work for them. The entire family came to love and admire Isom. The Negro cowboy never lost his fondness for all children. He enjoyed playing the fiddle for them and teaching them his expert skill with horses and ropes.

Good looking Madison "Matt" Rash, who was born in Texas in 1865, and Isom Dart, who was born in Texas in 1855, were long-time friends. Matt had been the trail boss of the herd of Texas cattle that had brought both Isom Dart and Matt north to the Middlesex operation.

Matt Rash worked for a while for the Middlesex, then became foreman for Tim Kinney's Circle K Cattle Ranch. He didn't like the Middlesex. It was large and hungry, and bent on acquiring all the land it could. The Brown's Park people joined together to fight it and its flood of cattle. Only Jack Gunn was willing to sell his place.

When the Middlesex forced Tim Kinney out, he sold his land to the company, but bought sheep and turned them loose on his old range. Jack Gunn also bought sheep, and along with Griff and Jack Edwards put even more sheep on the Middlesex range. During the bad winter of 1879-1880, rustlers and the grass-grubbing sheep nearly put the Middlesex under. In 1884 cattle prices dropped sharply. The Middlesex investors in Boston were screaming and the Middlesex was gasping for breath. The rough winter of 1886-1887 finished the outfit. Buffalo Jack Rife's brother, Ed Rife, bought what cattle was left. Soon the only reminders of the large cattle operation were rotted cattle carcasses and the name of Clay Basin that was given to the sloping, curving country north of Brown's Park. The Brown's Park people were not sorry to see the Middlesex go under. J.S. Hoy was the exception. He often regretted not selling when he had the chance.

Matt Rash had shown up in Brown's Park with a small herd of

57

cattle after Tim Kinney sold his place. He stayed with the Bassetts for a while, then built a cabin, bought Frank Goodman's cattle, and settled into a life in the valley.

Isom Dart built a cabin at Summit Springs on Cold Spring Mountain. By breaking and selling wild horses, he got the money to start his own herd. Both Isom and Matt worked closely with, and were good friends with, the Bassetts.

While Herbert busied himself around the home place, Elizabeth tended the growing cattle herd from the side saddle on her favorite horse, Calky. Their operation grew steadily. Soon a bunkhouse was required to sleep the hired hands.

One ranch hand, Jack Rollas, was a polite, young cowboy who wandered in from Texas in 1882. Good with horses, he was hired by the Bassetts to gentle some broncs.

Late that fall, Elizabeth was outside near the spot where Herbert, Harry Hindle, and Perry Carmichael were busy whipsawing lumber. Jennie Jaynes had been hired to be ranch cook. She was in the kitchen with her dress sleeves rolled up, cooking the noon meal. When she looked out the window, Jennie saw three men riding in. She went to the door to greet them.

"Well, you fellows are just in time. You're welcome to eat with us here in a few minutes if you're hungry."

"No thank you, we were just wonderin' if maybe Jack Rollas was around someplace."

"Why yes, he is."

Jennie pointed toward the corral and said, "That's Jack over there, saddling up that horse."

Without another word, the strangers turned and walked three abreast toward the corral. Because his back was turned, Jack was unaware of their presence. As the unsuspecting cowboy reached for a bridle, one of the men pulled his pistol and fired. Jack jerked forward, then ran for the back of the barn. There he fell. Jennie flew from the kitchen, gathered the saucer-eyed Bassett children and swept them into the house. Elizabeth, Herbert, Perry, and Harry ran for their guns. In a few seconds, sawed-off shotguns were leveled on the strangers.

After the men threw down their guns, Herbert and Perry Carmichael ran to the aid of the wounded man and carried him into the bunkhouse. The three strangers were herded along behind and lined up against the wall. Elizabeth's face burned in anger.

Elizabeth held one of the retrieved Winchesters steady and demanded, "Who are you and why in the world have you come in here and shot Jack like this?"

The one who had done the shooting answered, "My name is Hambleton. That man killed my brother two years ago in

Abilene! It's taken me this long, but I finally got my chance to settle things."

Elizabeth answered, "Well, you don't come in here and shoot an unarmed man in the back! I don't care what your reasons are. You just don't do it!"

Weakened from the loss of blood, Jack murmured, "I did kill a man by the name of Hambleton two years ago. He married my sister then he turned mean. He beat her something awful and I just couldn't stand it!"

"Here, Jack," Elizabeth said, as she held the gun out to him. "Go ahead and kill that thing who shot you. Kill every one of 'em if you want to."

Jack, already too far gone, never took the gun. Harry Hindle left to find the justice of the peace, Charles Allen. Herbert and Perry took the three captives to the house. Elizabeth and Jennie stayed with Jack, to do for him what they could. Once in the house, Herbert became more and more nervous. He didn't know what might come of things when news of the back-shooting reached the other settlers.

Later, when the neighbors began to arrive at the Bassett place, they learned that poor Jack had died and his murderers had escaped. Herbert had little to say. Knowing his decision would be in direct conflict with his wife, it was a long time before he admitted what he had done.

After Herbert had paced the floor for a while, he had told his prisoners to go to their horses and ride hard for the county seat at Hahn's Peak and turn themselves in. Of course, the three never went near Hahn's Peak. Still Herbert felt sure he had prevented further tragedy.5

Releasing those men would probably never had occurred to Elizabeth. Though she was a woman with a lot of style, she was also tough. She got tougher as her ranch grew. With her loyal cowboys at her side, Elizabeth did what she felt had to be done for her ranch. A pile of shriveled cowhide and bleached bones at the bottom of a high Lodore Canyon cliff gave credence to the story which circulated around the country about Elizabeth. It was said that the cattlewoman, cornered with a herd of ill-gotten cattle, chose to run the animals over the cliff's edge rather than be caught.

One day, Herbert knew there was activity at the corral. He didn't pay much attention to it until he noticed the worried bawls made only by separated cows and calves. When the bawling continued, Herbert went to see what was causing the ruckus. As he neared the corral he saw several head of cows pacing around it. Saliva streamed from their mouths as they bellowed at the bunch of calves locked inside. Then Herbert saw that not one of the cows wore the Bassett D-K brand. Instead they carried a variety of other brands. In the middle of the slick (unbranded) calves in the corral, was his bustling wife with a hot iron in her hand. Herbert stood gaping for a moment, then he clicked his heels together, turned, and walked swiftly away.[6]

Molly Sears   Charlie Sears
                        (Courtesy of Stanley Crouse, Jr.)

Chapter XI
JOHN JARVIE

John Jarvie began his life in 1844 in the green hills of Scotland. In his youth he labored in the damp darkness of a Scottish mine until the day his hard-nosed supervisor beat him nearly to death. John never went back to the mine. When next a ship sailed from the coast of Scotland for the shores of America, she had at least one young Scot stowed away.

In time John Jarvie chose the Wyoming territory to go into business. In 1871 on North Front Street, just across from the Union Pacific depot in Rock Springs, the Will Wale Saloon became the Jarvie Saloon. John's little business consisted of a kitchen, dining room, and a storeroom. He was licensed to sell wholesale and retail liquor and to operate a billiard table. On October 8, 1875, John Jarvie became a naturalized citizen of the United States.

John continued in his saloon business until 1880 when he met twenty-two year old Nellie Barr. Nellie had the most exquisite singing voice, and was so pretty, sensitive, and kind, that John loved her immediately. On June 17, Nellie proved she loved John just as dearly when she became his wife.

In a short while the newlyweds left the busy goings-on of Rock Springs for a life in a cove, sheltered by the hills and mountains in Brown's Park. Their plan was to put up a store on the north bank of the Green River near the old military road. For temporary shelter, while they built their log home and store, they lived in a dugout. The dugout was built for them by red-haired Bill Lawrence.₁ It was a spacious, two-room shelter with squared sides and log supports. The split cedar posts supporting the dirt ceiling were hefty ones, measuring more than a foot across. A shaved piece of cottonwood tree trunk was fitted to the entrance for the door. To make such a dugout more cozy and homey, the earth walls were probably covered with muslin. In such dugouts, the floor was usually spread with a thick layer of chopped cattail rushes, which was then covered with a multi-colored rag carpet.

The sagebrush grew extra tall there, with a few wild cucumber vines tangling around some of their bushy arms. Thin-branched willows, tall cottonwoods, clumps of salt grass and wispy, pinkish tamaracks grew along the nearby river shore. The dugout was so close to the river that the Jarvies could listen to its soothing roar as it smoothly flowed by.

When John and Nell were able to move from the cozy, dark dwelling into their clean new home, they turned the dugout into a storage cellar. It was an important time for the Jarvies, and the Brown's Park residents, when the general store and trading post opened for business.

It would be hard to imagine the value of the close availability of food, supplies, guns, boats, saddles, or wagon parts to the isolated people. Of course, the whiskey barrel was not forgotten, but neither was the candy. The Jarvies and their store soon became welcome friends in the valley.

In 1881 their first child John, Jr. was born. That same year their neighbor from down and across the river, Dr. John Parsons, died. Dr. Parsons had served as the valley's first postmaster since October 23, 1878, for a salary of $19.30 a year. Dr. Parsons had also been important to the travelers going to and from Ashley Valley because he had operated a ferry. After the doctor died, John Jarvie relocated the post office and the ferry to his place up river.

As the Jarvie family grew with the births of Tom, Archie, and Jimmy, so did the Jarvie place. Business was good. Soon there were corrals, stables, a blacksmith shop, and a stone house for storage.

John "Jack" Bennett was hired to build the stone building. Bennett was an ex-convict from Arkansas who had learned stonecutting work while in prison. He did a fine job in constructing the cream-colored rock building.

Below the house was a little pasture which ran beside the river. The ground was fertile and in the spring the grasses came up in abundance. Before long though, the summer sun baked

John Jarvie

Nell Jarvie

John Jarvie

(All courtesy of Stanley Crouse, Jr.)

the moisture from the soil and the grass shriveled and browned.

John put his finger to the side of his nose and thought the problem through. Then he set to work building a waterwheel. It ended up a good-sized structure which turned round and round in a pleasant rhythm. Buckets attached to paddles filled with water, then raised into the air and dumped with a splash into a flume. The wooden trough carried the water to a little ditch which carried the river water to the field. As the water spread across the ground, the killdeer ran through it and sang, mosquitoes laid more eggs, and the grass jumped to life.

John loved to read. He had quite a collection of books and was happy to loan them out to his neighbors. The newspapers and other items which came through the mails kept him abreast of current events. He was always happy to share and discuss such things. Another thing John "read" was people's skulls. He would lay his hands on their heads, and from the shape of their skulls he could tell about their personality traits and their feelings.[2] The formal terminology for the practice is called "phrenology."

In 1887 John got disgusted with the postal service. He was asked to spy on a postmaster in Vernal who was suspected of mishandling his duties. John simply sacked up the inks, pens, and all else to do with the post office, and sent it back. In 1890 Herbert Bassett was appointed the new postmaster.[3]

John accumulated several pieces of ground in both Colorado and Utah. He was pretty successful in raising some cattle and horses, but prospecting never made him a dime.

When someone rode by to announce there was going to be a "shindig," it pleased Nell and John because they loved to join the fun. Nellie became "pretty little Nell" to their Brown's Park friends and she was often asked to sing. Sometimes John joined his wife in song, and at other times he accompanied her on the concertina or organ.

Other social gatherings went on in the Park. They bore no resemblance to the family dances with their gossip group and midnight suppers. They were the poker parties where the smell of liquor, tobacco, and sometimes tension grew thick in the air. Men like John Jarvie and Herbert Bassett had no interest in such gatherings. Men like Jesse Ewing did.

Before arriving in Brown's Park, Jesse Ewing had been a stage station keeper on the Overland Trail and a miner at South Pass. He later entered into a mining partnership with a former mayor from Cheyenne named H.M. Hook. Along with two other men, Ewing and Hook loaded their boats with supplies at Green River City and headed down the river. However, Hook never made it past a submerged rock in Red Canyon. It tore the bottom from his boat and threw him into the water where he drowned. His body was recovered and he was buried in Brown's Park, beside the river which had claimed him. The other two men lost interest in the valley after the tragedy. Jesse Ewing stayed and built a cabin at the head of a steep canyon which sliced through the red dirt of Mountain Home. There he worked among the cedars, digging a mine into the hillside.

Brown's Park knew Jesse Ewing as a quiet, slow-talking man who never laughed out loud. He was small, but wiry and tough-looking, and usually kept to himself. He didn't like to talk about his past. He seldom carried a gun but depended on his sharp knife. No one who knew him had any interest in provoking him.4

Up the river a ways from the Jarvie store, beside the military road which crossed the river at Indian Crossing, went along the rocky hillside, then up Jackson Draw and on to Ashley Valley, stood two or three log cabins and an old rock house. There were no windows in the rock building. It had slits in the rocks about six inches wide and two or three feet in length, just the right size for a couple of rifle barrels to fit through.5 Though the folks around called it the old saloon, it had apparently once served as a military outpost.

One mid-winter day several men gathered at the old saloon for a bit of poker. Included in the group of gamblers was Jesse Ewing and a teenager named Charlie Roberts. After several hours of poker playing, Jesse Ewing sat back in his chair and silently frowned. He eyed the pile of money in front of the teenager, which had grown as his own pile had dwindled. When Charlie quit the game and walked out into the night, his pockets were heavy with Ewing's money. He humped up a bit, against the cold night's breath, then walked off the bank and onto the frozen river. Suddenly, something hit him in the back, sending him sprawling face first into the thin layer of snow on the ice. Terror and pain screamed inside him, then flickered to nothing.

The next morning the Jarvies were busy preparing for the day. The store door opened and Jesse Ewing stuck his head inside and said, "Go on up the river a ways Jarvie, and you'll find the purtiest corpse you ever saw."

With that he shut the door and went on, heading back to Jesse Ewing Canyon and his red-haired woman, Madame Forrestal. As John watched Ewing leave, he noticed the man wasn't wearing a coat. But then, he never had known him to wear one. John bundled up and hurried up the river where he saw the crumpled form on the ice ahead. He later told, many times, what he saw that morning. "My goodness, the tracks in the snow were plain. Ewing had to have jumped a good fifteen feet to stab that boy. Don't know how he did it, but the tracks were there!"

No one seemed to know the Roberts boy very well, nor where he had come from. He was buried next to the old rock building in as deep a grave as the men could dig in the frozen ground. Then a bunch of river rocks were piled on top. Although there was a scant judicial examination of the case, Jesse Ewing pled self-defense and nothing much came of it.[6]

It wasn't long after that a husky man named Duncan showed up at the Ewing cabin. Duncan glanced at Ewing's silent mistress, then looked the older man square in the eye.

Duncan said, "If you could use some help around here, I could sure use a place to hang my hat for a while."

Though it wasn't really in Ewing's nature to like having anybody hanging around, he decided it would be nice to have an extra pair of strong hands digging in the mine tunnel.

Day in and day out the two men ate breakfast together then walked through the cedars to the black-faced mine. They talked some, as they worked side by side. One morning Duncan got up looking sickly.

"I don't see how I can work today. I feel like hell," he said.

Jesse Ewing went to work alone. He put in a full, tiring day. When his stomach told him it was supper time, he put down his tools and started back to the cabin. Suddenly his entire world exploded. He fell - and he died. Stepping from behind a cedar tree Duncan raised Jesse Ewing's Winchester and made sure Ewing would never get up again.

Duncan and Madame Forrestal rode quickly away with everything of value they could pack. They stopped by the Jarvie store and told John that Jesse Ewing needed him at the cabin.

John Jarvie later helped bury Jesse Ewing just below the Jarvie pasture beside the river.[7] As the months came and went, no word of the redhead ever came back to the valley. However, the man who had freed her from Ewing's grip showed up alone in southern Utah, where he took his own life.

For the Jarvies, times were good. While the stagecoaches made their scheduled weekly runs during the 1880's and 1890's between Green River and Ashley Valley, the drivers of the Southern Stage Lines sometimes stopped by the store for a ride across the river on the ferry. Most often though, Smokey, Pete Hines, and other drivers crossed at the ford up-river named Indian Crossing. The stagecoaches then stopped at the stage relay station at a spring on the flat above Jarvies, which would later be named Kendall Spring. Then the coaches continued up Sears Canyon and on to Ashley Valley.

Through the years at his well-kept store, John Jarvie provided employment for several men. He almost always had someone hired to take a wagon to Rock Springs or Vernal and freight new supplies back to his store. Operating the ferry was another job several different people did for the Jarvies. One such operator was a friendly black man named Albert (Welhouse) Williams.

Albert was said to have "run off and left a woman and six kids back in Virginia."[8] He first came to Brown's Park with a traveling minstrel show as their heel-clicking buck-and-wing dancer.[9] He settled in the valley and worked off and on for different places. He had a blotchy complexion and was called "the Speckled Nigger" or most common "Speck Williams." He was also called "Nigger Albert." Albert was always known to buy good horses. When he went into town he spiffed up in his suit. With a five or ten dollar bill sticking out of his pocket he expected to be, and was, called "Mr." Williams.[10]

Before he was very old John Jarvie's brown hair and whiskers turned as white and silky as a jack rabbit's fur in winter. He loved watching and molding his boys and he loved handing out goodies to all the children. Whether he was reciting a Robert Burns poem, playing a Scottish ballad on the organ, gliding along the glassy river on ice skates, or reading people's heads, he was adoring life. And Brown's Park adored him.

Chapter XII

CHARLIE CROUSE

In 1860 a nine-year-old Virginia lad, named Charlie Crouse, walked alone across the countryside. The dark-haired boy hated that his father had died four years earlier, and hated the fact that his widowed mother had married J. Frank Tolliver. He decided he would have no more of them. So he left, to make it on his own in an unstable country that was shaking with the tension of the impending Civil War.

Somehow he survived it all, including taking an older boy's place in the draft and being inducted into the Union Army at age fourteen. When the war was over Charlie was a private, serving as an orderly to a major, also named Crouse, in the Dakota territory. His only "war wound" was a missing left thumb he'd chopped off with a hatchet while making a wagon brake block.[1]

When his soldiering days were over, he hauled freight for a while across the Laramie Plains. He learned the languages of the Indian tribes with which he came in contact and could converse easily with them. He could also shoot them!

In the 1870's he arrived in Green River City. There he made two friendships. One was with the owner of the livery stable, Aaron Overholt, the other was with rancher Billy Tittsworth. Aaron Overholt and Charlie became partners in numerous undertakings. Some of those undertakings would include owning thirty-three pieces of property in Vernal and importing jacks and running mules year around on Diamond Mountain.[2] While staying at Tittsworth Gap, Charlie learned about cowboying and stock raising from Billy Tittsworth, and several others.

At age twenty-seven he met and married seventeen-year-old Mary Law, when she came to visit her sister at the Tittsworth place on Gap Creek. Then the couple was off to Charlie's rock cabin on Diamond Mountain. The cabin sat in tall sagebrush near a mountain spring.[3] It was about four miles above the head of a box elder, chokecherry, and elderberry filled canyon. The red-walled canyon had a natural salt lick just above it, with mountain lion stalking its ridges and a rushing creek that was thick with beaver. It was later named after Charlie and became Crouse Canyon.

Mary was a sweet-natured girl with long hair.[4] She was determined from the first to make Charlie a good wife. She had only been married a short while when she got her first taste of what life was going to be like as Mrs. Crouse. Charlie had some horse dealing business in Pinedale, Wyoming, and was to be gone five days. As it turned out, while he was on his way home, a band of Arapahoe Indians intercepted him. They stole his new saddle horses and nearly killed him. He avoided capture and probably torture and death by hiding during the day, eating bitter still-green berries, and picking his way along rocky pathways at night. Finally, after seventeen days, Charlie saw his cabin peeking out from the tall, silver-leaved sagebrush.5 Inside was his very worried and lonesome young wife. Mary would suffer periods of loneliness many times through the coming years.

In the rock cabin on Diamond Mountain - named for cattleman Jim Diamond - Mary and Charlie's first child, Stanley, was born. In about 1880, Charlie took over squaw man Jimmie Reed's place and began building a ranch. Charlie and Mary first lived there in a dugout, then moved into the nearby log cabin that faced south toward the tree and willow-fringed creek.

In 1882 baby daughter Minnie was born in that log cabin.6 Before Clarence came along, Charlie hired a man to help him build a new home. Pine logs were hewed square, then the ends grooved so they would fit tightly together. With an auger, holes were bored in the proper places then wooden pegs were pounded into them with a hammer. Other logs were split and their faces smoothed. Those logs were placed side by side for the puncheon floor. The roof was topped with a thick layer of soil which soon sprouted a few cactus plants and sprigs of grass. The sturdy home gave comfort and shelter to the Crouses, and to many others who followed them. It absorbed years of rich history in the decades it sat perched on the bank above Crouse Creek.

Charlie built a horse and cattle operation and called it the Park Live Stock Company. On the bench above the house he planted a nice-sized apple orchard against the base of Diamond Mountain. The saplings took firm root in the rich ground. In a few years the trees were bearing several kinds of large, juicy apples and some crisp golden-fleshed crab apples. In the early dawn, deer could be seen stretching their necks in the orchard. They nibbled at the tender leaves and fruit, then spread out to feed in Charlie's bordering grain fields. Into those same fields flocked hundreds of white-chinned Canada geese.7

Mary felt bad that Charlie had no communication with his family. One day she wrote her mother-in-law and told her about Charlie and their life in Brown's Park. Not long afterward, on the Crouse doorstep with baggage in hands, stood Charlie's family. There was his stepfather Frank, his mother, Sarah, half brothers Joe and Columbus, and his half sister Amanderville "Mandy." (Mandy had been born shortly after Charlie ran away from home, on July 19, 1861.) As it turned out Charlie was pleased to have his family there. He was good to the Tollivers and helped them settle into a life in the valley.

At first Frank and Sarah Tolliver lived in a cabin near the spring just above the bench. They raised a good garden and Frank collected a lot of amber colored honey from his twenty-four stands of bees.

Sarah got acquainted with the people around and made several friends in Vernal. Whenever she wanted to go visiting, Charlie loaned her Dexter, his favorite saddle horse. Dexter was an easy-gaited quarter horse with a white striped face. One day while Sarah was in Vernal, she was invited to dine with an acquaintance named Mrs. Young. When she arrived at Mrs. Young's, Sarah was dressed in her long, black dress and starched, white apron. Her mouth watered at the steaming bowl of rich-looking soup that was placed before her. In the middle of some light-hearted dinner conversation, she scooped a large spoonful into her mouth. She nearly gagged! Sarah hadn't realized, until she felt and tasted one of the rubbery little creatures, that the soup was oyster stew. Sarah hated oyster stew! She had a dreadful time wallowing the oyster into the side of her cheek until she could manage to secretly spit it into her hand. Carefully, she then slipped it into her apron pocket. It was awful at the time but later became a funny story to share with her granddaughter, Minnie.[8]

The Tollivers stayed a few years in the cabin near the mouth of Crouse Canyon. Eventually their son, Joe, homesteaded on the bench across the river from the Jarvie place; Columbus had a cabin on Sears Creek, then homesteaded down the river a ways; Mandy married a man named Mike Lombard and moved to his place on lower Beaver Creek; Sarah and Frank moved up the creek from Mandy, to a cabin at the mouth of Beaver Creek Canyon.

Although Charlie Crouse became an anchor, of sorts, in upper Brown's Park, there was a rough side to him. He grew up in the midst of Indian fights and a civil war. It was a time when a low value was often placed on a human life.

Above almost everything else, Charlie loved his horses. He raised, traded, and raced thoroughbreds. One day in Vernal one of his favorite thoroughbreds came in second to a slick-coated gelding owned and ridden by a teenage boy. When Charlie couldn't get the boy to sell the horse, he invited him to Brown's Park.

"There's going to be a big race in Rock Springs that you ought to run this horse in. Stop by my place on your way through and have a look at my other horses."

The teenager took Charlie Crouse up on his invitation, but he never made it to Rock Springs.

George Law, Sr.

Mrs. George Law

Frank and Sarah Tolliver

Stanley, Minnie, and
Clarence Crouse

72

Charlie and Mary Crouse at new home on the Brown's Park Live
Stock Ranch

Charlie Crouse and cat, Stella

Mary Crouse
(Courtesy of Stanley Crouse, Jr.)

William Tittsworth
(Courtesy of Stanley Crouse, Jr.)

"I don't know what became of that kid," Charlie said later. "He rode in here one evening, had supper, and stayed the night. He got up and headed for Rock Springs first thing the next morning. Then his horse showed back up here alone."

Several men made a search but never found a trace of the teenager. In Charlie Crouse's pasture, a new champion gelding munched on grass with the other horses. In upper Crouse Canyon, among the sun warmed boulders, a young body lay cold and forever alone.9

Charlie sometimes raced horses against the Utes. He talked with them in their tongue, and gambled with them. One time he got into a fierce argument with a half-breed.

Charlie had enough of the man and said, "Breed, you get on your horse and you get off my place, now!"

With smoldering eyes the Indian stared at the white man and swung on his horse.

"I will kill you and your woman!" he sneered.

Charlie glared at the half-breed Indian then said, matter of factly, "Don't you ever come back across that river!"

The Indian kicked his horse in the ribs and galloped away.

Later that evening a silhouette moving on horseback appeared on top of the hill which overlooked the river and the Crouse ranch. The half-breed nudged his horse to hurry down the steep slope through the creamy sand. He reined the pony into the willows bordering the river, across the moist sandbar and into the river current. In a few minutes the horse climbed, puffing and dripping, onto the opposite bank about a mile from the Crouse house. Suddenly gunfire boomed out in the quiet.

The half-breed was buried in a thicket of bitter-sweet smelling willows nearby. The Indian's pony was turned loose to graze with the other Crouse horses.10

Albert Williams, the speckled-skinned black man, worked for Charlie. The two men did fine together, when they were sober. When they drank they could both be unpredictable and mean.

One afternoon Albert and Charlie had been drinking when Charlie gave Albert orders to push some bulls across the river. The river was running a little high and the old bulls didn't like it. They would start off the bank, but only go so far. They would shake their big heads and blow snot as they spun and broke back. Albert was soon on the fight. He jerked out his thirty-two pistol and peppered bullets around the bulls. Just then Charlie ran out of the willows screaming.

"What the hell you think you're doing?"

Instantly the two were wrestling, grunting, and slugging. They were in a clinch, staggering along a sand mound when Charlie gripped the handle of his knife. In the same instant that his foot slipped in the sand, he stabbed outward with the knife and felt it cut deep into Albert.

A little later Charlie walked into the house. By his look Mary knew something was wrong.

"What's the matter, Charlie? Where's Albert at?"

"I've killed the black son-of-a-bitch!"

"You've what? Oh, Charlie. Where is he. Where'd you leave him?" Charlie hung his head and said "He's down below, in the white knolls by the river."

Mary rushed out the door, her little dog following at her heels. She hurried across the creek, through the pastures and willows. Her dog ran ahead and soon began to make a fuss. Mary ran toward the barking and saw Albert, awkwardly crawling on his hands and knees through the white sand. His front was soaked with blood and his entrails were bulging from the wound.

Mary hurried back to the house to get the buckboard. When she told Charlie that Albert was still alive, he went with her to help. After they made it back to the house with Albert, Mary cleaned the grass and dirt from the wound and stitched it up. She nursed the Negro tenderly until he completely recovered. In spite of the stabbing, Albert and Charlie remained friends and drinking partners.[11]

In about 1886, a light haired young man with gray-blue eyes went to work for Charlie. He called himself George Cassidy. He stood a slender 5', 10 ½" tall and had a captivating smile which often broke free across his squared-off face. He liked horses, dogs, and kids, and they responded to his manner. Yet, he always kept a piece of himself reserved from everyone.

A much anticipated horse race was planned in Brown's Park between Charlie Crouse's long-legged sorrel gelding and a black mare from Ashley Valley owned by Ken Hatch. A crowd gathered at the old Indian race track on the Hoy ranch. A lot of laughing and betting went on that day. When the horses were brought up to the starting line, it was George Cassidy who sat astride Charlie's sorrel. Amid shouts and flying dirt clods, George brought the sweat-streaked red gelding across the finish line in the lead.

There was a victory celebration nearby at Charlie's brother-in-law, Charles Allen's place. The women piled the table with food then called the men in from the corral.

"It's ready! Come on and grab a plate."

Mary Crouse noticed George wasn't in the line of hungry men as they filed past the table. She found him alone in the bunkhouse.

"George, it's ready to eat. You'd better come on and join us," she said.

George went with her to the house. He ate and was friendly to everyone, but soon returned to his solitary corner in the bunkhouse.

George Cassidy had been born Robert LeRoy Parker on April 13, 1866, in Beaver, Utah. Twelve more children were eventually born to his Mormon parents, Maximillian "Maxi," and Ann Gillis Parker. In 1879 when Robert (he was usually called Roy) was thirteen, his family moved to Circle Valley. Roy then hired out as a ranch hand near Milford. There he met Mike Cassidy, a talented, good-natured cowboy and cattle rustler. Roy learned a lot from Mike Cassidy, and soon took a new last name from his idol. Roy, now calling himself George Cassidy, drifted from one ranch job to another. It was during this time that he worked for Charlie Crouse. He made friends wherever he went. These friends, including ones made in Brown's Park, would many times mean the difference between being captured and riding free. He was a unique boy, on his way to leading a unique life.

On June 24, 1889, George Cassidy, Matt Warner, and Tom McCarty pulled a robbery large enough to put them in the newspaper headlines for the first time. Willard E. Christensen (alias Matt Warner) had spent several years cowboying and rustling in the Diamond Mountain country. He had for a time run the ferry for John Jarvie in Brown's Park. He had also worked for Charlie Crouse and was good friends with him. Seasoned rustler Tom McCarty was married to Matt Warner's sister, and had become acquainted with George down in Utah in the Robbers Roost outlaw country.

On a day in June, as the three men neared Telluride, Colorado, they rode their strongest, fastest, most sure-footed horses. Fifteen minutes later, with two sacks crammed full of gold and greenbacks from the San Miguel Bank, George and Matt ran for their horses where Tom held them. The three men galloped past staring crowds and out of Telluride in a dust. They gave their horses their heads and flew across the open country while a confused posse began to organize. The three robbers, chuckling and feeling they had it made, unexpectedly ran directly into two young cowboys heading to town. Later, Tom McCarty would wish he had shot them both. He knew that one of the cowboys recognized them and would undoubtedly reveal their identities.

Tom McCarty was right. It was that recognition that pitched the three small-time bandits into the notorious world of the outlaw, where they would feel they "had no way to live except by robbing and stealing."[12]

76

In a few days Brown's Park saw the three tired outlaws ride up to Charlie Crouse's door. They were welcomed into the ranch house and fed. Charlie caught three fresh horses and took the tired men and some supplies to the cabin where his mother and stepfather had earlier lived. The men were well hidden there, among the cedars, willow trees, and pines. They had plenty of fresh water at the nearby spring. They spent a few days resting and playing cards until one of Charlie Crouse's hired men rode in.

"You gotta get out of here on the run, boys. There's a posse down at the house, and they're after you!"

The men hurried for the safety of Robbers Roost. One of the horses they left behind in the Crouse pasture was a big gray gelding named Freckles. After he rested up, the gray was put to good use as a cow horse around the ranch.

One day Charlie put his young son, Stanley, on Freckles to help run wild steers on Goslin Mountain. Charlie was trying to fill a government beef contract. The wild steers were as quick as deer. Stanley and Freckles were running wide open after one tall lanky beef when it made a quick turn around a cedar. Freckles reacted and turned just as quickly, causing his young rider to fly out of the saddle. The boy's foot slipped through the stirrup and was firmly caught.

Off somewhere in the cedars, Charlie heard Stanley calling him in a scared voice. When Charlie reached his son, he saw the little boy hanging with his head dangling beneath the big gray's belly. Freckles stood still. He had not moved since Stanley fell.

A very thankful father retired Freckles that day. He gave the horse the best to eat, winter and summer, until the old gelding died at the age of thirty-three.[13]

In times after Freckles arrived, the three Crouse children grew accustomed to seeing strange horses show up in the pastures as others disappeared in the night. Brown's Park grew accustomed to seeing activity around the little hidden cabin and its nearby spring as riders of the Outlaw Trail (sometimes called the Hoot Owl Trail) stopped by for a while. Brown's Park hid the outlaws well at such places as the Crouse house, the Parsons cabin, the Jarvie dugout, and in strongholds within the cedars and rocks. Billy Bender and Les Megs, leaders of the Powder Springs Gang, spent several winters on upper Willow Creek. Many others, including the Tom Crowley Gang, Red Sash Gang, and the 'Doc' Bender Gang, came and went, all the while treating Brown's Park with respect.

The valley claimed both Colorado and Utah land and could almost touch Wyoming. The outlaws valued her for this, for the ease in which they could easily cross from one state's jurisdiction to the next. The lawmen were frustrated by it, and scorned the valley for her subterfuge.

One year in the 1890's, the outlaws, some of whom could be the finest of gentlemen, showed their appreciation to the Park people for their kindness of always supplying friendship, a hot meal, or a fresh horse when it was needed. The outlaws planned, prepared, and served them a Thanksgiving feast at the upper Davenport ranch on Willow Creek. Isom Dart helped some of the Bender Gang in the kitchen where a very special meal was prepared. Some of the Brown's Park people, all of who came dressed in their finest clothes, included the following: John Jarvie; Charlie and Mary Crouse; the Blairs; Tom and Alice Davenport and their son, Joe; Walter Scrivner and his date, Leanore Strickland, a schoolteacher from Canada; Harry Hindle; John Erickson from Sweden; Matt Rash; Uncle Billy and Auntie Bell Rife; Longhorn and Armida Thompson; several of the Bassetts; John Dempshire; Martin Guofonti; and the Spicer's nephew, Charlie Sparks.

The group was served an elegant meal of Bluepoint oysters, roast turkey with chestnut stuffing, mashed potatoes with brown giblet gravy, candied sweet potatoes, creamed peas, roquefort cheese, and salad. For dessert the guests enjoyed coffee with whipped cream, pumpkin pie, and plum pudding soaked with brandy sauce.[14]

After the meal was finished the group took their horses and wagons to the lower Davenport ranch. There they listened to the music and danced until dawn. It was an unforgettable time for all who attended. One of those was outlaw George Cassidy. During an earlier fall cattle roundup, George had worked as a meat supplier for the large group of cowboys. Such men who had that job were commonly called "butches." The nickname of "Butch" stayed with George and he became known as "Butch" Cassidy.

While in the Wind River Basin of Wyoming in August, 1891, Butch purchased three saddle horses from Billy Nutcher, possibly unaware that they were stolen. Because he had them in his possession, Butch was arrested for horse stealing and on July 10, 1894, was sentenced to two years hard labor in the Wyoming State Prison. Although Butch served his time without causing trouble, he grew bitter. He felt he had been framed by the large ranchmen in their attempts to rule the cattle range and rid it of nesters and mavericks. When he was released from prison he had made up his mind to become "the most dreaded, most hunted, and surely the most illusive outlaw that either North or South America have had to contend with yet."

It was then he began his search for the men who would ride

beside him, and they would become known as "The Wild Bunch." They were:

William Ellsworth "Elzy" Lay. Butch had become acquainted with Elzy in Brown's Park while Elzy was putting up hay for the Bassetts. He worked for Matt Warner on Diamond Mountain cowboying and breaking horses. He learned about horses from Charlie Crouse when he worked for him on the Park Live. Elzy, nearly six feet tall, dark and good looking, was extremely capable with horses and guns. Though he was quiet and charming, he was hungry for adventure. He became Butch's lieutenant.

Harry Longabaugh. He had gained the nickname "The Sundance Kid" after serving time in the county jail at Sundance, Wyoming. Similar to Butch in build and looks, but a bit darker, he dressed and acted the gentleman. He was a fast draw and a dead shot.

Henry Rhodes "Bub" Meeks. Like Butch, his family was Mormon. His father had been one of the first pioneers to follow Brigham Young to Utah. "Bub" was working as a Brown's Park cowboy when Butch first met him.

Harvey Logan "Kid Currey." He was very different from Butch. Although he didn't go looking for trouble, he was quick to fight and could kill without remorse. He was slender, with the hint of Indian blood in his looks.

Ben Kilpatrick "Tall Texan." He was a big, soft-spoken, dark-haired cowboy from Texas. The left of his light brown eyes had a flawed iris and looked as though it had two pupils.

Will Carver. He was a sandy-complected Texan who had first run with "Black Jack" Ketchum in the southwest. He was quiet and stayed to himself.15

Each gang member had his own problems and his own reasons for choosing to ride the Outlaw Trail. Under the leadership of a man who preferred to use his wit, rather than his gun, they found a common bond along with some high-priced fame.

In 1890 Charlie Crouse sold part of the Park Live Stock Ranch to Rock Springs banker, Augustine Kendall and Kendall's partners. Charlie gave Mary ten thousand dollars from the sale. Shortly thereafter she gave the money back to Charlie and he put it into a steer operation with Bill Aines, Pete Neilson, Frank Scoffield, and another man by the name of Hoight.

In the meantime the Crouse family moved to Vernal where Charlie and partner, Aaron Overholt, opened a saloon. The saloon quickly gained a reputation as a hangout for outlaws. Charlie did welcome Butch, and other old friends, anytime, into his establishment.

Once, when Matt Warner and friend Bill Wall were in the Vernal jail for a shooting incident, an angry lynch mob began to form. Charlie Crouse joined with Butch Cassidy, Elzy Lay, and Bob Swift. The four men formed an armed bodyguard outside the jail. Before violence erupted, the prisoners were transferred to the jail in Ogden, Utah.16

Back in Brown's Park, Charlie Crouse's half brother, Joe Tolliver, was living on a homesteaded meadow at the foot of Diamond Mountain. Instead of being with his family on Christmas Eve, 1891, Joe was at the Park Live Stock Ranch house with several other men. They had been playing cards and drinking whiskey half the night when Joe, very drunk, started picking on a slim, young cowboy.

"I don't want a drink, Joe!" Charlie Seger said. "You know I don't touch whiskey. I don't like it!"

The more Seger protested, the nastier Joe Tolliver became. Joe's eyes were cold when he jerked the cowboy to his feet and began knocking him around. Charlie Seger began to fight back then. Nevertheless, before he had a chance to put the bully in his place, Joe's white-handled pen knife stabbed him above the heart.

That night's carousing ended abruptly and Herbert Bassett was sent for to do the doctoring. Though he tried, there was little he could do for the dying man.

Herb later told Elizabeth, "I couldn't save him. Charlie was scared to death and he really hurt. His back was as black as black before he died. He bled inward. I couldn't do anything for him."17

After Charlie Seger died, layers of red sandstone ledge rock were stacked to make a large square border. Charlie's body was placed within the border, then the square was filled with dirt. Charlie Crouse helped get Joe Tolliver cleared of murder charges. The Brown's Park killing was barely investigated by the law and it was judged self-defense. Eventually Charlie's brother, Albert, was buried beside him in the grave. A large sagebrush grew on its top and a nest of blue racer snakes became guardians within the layered rocks.

When Brown's Park saw Charlie Crouse return to her, it was nearing the end of the century. He moved to a spot a couple of miles down river from the John Jarvie store, just below Dr. Parsons' smelter. He built the little establishment of Bridgeport and started a post office and combination store and saloon. He hired LeGrande Young, grandson of Mormon leader Brigham Young, to build a bridge across the river. Travelers of all sorts, including stockmen, Mormons, and Indians, paid Charlie for the use of the Bridgeport toll bridge.

Although the faces of his Wild Bunch changed, Butch Cassidy continued to ride the Outlaw Trail until 1908 when, to avoid capture, he and the Sundance Kid fled to Bolivia, in South

America. It was said that the two outlaws' lives ended there, when they were shot to death by a troop of Bolivian Cavalrymen. However, years later, evidence surfaced to prove that Butch left Bolivia alive. Some say he settled in Spokane, Washington, took the name of W.T. Phillips, and lived respectably until his death in 1937.[18] However, other historians remain unconvinced and contend that the way Butch Cassidy lived the final years of his life remains a mystery.[19]

Chapter XIII
THE LYNCHING

By 1898 the Bassett family had been through many changes. Four years earlier, during the month of December, Elizabeth started feeling sick. She was unaccustomed to illness, and had neither the time nor the patience to allow herself to be ill. She ignored the weakness and discomfort she felt when she saw that her milk cow was being swept into a passing herd of cattle. Elizabeth hurried outside, saddled her horse, and loped to catch up with the herd so she could bring her cow home.

At four o'clock the next morning, Elizabeth woke up in pain. She had a high fever, and her stomach hurt terribly. She got so bad that Herbert called the ranch foreman, Jim McKnight, and the other cowboys to help. The worried men did the only thing they could think of and applied heat to her stomach to relieve her agony. The heat did soften the pain, but in reality it was useless. Elizabeth had what was then called "inflamed bowels." She died shortly, from a ruptured appendix. Elizabeth, the center of the Bassett family, was buried on a hill above her log home.

Cowboys Jim McKnight, Matt Rash, and Isom Dart remained loyal friends. Matt Rash took over running the Bassett ranch. Herbert cared little for it, and spent more and more time in the cabin he had built for the Lodore Post Office. There he found comfort and enjoyment in the stacks of his reading material. Armida (the Bassett children called her "Auntie") Thompson eased things for the Bassetts when she came to help out as housekeeper and cook.

Being both father and mother was not an easy job for Herbert. Though his children gave him joy, they also frustrated him. At twenty-four Josie was an attractive girl with bright copper-colored hair and a freckled complexion. She had married blue-eyed Jim McKnight shortly after her mother's death, when she could no longer deny that she was carrying his child. By 1898 she had given birth to both Crawford, and his younger brother, Herbert "Chick." They lived on Beaver Creek, since Uncle Sam Bassett had deeded his cabin and land to Josie for a wedding present. He asked only that she keep a place for him for the remainder of his life. Josie did so, and cared for the old mountaineer until his death six years later.

Herbert's daughter Ann had always been willful. She had very little patience with what was going on in the kitchen, especially if there was a horse to be ridden or a steer to be roped. As a young girl she ran through the brush, climbed Brown's Park's hills, and sneaked to the bunkhouse to become part of the cowhand's world. Because of the wildness she felt, she sometimes wondered, "if more than milk was not imparted through those months of feeding" from her Indian wet nurse. She had been the only one of Herbert's children whom he had physically punished. One day when she was little, tom-boy Ann pushed her kind father too far. Herbert had left his sharpened axe leaning against a log and returned to find Ann busy giving the log a shave with it. Herbert was horrified. He yelled for her to put the axe down.

Ann yelled back, "No, you son of a bitch! I'll do this if I want to!"

Herbert's face was stern when he took hold of Ann and gave her a spanking while telling her she had done "enough for a time."[1]

By 1898 Ann was a beauty. She was twenty years old, had a dash of freckles, grayish green eyes, and rich folds of cinnamon-colored hair. Like Josie, Ann had been given fine educational opportunities. She studied not only in Brown's Park and Craig, but also at St. Mary's of the Wasatch Catholic School in Salt Lake City. Although she always had a rebellious undercurrent, at twenty she could be the most proper of ladies in dress, speech, and manner.

Herbert's boys, Sam and George, were easy-going and kind-natured like their father. At seventeen, Herbert's other son Eb was a handsome fellow with thick black hair and gray eyes. He was good-hearted, but like his sister Ann, was a bit of a rebel.

In February, 1898, an event took place at the Bassett Ranch which forever changed Brown's Park, and Eb Bassett.

Valentine Hoy had started the Red Creek Ranch in 1890. The ranch headquarters were just north of Brown's Park in Wyoming. All of the Hoys had known the 1890's as hard times in the cattle business. Possibly that is why, in 1893, Valentine signed a warranty deed on the place to his wife Julia.[2]

In the fall of 1897, the Hoys saw no cash profit after shipping time. What money they made from the sale of the cattle was turned directly over to the bank for loan payments. That news made Pat Johnson mad. He wanted to collect on a debt Valentine owed him. He knew he couldn't get blood from a turnip, but he figured he could get part of the turnip! He partnered up with "Judge" Jack Bennett and started rustling Hoy cattle.

P.L. "Pat" Johnson had always had the makings of, and the yearning to become, an outlaw. In 1892 he had reportedly killed a man in a bar fight.

Jack Bennett, who had peddled liquor to the Indians and served some time in prison, wore about the same stripes a:

Johnson. He had gained the title of "Judge" in April, 1897, from Butch Cassidy and his gang. After pulling off a robbery at Castle Gate, the Wild Bunch had arrived in Baggs, Wyoming, for a celebration. When outlaw "Old Man" Bender got sick and died of pneumonia, a kangaroo court was set up in the Bull Dog Saloon to put the doctor on trial. Johnson and Bennett were in the bar and Bennett was appointed judge. The doctor was not harmed, and Bennett took his nickname with him when he left Baggs.[3]

In the meantime, a prospector by the name of Strang and his sixteen-year-old son Willie had moved to Brown's Park hoping to find something worth prospecting. Albert Williams was operating the Jarvie ferry one morning when Mr. Strang and Willie stopped by.

"Albert, do you suppose it would be all right if I left my boy here with you for a few days?" Strang said. "I've got to make a trip to town and thought Willie could help you around here 'till I get back."

Albert was always good to the youngsters and agreed to let Willie stay for as long as he wanted.

All was well until Pat Johnson happened by, whistling and throwing loops with his rope. Before Albert knew Willie was going, he had disappeared over the hill with Johnson. The teenager couldn't resist the invitation to "go rope a few steers" with the older cowboy. When they later arrived at the two-story Red Creek Ranch house, Willie met Hoy's hired man, young Charlie Teters, William Pidgeon, and Johnson's friend, Judge Bennett. The kid must have thought he was really having a big time getting to spend the night in the drinking, laughing, and card-playing company of such men.

The next morning Johnson was in no mood for Willie's pranks, but Willie was still full of fun. Johnson was getting a drink of water when the teenager jokingly bumped the bottom of the dipper. The water went in Johnson's face, up his nose, and down the front of his shirt. At first Willie howled with laughter but suddenly got frightened and ran for the door when he saw Johnson start after him. Willie bolted from the house, dashed down the steep hill, and ran for the horse barn on the other side of the creek. Just as he stepped onto the footbridge, Johnson lifted his revolver and fired. Although it is likely that Johnson only meant to scare the boy, the bullet hit Willie in the backbone and he fell, face first, onto the bridge planks.

Valentine Hoy's in-laws, the Blairs, had spent the night in one of the upstairs bedrooms. They heard the shot, saw the injured boy, and hurried to help the men bring the bleeding boy into the house. They all tried to help him, but Willie soon died.

Johnson regretted what had happened, but his dealings with

the law had not put him in its favor. He didn't want to face any lawmen with the story of shooting a kid in the back. Within a few minutes, Johnson and Bennett rode away together, on Hoy horses. Bill Blair left soon after to sound the alarm.

Johnson and Bennett ran for Powder Springs, located northeast of Brown's Park on the Colorado-Wyoming border. It was frequently used as a stopping-off point for outlaws riding between Hole-in-the-Wall in Wyoming and Robbers Roost in Utah. When Johnson and Bennett arrived at Powder Springs, they met and joined two recent escapees from the Utah penitentiary. Johnson and Bennett had taken a dangerous step. One of the men was a hard-core criminal by the name of Harry Tracy. Tracy was with convict Dave Lant.

Between them, the four decided that Bennett would ride to Rock Springs for supplies. He was to meet the others later at the eastern edge of Brown's Park, near Lodore Canyon. From there, they planned to head for the Silvertip Spring at Robbers Roost.

Because Valentine Hoy had earlier sworn out a warrant on Johnson and Bennett for stealing Hoy livestock, two Colorado lawmen traveled toward Brown's Park. Sheriff Neiman and Deputy Farnham were unaware of the Strang boy's murder. Although they had spotted the three men just before arriving in Brown's Park, they had no way of knowing they were two escaped convicts and a man who had just killed a teenaged boy.

Chick McKnight   Herb Bassett   Ann Bassett   ?   ?
(Glade Ross collection)

86

Bridge at Red Creek Ranch where Willie Strang was shot as he ran to the blacksmith shop on the other side.

Meanwhile, when the news of the murder of Willie Strang reached Vernal, Willie's brother, John Strang, set out for Brown's Park with two lawmen. The following article appeared in a 1932 edition of the **Vernal Express**. It describes, from John Strang's memory, the posse hunt for the bad men and the death of Valentine Hoy.

It was in 1898 and hearing of the death of his brother Willie Strang, 16, shot by "Pat" P.L. Johnson, Mr. Strang, then 17, who was in Vernal, accompanied Sheriff Billy Preece and LeGrande Young, deputy United States Marshal, to Brown's Park.

Leaving Vernal the trio went as far as the Bill Spack ranch on Brush Creek where they stayed for the night. The next day they made their way over Diamond Mountain in deep snow arriving at the Charley Crouse ranch, located about midway of Brown's Park, late in the evening only to find that Johnson had left the country on his way, it was thought, for Wyoming points.

Evidently later Johnson had caught up with Dave Lant and Harry Tracy and headed for the desert country.

Mr. Strang states that Sheriff Preece and U.S. Deputy Marshal Young, not finding Johnson there returned to Vernal the next day for purposes not known to Strang, who stayed at the Crouse ranch.

Crouse, so Mr. Strang relates, sent him to the Ladore post office to find out which way Johnson had taken or to see if he had secured any mail.

That evening Sheriff Charles Neihman of Routt County, Colorado came to Ladore and stated he was sure Johnson was on Douglas mountain with Lant and Tracy, or so he thought, for as he rode by and started towards them they had waved him back. He had attempted to find out who they were and what they were doing in that section. It is not known whether they recognized him as an officer or not.

Sheriff Neihman told Strang to notify all that he could to form a posse and they would ride the next morning to head off the bandits.

In the posse, so hastily secured, was Valentine Hoy, James McKnight, Joe Davenport, Boyd Vaughn, Bill Pidgeon, Ed Bassett, 17, a boy friend of Strang's, and Isham, a negro.

As they rode up to the outlaw's camp the posse surprised them as they were cooking breakfast, Mr. Strang says. They had camped in a ravine not far from Ladore canyon at the foot of Douglas mountain.

When they saw the posse they scattered to the shelter of the nearby rocks leaving the food, saddle horses, and camp outfit even their overshoes. All this and three pack animals were taken by the posse and sent to the Bassett ranch in charge of the negro Isham. Except for their firearms the outlaws were now at the mercy of the posse, who were determined to get Johnson, who had murdered young Strang.

All day they had attempted to get them to surrender, so Mr. Strang says, but being at a distance tending to the horses he could not distinguish their talk. As evening approached Hoy started into their stronghold and had beckoned for the group to close in. As he was close to them behind a rock Tracy it is thought, shot Hoy

88

who fell shot through the heart, out of reach of his companions. Strang was bringing up the horses and was on lower ground near Hoy when he fell.

They returned to the Bassett ranch for the night.

That same day Valentine Hoy was killed, Eb Bassett was alone gathering fresh horses for the posse. He was on his way home with the horses when he spotted John Bennett. Bennett had camped to wait for his companions as planned. He was unaware that a posse was after his friends or that Valentine Hoy had been shot.

When the posse learned that Eb had found Bennett's location, the agitated men formed a plan. Eb Bassett would be its key.

John Bennett knew Eb well and considered him a friend. He was not alarmed when the teenager rode into his camp that evening.

Bennett was pleased with the offer to get inside from the cold when Eb said, "There's nobody home, so I'm alone over there. Why don't you come on back to the house for the night and we'll play some cards."

When John Bennett stepped into the Bassett house and into the sites of all those cold-barreled guns, he never had a chance. He was astounded. He not only felt betrayed by a friend, but he firmly believed he had done nothing wrong. He figured the worst he had done was to ride away from the Red Creek Ranch with Johnson. He was mad at the way he was being treated. He cussed his captors and called them cowards. Although Herbert Bassett had tried to calm the men, their already hot tempers burst into flame. The group rushed Bennett and grabbed him.

As they pushed him out the door Bennett screamed, "Herb Bassett is the only white man in Brown's Park!"

In a short time the commotion was over and everything was quiet. Judge Bennett dangled hideously at the end of the rope where it had been looped over the crosspiece of the yard entry gate.4 The yard gate had not been high enough for a proper hanging; Bennett's death had been slow and sickening.

The men returned to the Bassett house. There they agreed that a masked group of men had ridden into the ranch and done the lynching.5

As for Bennett's partners, lawmen from Utah, Colorado, and Wyoming worked together in the pursuit of Tracy, Lant, and Johnson, and eventually the three were captured. The **Vernal Express** wrote the following account of the story:

The posse that went to Brown's Park after the murderer of Willie Strang came back to Vernal Tuesday night. The whole gang was caught and Bennett was hung by a masked mob of about thirty men.

The men who were on the trail of the murderers followed them up as close as possible. The trail was rough, the snow deep and the men had to go in single file leading their horses which were tied head and tail. V.S. Hoy had just made a change with the leader and as he was climbing over a rock, two shots were fired and Hoy dropped back dead. The others laid low and watched for the outfit about two hours, when night came on they moved down off the mountain into camp and sent to Vernal for more help.

The next day seven more men joined them and they went back and found tracks of the gang and followed them until darkness preventd them from doing any further trailing. The next day they followed them to the G horse camp near which the gang had killed a colt to appease their hunger, being cut off from all supplies by their pursuers. The posse camped at the horse camp all night and the next day they again took the trail and overtook the outlaws in a flat near Powder Springs.

The first man to give up was Johnson, who threw his gun down in the snow; threw both hands up and begged for mercy from his captors. John Strang, the brother of the murdered boy, was determined he would kill him, but the posse shielded the outlaw. After some parleying Tracy also gave up.

After the prisoners were taken the posse started back to Ladore, which is located in the lower end of Brown's Park. Lant and Tracy were taken to Hahns Peak by the sheriff of Routt county and the sheriff, Peter Swanson, U.S. Marshal Laney and two deputies took Johnson and started for Rock Springs, but it is doubtful whether they ever got to their destination with a live prisoner.

John Strang was the first to arrive in Vernal and give the news of the capture of the outlaws and about an hour afterward the majority of the posse got in and confirmed the report of Strang.

Shortly thereafter, Utah Governor Heber Wells hosted a conference in Salt Lake City with Governor Richards of Wyoming and Governor Adams of Colorado. The three decided to join forces in appointing special officers to break up the outlaw gangs who were overrunning their three states. The incident in Brown's Park had proven that their cooperative action could be very effective.

Pat Johnson stood trial in Wyoming for the shooting death of Willie Strang. He was found innocent. He served two years of a ten-year sentence for his part in Valentine Hoy's murder. After twice escaping from Colorado jails with Harry Tracy, Dave Lant surprisingly went on to receive a citation for military bravery while serving in the Philippines.

Harry Tracy became infamous in a murder and robbery spree across the northwestern United States. Finally trapped in a cornfield by lawmen, he shot himself through the head.

Eb Bassett never forgot the hanging of the man who had called him friend, nor the part he had played in it. It would remain inside him, eating at him, for the rest of his life.

Years later Eb told a young friend, "I see that man's face every night . . . every single night in my sleep."[6]

The law had come in force to Brown's Park. Now fewer and fewer outlaws dared ride along her ridges. They could not feel very safe with her, ever again.

Albert Seger (old Bassett P.O. in background)

91

Chapter XIV
THE CONFLICT

Cattlemen had free rein to run their livestock almost entirely on government land in the 1870's. This method was taken full advantage of by those with money enough to stock the range. As the herds expanded, the cattle spread out and the barons claimed large areas of land. They centered their massive operations around a river or some other substantial water supply. One cattleman's range was typically separated from another by a mountain range or some other natural boundary. Occasionally the stockmen made a token gesture of legal claim and filed on a few acres of ground at their main water source.

Under one or a combination of the Pre-emption Act of 1841, the Homestead Act of 1862, the Timber Culture Act of 1873, and the Desert Land Act of 1877, a pioneer cattleman could gain legal title to small portions of land along streams at his ranch headquarters. However, these laws for acquiring land were not satisfactory to livestock men. They needed about forty acres per cow in the sparsely grassed rangelands. They could obtain no more than a total of 1,120 acres if they utilized every one of their legal privileges. Therefore, most of the land they needed was simply claimed as their private domain. Cattle baron Abel "Shanghai" Pierce once ran more than fifty thousand head of cattle while owning only eleven acres of land. He controlled over one million acres.[1]

The huge and growing herds, adding up to millions of cattle, meant big business with big expenses. When more capitol was needed, rich investors were sought. They were found in the eastern United States, as well as in England, Scotland, and other European countries. While the barons and their investors were looking for profits, the small ranchers were looking for homes and began elbowing their way onto the range.

The big cattlemen had to start making plans. They had already seen the elimination of other pests that had usurped their range. There had been the grass-hogging buffalo, the Indians, and the Comancheros. (The Comancheros, made up mostly of Mexicans, had encouraged the Comanches to steal cattle from all across the country, then they traded the Indians whiskey and other goods for the stolen herds.) Now the big ranchers were having to deal with the growing number of nesters. They saw the nesters as intruders living in covered wagons, dirt dugouts, and cabins with squalling, barefooted kids, and thieving lariats. The newcomers were filing on one chunk of ground after another, steadily chipping away at the grazing lands with each homestead application.

The barons, believing they had first right to the public land which they had been using, strung mile after mile of barbed wire to secure their illegally claimed empires. They backed their claims with bullets and nooses.

The complaints of the small farmers and ranchers were heard in Washington. President Grover Cleveland ordered the illegal fences down and the fencers prosecuted. Eventually the fences did fall. However, then came the large scale abuse of the Homestead Act and other acts. The big cattlemen used their cowboys to gain possession of countless acres of land. They had them file on homesteads and when the cowhands secured the title, the cattlemen were able to buy the land from them for a small fee. They also contacted widows of Civil War veterans and convinced them to file for land under special land-bonus privileges (scrip) of the 1872 amendment to the Homestead Act. The widows were then paid the sum of between two hundred and four hundred dollars for title to that land.

Though large operations, such as Wyoming's Swan Land and Cattle Company, did gain many acres of ground, sometimes the plan backfired. The cowboy sometimes decided he did not want to turn the homestead over to his boss, and would keep the land, which was legally his, and begin building a little place of his own. Often by mavericking, he started his cattle herd.

After the Civil War, almost every cowman got his start by rounding up and branding wild cattle. Mavericking, or gathering unbranded slicks, was accepted as common practice. Now, since the mavericks were most likely offspring from their herds, the big cattlemen suddenly looked on the practice of mavericking as pure cattle rustling.

By the late 1860's, associations were organizing and stock detectives were being hired for protection against maverickers and thieves. By 1872 Wyoming was closely observing the two protective associations which had formed in Colorado. By the 1873 general spring roundup, Wyoming ranchers had organized the Laramie County Stock Growers Association. In 1879 the organization was re-named the Wyoming Stock Growers Association. With strong connections to Cheyenne (the State Legislature) the association quickly gained power. Although the stock detectives were not legal law-enforcement officers, they acted as though they were. They began not only arresting men, but shooting them if they resisted. Many of the settlers were justifiably concerned with the methods and the increasing power of the Wyoming Stock Growers Association. As a matter of fact, "the settlers feared the Association and its armed range riders much more than the rustlers or the outlaws did."₂

The Wyoming Stock Growers Association, made up almost exclusively of big ranchers, became a powerful force in Wyoming and the surrounding cattle range. In 1884 it saw to it that the territorial legislature passed the Maverick Law. This law gave the Wyoming Stock Growers Association complete control of the big roundups and the mavericks. Profits from the maverick sales went into a fund to hire stock detectives and inspectors to protect the Association against thieves. Though some minor changes were made in the Maverick Law in 1886, it was still hated by the small ranchers. The law was eventually repealed in 1888 and the roundup supervision went from the Association to the Board of Live Stock Commissioners. However, as it turned out, the territorial, and later the state boards, were controlled by leading members of the Wyoming Stock Growers Association.

Without a doubt, rustling was going on. It was common for a cowhand on the open range to ride with a running iron tied to his saddle. When there was something he wanted to brand he built a small tepee of sagebrush and lit it afire. Above the glowing cherry redness of the coals, the metal ring was hung on a stick or thrown in the fire and heated. When the ring was hot it was held firmly between two crossed sticks and could be used to make or alter almost any brand. Cowhands found the iron a handy tool. So did the rustlers.

Rustlers adding to herds with a running iron or with detestable tricks like slitting calves' tongues so they would wean off early, or killing mother cows in some hidden spot and taking the calves, gave big cattle ranchers valid reasons for action. But court convictions of rustlers were found to be difficult. Jury sympathies were not with the wealthy cattlemen. No middle ground between the big and the small could be found.

A blacklist was made up of alleged rustler brands. It apparently contained the names of ranchers whom the Association looked down on, whether they were proven rustlers or not. Unfairly, former cowhands who had gone out on their own were automatically on the list. Often men on this list could not acquire a brand. If they did, the roundup inspectors would not recognize it as valid. Such branded stock was secured by the Association and sold as mavericks.

In united opposition to the big outfits, small settlers organized the unofficial Northern Wyoming Farmers and Stock Growers Association. They planned a roundup of their own to begin May 1, 1892. That date was well ahead of the official scheduled roundup. It was inevitable that there would be trouble.

On April 5, 1892, horses, supplies, twenty-five hired Texas gunmen, and twenty-four Wyoming men, including large ranch owners, ranch managers, inspectors, and detectives, traveled in a special train out of Cheyenne. With the apparent knowledge of some Wyoming congressmen, Union Pacific officials, and newspaper men, the group - they called themselves the Regulators - headed toward Johnson County. They had a list of seventy names. Each man on the list was to be eliminated.

It was later called the Johnson County War. Quick organization of the Johnson County people - called the Defenders - along with Colonel J.J. Van Horne and a detachment of cavalry, managed to halt the invading Regulators before a great many lives were lost. However, it showed how determined and desperate the highly financed cattlemen were to continue controlling the rangeland they saw slipping away. It most certainly was a war. The huge cattle outfits and hired assassins, such as Tom Horn, were fighting against the United States Government and the small homesteaders.3

It has been debated whether or not Tom Horn was working in Wyoming as a stock detective during the Johnson County War. For certain by 1894 he was employed by the Swan Land and Cattle Company. It was said that he was later fired as a Wyoming Stock Growers Association stock detective because he was too quick to use his gun. For that same reason, Horn was hired privately by some of the big outfits, for a fee of five hundred dollars per enemy downed.

Tom Horn's mother had been kind, but because of his tough-fisted father, he had run away from his Missouri home at an early age. He worked his way west and through the years he grew into a tall, lean, broad-shouldered man with a caramel complexion. His hair was black and his eyes were dark and penetrating. He was, at one time or another, a mule tender, teamster, ranch hand, and a prize-winning rodeo contestant. He also lived with the Apaches and learned their ways. Then he fought them and scouted against them for the army. He served for a short while in Cuba during the Spanish-American War before contracting malaria. Later he worked as a Pinkerton agent in Colorado. By the time he became a Wyoming stock detective, he was a hardened assassin and applied for jobs with the statement: "Killing is my specialty."

Isolated Brown's Park had watched her ranches build steadily with very little outside interference. Though the Middlesex had made an effort to push in, poor management, bad luck, weather, and the cooperative efforts of the Brown's Parkers, had caused the big outfit to topple in a short time. Although there was bickering back and forth, for the most part the valley's stockmen, including some sheepmen, worked together. They showed good judgment and kept the valley grasses and the upper summer country grasses, healthy and able to reseed yearly.

It was the mid-1890's when Hi Bernard rode into Brown's Park. Years earlier the pockmarked cowboy had quit his life as a Texas trail boss to become a successful ranch foreman. He had worked for several large outfits and was now a new foreman for wealthy Ora Haley. He would be running the Two-Bar extension of the Haley Livestock and Trading Company. He headquartered at the recently purchased Salisbury and Major Ranches located on the lower Snake River in Colorado, about thirty miles east of Brown's Park. Ora Haley had a talent for hiring extremely competent managers and blue-eyed Hi Bernard was no exception. Hi had intentions of working out an agreement with the ranchers of Brown's Park. He wanted their stock to be gathered with everybody elses during the big roundups. In Colorado, as in Wyoming, a general roundup controlled by the big outfits was common practice. He perceived no problems in convincing the little Brown's Park ranchers that they should be in agreement.

Hi Bernard was mistaken. The Brown's Parkers wanted no part of his roundup. They had seen the avalanche of Two-Bar cattle slowly moving nearer. They knew more and more would soon be spilling over onto Brown's Park range. They knew they had to hold back the flood or their range would be nothing but grubbed stubble, while their grasses filled the bellies of Two-Bar cattle. They did talk to the Two-Bar foreman, and an agreement on how they would manage their herds was reached.

A territorial boundary line called the Divide was designated along a distinctive limestone ridge between Vermillion Creek and Little Snake River. Brown's Park cattle were to stay to the west of the Divide and the Two-Bar herds to the east.4 Also, the Brown's Park ranchers agreed to discourage sheepmen from moving in on their range, with the insistence that an exception be made for those few already a comfortable part of the valley.

Hi Bernard accepted the agreement knowing it was the best he was going to get from Brown's Park. He had not felt completely welcome there. He felt less so when he received a letter from Ann Bassett. She was extremely protective of the country where she grew up, and informed him that to her "the tracks of Two-Bar horses, or cattle, were obnoxious."5

The Brown's Park Cattlemen's Association was formed and Matt Rash was elected its first president. The Association built a cabin near the Divide and made sure someone stayed close to keep Brown's Park cattle from meandering across the line, and to push back intruding Two-Bar cattle. At the same time Hi Bernard had men patrolling his side of the Divide. Everything remained relatively quiet in Brown's Park for a while.

In the meantime, the blatting, nibbling sheep herds were multiplying and spreading in woolly waves across more and more western cattle country. The sheep owners ignored the cattlemen's claim that they had established prior use rights to the public domain grazing lands. Cattlemen got together in a united force in many areas. They warned sheepmen to stay out of certain territories and not to cross their designated "dead lines." When sheepmen stubbornly refused to back down, the conflict often erupted in bloody violence. Sheep, and sometimes their herders, were abused or brutally killed.

In 1897 Brown's Park got her first jolt of real interference from the powerful ranches growing in Colorado. Seven supply wagons rolled in behind a large group of Routt County cattlemen. Regardless of the agreement with Hi Bernard, they wanted all sheep grazers out of the country. They meant it!

A short time earlier a group of vigilantes had nearly hung Jack Edwards in Colorado after they had clubbed his sheep and killed two herdsmen. The few sheepmen in Brown's Park were justifiably intimidated. Though the Davenports kept a little band of sheep, Frank Goodman sold his place to Matt Rash and moved on. Not many sheep were seen in the area for a while.

The power behind the push against the northwestern Colorado sheepmen was the Snake River Stock Growers Association. It was controlled by the Two-Circle Bar (Yampa Livestock), the Two-Bar (Ora Haley), The Bar Ell Seven (Charley Ayer), the Sevens (Pierce-Reef), and the Reverse Four (Clayton -Murnan). They had many of the same problems in controlling the range as did the big ranchers in Wyoming. Unfortunately, they also had many of the same solutions. The feeling in the Snake River Association was that the Brown's Park residents had not been very cooperative. It was, after all, common knowledge that they let outlaws come and go at will. Letters from J.S. Hoy, one of the valley's own residents, condemned the place as a nest of rustlers. On top of all that, the Brown's Park range was considered under-utilized and most certainly was ideal for wintering cattle. Top members of the Association met at the Two-Circle Bar. It was decided that Two-Circle Bar manager, J. Wilson Carey, would collect one hundred dollars every month from each member and turn it over to Charley Ayer. Ayer was to hire a man to move into Brown's Park and gather evidence of rustling.[6]

In the early spring of 1900, a tall, broad-shouldered man with the dark coloring of a Mexican rode into Brown's Park leading a pack horse. He introduced himself as James Hicks. He explained he was a rancher from New Mexico and was on the scout for some good horses or a ranch to buy. He was welcomed to camp on Bassett ground while he looked the country over.

Neither Josie nor Ann liked James Hicks and did not trust him. He had an underlying vulgarity which grated on the women but seemed to go unnoticed by the men. He boldly slid his eyes over Josie the first time he met her.

"How old are you?" he kept asking her.

Josie refused to answer the question and ignored his other off-color remarks. She wished her brothers would send him on his way.

Josie told her dad, "That man's no horse buyer. If anything he's a horse thief. He can't even hit the ground with his rope. That fellow is a mistake, that's all!"[7]

Ann had been away at school. When she came home to help with the spring gathering, she met Hicks. Matt Rash had hired him for the roundup. Hicks didn't seem to know much about working cattle, so Matt put him on as cook. Where Josie had avoided the mustached man, that wasn't Ann's way. She told him off when he made her mad with his boasting, in blood-stained detail, about the Indians he had fought and single-handedly butchered.

Matt Rash and Ann had grown closer in the recent years. There was a strong likelihood that the two would marry. Matt understood Ann's fiery nature and tried to calm her belligerence against James Hicks.

Matt grinned at Ann and said, "Most all of the big Indian battles were fought around the campfire as men smoked and talked."[8]

James Hicks moved among the ranchers, ate with them, and laughed with them. When he loaded his pack horse and rode out of the valley, little attention was paid to his leaving.

Then one morning in early June, an unpleasant shiver rippled through the valley. Matt Rash, Isom Dart, Joe Davenport, Longhorn Thompson, and some other men had wakened to find they had had a visitor in the night. Hung on their fence posts or doors each found a note of warning. The unsigned messages made it clear that the ranchers named were to be moved out of the valley in thirty days time.

That such a grim messenger had lurked around as they slept was frightening to everyone. Though they were all uneasy and grew very cautious, Brown's Park was their home. No one left.

On July 7, Matt Rash, riding back from town, stopped by the Bassett ranch. He visited for a while then rode on home. At first light the next morning, he saddled up and rode to his cabin on

Cold Spring Mountain. It was always pleasant to trade the dried out midsummer heat of the valley for the smell of pine and flower-sprinkled meadows.

Matt's lunch was on the table, his boot pulled off his sore foot, and his back to the door when the first bullet struck him. He spun around and a second bullet plowed into his right breast, knocking him to the floor. Matt was alone when he woke up. With what little strength he had, he dragged himself to the softness of his bed.

On June 10th, with barely a care in the world, fourteen-year-old Felix Myers and his friend, George Rife, decided to stop by to say hello to Matt. As they rode to the cabin, the smell of carrion was heavy in the air. They saw a young bronc lying dead and covered with flies in the corral. Blood from a bullet hole just above the point of his nose had dried and turned dark. Puzzled, Felix walked to the cabin. He pushed the door open and was knocked backward by the sight and smell of death.

When volunteer Deputy Sheriff Charlie Sparks and the other men carried Matt's body from the cabin for burial, they were forced to wear carbolic acid soaked handkerchiefs over their noses and mouths. They found Matt's saddle horse running loose with a new rope around its neck. Before long, Matt's father and brother arrived in Brown's Park. They exhumed the body and took Matt home to Acton, Texas. Felix Meyers had been so badly shocked that he developed a jerking twitch and a need to be alone. Both remained with him always.⁹

In deep mourning, Ann cried out that James Hicks was behind Matt's murder. She was certain of it. However, a letter arrived for Matt from Hicks, stating that he would be returning to Brown's Park. It was mailed from Denver on the day of Matt's death. Ann alone clung to her suspicions. After all, she figured, it would have been easy enough for Hicks to have had someone mail that letter for him.

James Hicks did return to Brown's Park. He told anyone who would listen, "I'll bet it was Isom Dart who did that job. I was with Matt one day when him and that nigger got into a hell of a fight."

But, no one paid much attention to Hicks' story. Before long he left.

By October the aspen leaves on Cold Spring Mountain were frost burned around the edges and had turned yellow and orange. The cooling breezes fluttered them more often and they shimmered along the creeks and down the slopes. George and Sam Bassett, Billy Bragg, and others had spent the night on the mountain at Summit Spring at Isom Dart's cabin. The next morning, George and Isom stepped outside and had walked about twenty steps when a rifle shot echoed across the morning. The middle-aged negro fell and never moved again. Terrified, George ran for the cabin. The boys stayed hidden inside and watched through safe peepholes for any movement in the trees. When they eventually went outside, the killer had long since gone. Two .30-.30 cartridge cases were found at the base of a pine about 120 yards from the cabin. They all knew that Hicks packed a .30-.30 rifle.

As stories came together from surrounding cowboys, it became evident that James Hicks was Tom Horn. One such report was that two or three days before Isom Dart was murdered, Tom Horn had spent the night in the Two-Bar bunkhouse.

Sam Bassett, who had sold his share of the Bassett cattle, left Brown's Park and never returned. Joe Davenport went to Missouri for the winter. On Thanksgiving Day, Longhorn Thompson survived an ambush in a clump of winter-reddened willows on his home place. He and his wife soon moved to town.

The violence of the past months had disintegrated the Brown's Park Cattlemen's Association. The men ceased sending anyone to hold back the Two-Bar cattle. But with obsessive vengeance prodding her, Ann Bassett saddled her horse, grabbed her rifle, and rode to the Divide. Alone, she made the patrols. There were times when her hatred of the Two-Bar made her spur her horse and run trespassing cattle until their mouths hung open. They either jumped into the Green River and hit the other side running for parts unknown, or struggled to their deaths in the current. There were other times when Ann didn't bother. She simply raised her rifle and shot the cattle where they stood.

One night while a summer rain patted against the house, Ann was almost struck by a bullet as she sat at the Bassett kitchen table. She blamed Ora Haley.[10] She did feel some vindication when Tom Horn was hanged in Cheyenne on November 20, 1903, for the murder of teenager Willie Nickell. However, it turned her stomach in 1909 when J.S. Hoy and Valentine Hoy's heirs sold the Tommy White Bottom to Ora Haley, giving the Two-Bar a legitimate base in Brown's Park. (J.S. Hoy later moved with his wife to Denver, Colorado, where he worked on the Hoy Manuscript.)

Ann bought a place of her own at the base of Douglas Mountain. Along the meadow at the headquarters stood the huge ovens of Griff Edwards' -Griff died of a heart attack in 1897 in Nebraska- abandoned copper smeltery. The ranch, known as the Smelter, became her summer home and range. She wintered in Brown's Park at the old place.

In June, 1900, Ann's sister Josie divorced Jim McKnight. Following advice from her father, she sold her place on Beaver

101

Creek and with her two boys moved to Craig, Colorado. In 1902 she married the town's druggist, Charles Ranney. Two years later, at the age of twenty-six, Ann surprised many when she married Two-Bar foreman Hi Bernard.

Ann was very happy with what she considered a good business arrangement with a brilliant cattleman and another way to get to Ora Haley. Hi Bernard was infatuated with the complex young beauty. He was very pleased with the marriage regardless of his new wife's reasons. Ora Haley was not amused. He fired Hi Bernard within days.

Ann and Hi's marriage worked for a while. Hi bought some land adjoining Ann's Smelter Ranch. They leased the Harry Hoy Ranch in Brown's Park and together began to build a successful ranching operation. Nevertheless, the marriage soon began to crumble and in 1910 it ended in divorce. But Ann's fight with the Two-Bar was far from over.

Chapter XV
THE GENTLE AND THE ROWDY

The passing of the one hundred years of the nineteenth century barely aged Brown's Park, but it was a time of change for her. She watched as the mountain man and outlaw eras quickly came and went. She felt new trails and a road or two make subtle etchings across her. When the cattle herds arrived she listened to the bellowing of fighting bulls and of bull-headed men. She saw tepees replaced by log homes happily tucked into her prettiest niches and little orchards begin to bear fruit. She saw a few less of her cozy hillside wolf dens and she watched the free roaming of her long-time Indian friends become government regulated trips between reservations. The valley watched some of her landscape change as brush covered flats became grain fields and alfalfa hay meadows. She still had some of her old friends from the last century with her. Some were gentle and others were rowdy by nature.

By 1902 Charlie Crouse, with the help of his boys and hired men, had grubbed a lot of greasewood and sagebrush below Bridgeport. They also had worked hard digging a ditch to irrigate it. Above the Jarvie store, Charlie built a dike of cottonwood, cedar, and rocks across a channel made by an island in the river. The diverted river water gushed into the ditch and followed the surveyed route past the Jarvie place, directly over Jesse Ewing's grave, and on to Bridgeport.[1]

It was near Bridgeport where Charlie Crouse managed to get Joe Tolliver out of trouble once again. His half brother had picked a fight and seemed determined to take on Mike Flynn. Charlie knew Mike and his reputation very well and he knew that Joe was fooling with the wrong man.

Mike Flynn was a bit of a cowboy and a bit of a scoundrel. He had a summer place on Diamond Mountain on Pot Creek and wintered his cattle at his cabin a few miles down river from the Park Live. His wife Mercy Green Flynn was a tough little redhead. Together they made a matched team.

Charlie Crouse was well acquainted with the Flynns and he was especially good friends with a cousin of Mercy's, Charlie Green. Mercy and Charlie Green were alike in that they chose spicy lifestyles in spite of a staunch Mormon upbringing.

Charlie Green was an average built critter with a thick sprout of red hair that usually stuck up in back like a rooster's tail. He stayed busy prospecting in and around Brown's Park and making moonshine whiskey in Little Brown's Hole. He told his friend Charlie Crouse about witnessing a run-in about some stolen horses between Mike Flynn and the Burton boys.

The fight had happened one evening when Mike and his family were headed to Pot Creek in their platform spring seated wagon. When Charlie Green met up with them, Mercy was on the seat to her husband's left and their two boys were in the back. Mike's Winchester was upright in the front of the wagon box, between his feet. Intending to visit with Charlie Green for a few minutes, Mike stopped the team and pulled back on the wagon brake beside him. They had barely said their hellos when the Burtons from Greendale rode over a ridge. As they trotted up to the wagon, they were hard-faced and plainly on the fight.

One of the men drew his pistol and said, "Mike Flynn, we're going to kill you, you thievin' son of a bitch!"

Mike never said a word. He looked coolly from one man to the other and kept grinning all the while. Hidden from view beneath the wagon dashboard, the toe of Mike's boot inched slowly until it was beneath the trigger guard of his rifle. Suddenly, in one swift blurred movement, Mike threw the reins to Mercy, kicked the brake loose with his right foot, jerked his left foot upward pitching the rifle into his hands, tumbled backwards into the back of the wagon, and shot twice. By then Mercy had the team running for home while the Burton men were ducking for cover.

Charlie Green had to laugh out loud as he hurried on his way. He'd seen a lot, but he'd never seen anything quite like that.

Now at Bridgeport a couple of years later, Charlie Crouse probably remembered Charlie Green's story as he walked up to Mike Flynn and Joe Tolliver. Charlie was just in time to see his foolish half brother pull a gun. Mike sat still in his buckboard and never said a word. He just grinned.

"Give me that gun, Joe." Charlie Crouse said.

Joe looked surprised and said, "No! I'm goin' to kill him right here and now!"

Charlie moved quickly beside Joe and grabbed the gun away from him. He looked up at Mike Flynn and said, "Go ahead Mike, you go on your way. I'll take care of Joe."

As the harness jingled and the buckboard rolled away, Joe spun to face Charlie.

"Why the hell didn't you stay out of it? I was about to shoot him!"

Charlie looked sideways at his half brother and said, "Joe, that man would have killed you in just a little bit. He would have either got you with his Winchester or with that knife of his. Don't tell me you were going to kill him. You never would have had the guts to pull that trigger. I knew it and so did Mike Flynn."[3]

It wasn't long after that, when Joe moved to Vernal and became a deputy sheriff. He apparently made a pretty good lawman, when he was sober. One day he went to the barber shop and lounged back in the chair to get a shave. He made the barber nervous because he kept taking his revolver out of his hip holster and messing around with it.

The barber spoke up. "Joe, you'd better put that damn thing away and leave it alone before somebody gets hurt."

Joe Tolliver looked up at him and said, "What, with this?" Then he brought the gun up to his own temple and pulled the trigger. Charlie Crouse was not able to help his half brother this time, nor ever again.

In 1902 Bridgeport was doing a reasonably good business, with the toll bridge drawing many travelers. Up river, John Jarvie wasn't doing so well.

John was alone. In 1895 his Nellie had died of tuberculosis while in the comforting embrace of her dear friend Lizzie Allen. After Nellie was buried in Ogden, Utah, where the Barr family had settled, John took on the job of raising his boys alone. Although there were many offers of help from neighboring women, it was a responsibility he felt was his alone. He nurtured them in every way he knew. He even sewed for them on Nell's treadle sewing machine.4 He gave them his knowledge and taught them independence. However, when it came time for them to exercise that independence, he hated to see them leave. In a letter to son Tom, he wrote:

I must say it was a hard blow to me when you all left, and hurt me more than ever I said, but for all that, it would have pleased me very much to have seen you all doing well, behaving yourselves as gentlemen, and getting ahead in the world . . .5

Charlie Crouse's bridge, saloon and store, located only a couple of miles down river, was hard on John's business. Almost no one used the ferry anymore and in the spring of 1902 John didn't even bother to repair any winter damages. He let it lay on the river bank like a rotting fish. On May 28 he wrote to John Jarvie, Jr.:

Crouse has a Bridge where Gray's Ferry used to be, and a P. Office and store. So I have very little to trade, and the ferry has not run for two years, but it does not take much to keep me here.

105

Charlie Crouse ditch

Some Brown's Park cowboys
Bill Davenport, Bob Franklin, Charlie Ward, Joe Davenport, Jim Warren

In that same letter John's words show the pain of a dedicated parent left with an empty nest. He wrote:

> I am well, also individually alone. The boys appearingly have all made a mistake when they chose me for their father. And each and every one, as soon as they were able, or thought they were able to be a father to themselves have left, and I candidly believe that all left with the idea that I was unfit to be father to them. Perhaps they are right, I admit I was hard to please, and wanted to see everything done away ahead of what the average boy could do. I sure had a strong desire to see my children excel in everything that was good and clever, and while everything has been backwards with me since I entered into the mining or prospecting business, yet not anything has hurt me mentally like my boys all repudiating my right to boss, or that I was capable of directing them. Yet I still think, that it will all come out for the best.[6]

Of all his sons, John, Jr. seems to have been the most lighthearted. He got a kick out of joshing his friends and had eyes which sparkled with humor and wit. His father loved his first born dearly and wrote him: "I think you will be pretty hard to beat as an all around efficient man for almost anything . . ."

One time John, Jr. and his youngest brother Jimmy went to visit Harry Hindle where he was living on Beaver Creek. Harry had put on several years since he had helped Herbert and Elizabeth Bassett capture the three Texans who had shot Jack Rollas. When John, Jr. and Jimmy stopped to see him, several other men stopped by as well. Soon a drinking party was on. The group was good-humored and laughter echoed from the log house.

The more Harry Hindle drank, the more determined he was to pay Mrs. Jim Warren a visit and give her a bawling out. He had gone up the creek to see the Warrens a few days earlier and had gotten into a tiff with Catherine Warren.

Harry said, "She told me that if I ever came back, she was a goin' to scald me with the tea kettle!"

The drunk man took one step forward and two steps back and slurred, "If you boys'll prepare my team and buggy, I'll go see Mrs. Warren and give her a cussin'!"

Most of the men present were wild horse runners. Several of their captured horses were eating in the nearby pasture and a few head were standing in the corral. John, Jr. and the others whispered together and snickered as they hurried outside. Several minutes later, the cowboys returned to the cabin and steered the pie-eyed old man out the door. With some effort the men got Harry onto the buggy seat and gave him the lines. They handed him a whip, which was a great long birch sapling cut from along the creek.

Harry Hindle sat down, leaned forward in the seat, and let fly with the birch. It came down stingingly across the horses' rumps. At that instant, Harry was thrown backward as the horses bolted forward. They commenced kicking and bucking causing the wagon and Harry to be jerked in all directions. The harnessed pair were not Harry's gentle team but two wild broncs fresh from the mountain. The frightened horses broke into a gallop and rushed down the dusty road with the buggy wheels spinning and bouncing. Suddenly Harry stood up, threw the lines away and took the birch in both hands. Harry was pouring it on with the birch sapling whip and whooping like a drunken sailor, and the wild horses were doing their level best to run, when the comedy went around the hill and out of sight.

John, Jr. and the other men roared with laughter. Their sides were still aching from laughing about five minutes later when they saw the horses and buggy come back into sight. All the fun stopped. The buggy seat was empty. Then they saw Harry dragging under the buggy, his feet tangled in the leather lines. The men, suddenly sober, ran and headed off the puffing, sweat-soaked horses. When they got Harry loose, he was skinned and beat to a bloody mash. They got him in the house and he was so near death that it was hard to find any life at all. All of the men, except for John, Jr. were frightened of what they had done to Harry. They hurried to their horses and rode away. John, Jr. cleaned Harry up, stayed by his bedside, and did for him what he could. John was certain the old man would die within hours, but the next day Harry surprised him and woke up. Harry healed quickly and before long he was fine. John shook his head and guessed that the tough old fellow had survived the wild wagon ride because he had been whiskey-numbed at the time.7

Back at Bridgeport in the year of 1904, Charlie Crouse's life changed more drastically than he ever anticipated. He had loved and depended on his wife Mary, but never realized how much until it was too late to tell her. When she died, a big part of him died with her. He was never the same.

Although the Crouses had been John Jarvie's competitors in business, they were always his friends. He liked Charlie and the boys, Stanley and Clarence. He truly loved young Minnie and her kind mother, Mary. At Mary's burial near the river at the

Farm Ford, Brown's Park listened as John Jarvie spoke these words:

> Here in this world where life and death are equal kings, all should be brave enough to meet what all have met - from the wondrous tree of life the buds and blossoms fall with ripened fruit and in the common bed of earth patriarchs and babes sleep side by side.
>
> It may be that death gives all there is of worth to life. If those who press and strain against our hearts could never die perhaps that love would wither from the earth. Maybe a common faith treads from out the paths between our hearts and the weeds of selfishness and I should rather live and love where death is king than have eternal life where love is not. Another life is naught unless we know and love again the ones who love us here.
>
> The largest and nobler faith in all that is and is to be, tells us that death even at its worst is only perfect rest - we have no fear; we all are children of the same mother and the same fate awaits us all. We, too, have our religion and it is this: "Help for the living, Hope for the dead."
> 8

Shortly after Mary died, Clarence and Stanley left for lives of their own. Minnie became the lady of the house and took care of her father. Within a short time the Bridgeport bridge was torn and twisted into splinters by a rampaging ice jam. Charlie never found the heart to rebuild it. He stopped selling almost everything but whiskey. He took quite a bit of that supply for himself.

As for John Jarvie, although no amount of coaxing could get the Jarvie boys back home to live, they hadn't strayed far and usually worked nearby. It pleased John Jarvie that once again his ferry was on the river, that his store business had picked up, and that his boys came to see him often.

Chapter XVI
C.M. TAYLOR

Charles Melvin "C.M." Taylor was an uncommon man. A self-styled perfectionist, he was tall, as rugged as a wild horse, yet gently sensitive. He was born in Hamburg, Iowa on March 21, 1876. His folks, Samuel and Nancy Taylor, later moved their family to Ainsworth, Nebraska. There C.M. grew up with his brothers Frank and George and a sister Eliza. C.M.'s parents never had much money, but they were kind and happy people. His wide-girthed mother showed a touch of Indian heritage in her heavy browed eyes. She smoked a corn cob pipe and often folded her children in great soft hugs. C.M.'s English father was tall and slender. He wore a long beard and brought C.M. and the others along with a gentle hand.₁

In time, C.M.'s thick-set brother, George, grew a droopy mustache. With his hat scooted back on his head, he looked the part of the Nebraska sheriff he became. Eliza married and lived nearby. Frank was different. He dressed in the finest suits and slicked his hair back from his handsome face. He became a professional gambler finding pleasure in the company of dance hall "chippies." C.M. shook his head at the shame Frank's lifestyle brought to his quiet parents.

C.M. helped work, plant, weed, and harvest the fields of the family farm. He enjoyed watching things grow. But as C.M. grew, he couldn't stop looking west and wondering about the mountains and the cattle ranches located there.

By the time C.M. was a young man, he was an engaging combination of lighthearted charm and strong good looks. He knew how to handle a bullwhip and his pearl-handled six-shooter and he always wore a big hat. He was slim-hipped but showing signs that he was going to be a big man. His eyes were bluish gray and their gaze was magnetic. He lit soft flames of romance in the hearts of many young girls, but Nina Cole was something special, even if she did act a bit too proper.

Nina Floy Cole was born at Oxford Mills, Iowa, on August 21, 1882. She was the third of ten children born to the union of Ruth Edith May Smith and George Andrew Cole. When Nina was about four years old, her family moved to Ainsworth where they farmed and prospered.

As a teenager, Nina had chocolate-brown hair that hung long and wavy. Her eyebrows arched above large dove-gray eyes. A slender girl, she carried herself as gracefully as a doe in a meadow.

Nina Cole   C.M. Taylor

C.M. was twenty-five, and Nina was nineteen, when most of their dances began being reserved for each other. They grew steadily closer and found excuses to be together as often as they could. Then after she had lain with him, and her shoulders had trembled with sobs when she told him of the child, C.M. knew he would love and care for her always. They were married on January 29, 1901.

By 1906 C.M. and Nina were the parents of five-year-old Jesse Gerald and two-year-old Nancy May. It was on a bright June morning and the family was busy stripping the last of their belongings from the little farm house and packing everything, just so, in a covered wagon.

C.M. had tried to be satisfied on the Nebraska farm. But every little while his thoughts turned to his dream of owning a ranch in those far off mountains.

In the spring of 1906 during calving, he got up early to check on a cow he knew was close to having her calf. When C.M. stepped from the house, he was sickened by the sight of a neighbor's huge boar hog eating on the newborn calf. The final strap holding him in Nebraska snapped.[2]

C.M. had corresponded with the postmasters in Rangely, Colorado, and Vernal, Utah, to learn about those areas. It was the Vernal country he and Nina decided upon. Nina was sad to leave her family, but she was ready for an adventure. The couple sold the farm and all the livestock except for the gray team and C.M.'s bald-faced bay saddle horse.

Jesse Taylor

Finally, with seven hundred dollars cash in their pockets, they were ready to go. The tearful family goodbyes had been said; a route had been mapped out with the bridges, fords and fresh water stops clearly marked; the wagon was packed; the bay gelding was tied on behind; and the children were snug in the back.

C.M. climbed onto the wagon seat and picked up the reins. Then he winked at Nina and grinned.

"Well, family, we're on our way!" C.M. said. Clapping the leather lines across the rumps of the gray team, he turned them southwest.

Blonde, curly-headed Jesse and his dark-haired little sister, Nancy, watched out the egg-shaped hole in the rear of the canvas wagon covering and urged Jack, the big greyhound, to hurry and keep up. They waved goodbye to the whirring windmill and the empty farmhouse. Their blue eyes watched the farm get smaller and smaller until it faded from sight. Then Nancy played with her doll and Jesse kept his toy silver pistol handy to shoot any buffalo or bear they might chance to meet on the trail.

The Taylors didn't try to make too many miles in a day, so animals and humans fared well. When they stopped to make night camp, the first thing C.M. did was make sure that the horses were well tended. When he removed the heavy harness, the horses usually sniffed at the ground, then buckled their front legs under them and rolled onto their sides. They squirmed onto their backs and kicked their legs in the air to rub the itchy sweat of the day's work away. Then they got to their feet with a groan and shook the dust free.

Jesse gathered whatever seasoned firewood was available. When he could find cow chips, he would kick the dried manure clumps loose from the ground and pack them back to camp. The chips made a lot of smoke, but they burned slow and hot, making a dandy cooking fire. It didn't take Nina long to have a kettle of beans and salt pork bubbling beside a skillet of frying potatoes. The sliced potatoes sizzled to a golden brown in plenty of flavorful pork grease. Other times the family would dine on fresh sage chicken or rabbit. Whatever the supper was, it almost always included a dutch oven filled with thin-crusted baking powder biscuits.

A handful of Arbuckle's coffee beans were ground daily in the coffee mill. The fresh grounds were added to a coffee pot filled with cold water, then the pot was placed on the fire. As the water simmered, the steeping grounds sent delicious tufts of steam into the air. At last a little dab of cold water was poured on the foamy top to settle the grounds.

When supper was ready everyone took a filled plate to some comfortable spot. Occasionally they sat in the grass and at other times they chose a log or a rock or sometimes the wagon tongue. For dessert, they often had a square of sorghum and raisin flavored coffee cake.

When it turned dusk, C.M. lit the end of the braided rag placed in a pie tin filled with grease. Aside from the campfire, the flame of the smoking "bitch lights" were their only lamps. Bedtime usually came soon after. Snuggling into soft blanket-covered featherticks inside the wagon was a welcome time. Sometimes in the night they were awakened by the soft patter of rain on the canvas roof and a sweet dampness touching their noses.

When dawn came the family was up and busy. They all washed in the blue enamel wash basin and Jesse and Nancy winced as Nina combed the knotted tangles from their hair. After a breakfast of salt pork, which had been fried crisp, and a stack of hotcakes with syrupy molasses, they were ready to meet a brand new day.

The day they first spotted the Rocky Mountains, C.M. wasn't sure whether to feel excited or not. Nina, who always called C.M. by his given name, asked, "Charles, are those clouds way over there?"

"I'm not sure," C.M. answered. "I was just puzzling on that very thing." Then with a sparkle he said, "By gosh, Nina, I believe those are mountains!"

As the wagons wheels turned round and round, the family watched the silent giants grow on the horizon. It had been a long haul but C.M. was certain that by the next day they would be making camp at the foot of the mountains. When they came upon some men working a short distance from the road, C.M. handed Nina the reins. He set the heavy iron brake lever so that it fit into the ratchet frame, and hopped down from the seat. He walked over to the men, visited a few minutes, then came back to the wagon shaking his head and laughing at himself.

"Well, it seems I have a lot to learn. Those fellows said that at the rate we're traveling, we'd be blamed lucky to reach the mountains in three or four days time!"

As the Taylor family passed to the north of Ft. Collins, Colorado, they were entertained by the United States Cavalry. C.M. pulled the team to a halt and they watched a company of mounted soldiers practice their maneuvers. The soldiers walked, trotted, then galloped their groomed mounts in formation. Then, upon a given order to charge, the cavalrymen spurred their horses to a full run. It was a new and memorable experience for the travelers.

When they finally reached the mountains, C.M. was not disappointed. He was won over by the beauty of ledgerock and pine, mint green meadows, chattering squirrels and showy sprays of wild flowers. The higher the wagon road took them, the sweeter and cooler the air became. As they made their way over Rabbit Ears Pass they saw the twin granite peaks from which the pass got its name, jutting high into the sky.

Although it was mid-summer, the Taylors noticed patches of lingering snow. Suddenly they were halted by a huge drift blocking the road. The snow had a crust, but refused to support the weight of the horses or heavy wagon. The family worked together to unload food, utensils, clothes, pictures, books, and bedding. With their burden lightened, the horses managed to break trail through the drift and pull the wagon to dry ground on

115

the other side. Everything was then carried across the snow bank and repacked in the wagon. There was one more big drift waiting for them on down the road, and they patiently repeated the same routine.

As they started to descend the mountain, the ground grew slippery and the grade sharply steep. Holding the team and wagon steady was a touchy job. When C.M. felt the wagon was in danger of sliding out of control, he very gently stopped the horses and set the brake.

C.M. said, "Nina, we'll get you and the children out of the wagon first, then I'll see what I can do to give those poor horses some help."

As Nina and the kids watched from solid ground, C.M. rigged up a "rough lock." He hooked the end of his big chain to the wagon box, then wound it around one rear wheel, between the wooden spokes. When C.M. urged the horses to move slowly forward, the chain had the effect he had hoped for. It prevented the wheel from turning, causing it to drag. Also, it dug constantly into the ground for added traction. C.M. took the team and wagon down the slope while Nina carried Nancy. Jesse walked along with his dog, Jack. It was a slow, but safe, trip. Although the mountain had caused a few hardships, C.M. barely noticed. He understood why he had been drawn to this country for as long as he could remember.

Destiny is a fragile thing. For the Taylors it was as fragile as the bridge which lay broken and scattered along the banks of the tumbling Yampa (Bear) River. They could see the little town of Maybell, Colorado, but they couldn't ford the churning river to get there. They made their way around the hills and camped for the night. The next morning, C.M. crossed the river in a

C.M. Taylor family the day they left Nebraska

116

Mr. and Mrs. James Greenhow, taken during the winter of 1907-1908

borrowed rowboat and walked to Maybell to find out how they could possibly continue on to Vernal.

Basin big sagebrush can grow extremely tall. It was within the shelter of these grayish bushes that the Taylors had made their camp the night before. Having forbidden the children to go anywhere near the river, Nina busied herself with camp chores. She threw out the last of the dishwater and made the two beds in the wagon. Lost in her own thoughts she jerked when two men on horseback rode out from the brush. Although they were alert and watchful, they treated Nina with respect. They stayed only long enough to accept a quick cup of coffee and some cold biscuits.

As they rode out, one of the men turned in his saddle and said, "Since you folks can't get across the river, you might think about heading toward Brown's Hole." Then they disappeared as quickly as they had come.

It was evening when C.M. returned. He was still undecided about what to do. Nina was just glad he was back for she would always believe that the two men who stopped that morning were outlaws on the run.[3]

Just about the time supper began to steam on the fire, a young cowboy named Bill Braggs rode in. He was leading two pack horses and an extra saddle horse. He was made welcome to stay for supper. Later he decided to take off his bat-winged chaps and stay until morning.

"Why yes," he said, "I know of Brown's Hole, or Brown's Park.

117

People call it both. Anyway, that's where I've just come from. I graze some cattle there sometimes."

Nancy and Jesse were put to bed. The adults sat up talking about the valley long into the night.

After they parted company the next morning, it was Billy Braggs' directions the Taylors were following when they crossed the bridge on Snake River. They made noon camp just above the bridge in a grassy meadow.

For lunch Nina brought out some biscuits left over from the night before and opened a two-gallon wooden keg of herring. C.M. was busy making sure the three horses were fixed so they could get a bite or two of grass. He was fascinated by some cowboy activity going on up river. He could see three horse-backers working more cattle than he had ever seen in one herd. Just as Nina called that it was ready to eat, C.M. saw one of the riders rein away from the others. The horse trotted along the river bank, heading for the Taylor wagon. A minute or two later an attractive woman with dark red hair and greenish gray eyes stepped easily from the saddle. She was dressed in chaps and hat.

The woman stuck out a friendly hand and said, "Hello there, I'm Ann Bernard."

Ann Bassett Bernard happily shared the noon meal with the Taylors. When she discovered that they were heading for Brown's Park, she spilled over with stories about the valley where she had been born. Before she left she gave them some final directions told them just where to cross muddy old Vermillion Creek, and waved a wide goodbye as she rode out in a dust. Nina and C.M. had made a new friend and five-year-old Jesse had developed a special admiration which stayed with him always.

A couple of days later, on a heat rippling August afternoon, the covered wagon moved to the top of a little rise and the Taylors saw the valley of Brown's Park sweeping westward with a quiet beauty. To their distant right were the creamy cliffs of Irish Canyon. Close on the left towered the red rocks of Lodore Canyon. Traveling a bit further the Taylors saw that Diamond Mountain crinkled toward the lowering sun with more shades of blue than they had ever known existed.

The next day's travel took the Taylors about eleven miles into the valley, to the George Sterling place. The Sterlings were a friendly couple with three children named Rex, Cyrill, and Will Rose. After a few shy minutes, Nancy and Jesse went off to play with their new friends. The two families spent a pleasant evening and it was decided that the next morning C.M. would ride his horse up the valley to scout things out. Nina said she would be thankful for a day to rest and visit.

118

Not long after daybreak the next morning, C.M. put on his wide-brimmed Stetson and saddled the bay. By the time the sun began to rise behind them, the gelding had covered quite a bit of ground. C.M. was an observant young man and was bound to notice just about everything as he rode toward the upper end of Brown's Park. Among the sagebrush he saw the bunches of shadscale growing low with its flat leaves and spikey twigs. There also were the dried stems of cheat grass bleached tan from the summer heat and the furry yellow blossoming rabbit brush. The tall blue blades of western wheatgrass and stemmy needle-and-thread grass were maturing to what would be nutritious winter forage. He saw that along the river, most of the bottoms were productive hay meadows bordered by cottonwoods and bushy greasewood.

C.M. rode through the cedars and over old scorched Indian fires. He was followed and scolded by black and white magpies. He heard the chirping of yellow and gray kingbirds and saw the flitting of many other cedar birds as he passed over busy anthills and various animal tracks. The gelding walked and trotted through gullies and over knolls, some were red-tinted and rocky and others, powdery and chalk white. Horse and rider traveled through Goodman Gulch, past the Hoy and Spitzie river bottoms, through Spitzie Draw, then past Hog Lake.

C.M. rode into the Willow Creek Ranch a couple of miles after crossing out of Colorado and into Utah. At that time the place was owned by Augustine Kendall of the First National Bank in Rock Springs and was being run by a former blacksmith from Rock Springs named James Greenhow. C.M. first got acquainted with Mr. Greenhow then met his plump wife and her son from a previous marriage. The boy's name was Jim Graham. Jim was a wiry teenager with penetrating pale blue eyes and a quiet manner. The sandy-haired boy had just returned with a string of trout from the creek.

The Greenhows took a liking to C.M. and in an effort to brag on things a little, took him over to Birch Creek to the George Celvington place. There C.M. met Albert Williams. The orchard George had planted years earlier smelled of ripening fruit. C.M. picked a plump nectarine, the first he had ever seen. The instant he bit into the sweet, juicy, sun-warmed peach, he made his decision to stay.

The next day C.M. swung out of the saddle and said, "Well, Mrs. Taylor, we're going to pull the wagon up here about twenty-five miles and that's where we're going to stop."

When they left the Sterlings, Jesse sat in the back of the wagon, pouted, and listened to his father's excitement about there being work at Bridgeport. The boy couldn't have cared less about work, he just wanted his favorite silver pistol which

119

had mysteriously disappeared in the night.

It was just after dark when the Taylors pulled into the Greenhow place. They discovered a house full of men playing poker and enjoying a few glasses of whiskey. C.M. joined the conversation, but he didn't join the game. He didn't begrudge others their fun, but because of his brother, Frank, he had no use for a deck of cards. However, jolly introductions were made all around and the men wholeheartedly welcomed the Taylors to Brown's Park.

Later on C.M. asked, "Mrs. Greenhow, where's your boy Jim tonight!"

The heavy-set woman put her hand to her chest and whispered, "Oh, he's holding the money stakes, don't you know. He's run to hide down in the willows." She patted her chest. "Oh, my, I have a weak heart you know and I don't like this. But Jimmy knows that Albert Williams and Charlie Crouse are drinking and he'd better stay hid 'till morning."

The evening passed in good-humored fun. However, it was dawn before the teenager showed up with the poker stakes safely tucked in his pockets.4

Later that day the Taylor wagon creaked to a halt next to the bunkhouse and beneath the shade of the cottonwood trees at Bridgeport, Utah. The family was greeted warmly by Charlie Crouse and his daughter Minnie. The river purred in a swift, steady motion as Charlie bent slightly and spoke to Jesse.

"Now that river's up young fella, you be awful careful if you go down around it."

Charlie showed the Taylors his solid little establishment. Bridgeport was made up of the main house, bunkhouse, meat house, blacksmith shop, and corrals. A combination store and saloon existed in a low-slung dugout.

C.M. turned to look the country over and was strongly impressed by the extreme closeness of the mountains. Among the foothills, standing alone and looking out of place, was one with vertical golden cliffs. It would have looked more at home in the desert with a Navajo tribe camped beneath it. Behind the hills, Cold Spring Mountain swept upward. Squarely in front of C.M., just across a sagebrush flat known as Bake Oven, Jesse Ewing Canyon sliced through dusty-rose colored Mountain Home. When he looked up river, he saw Diamond Mountain folding in pretty bluish green peaks.

C.M.'s love for Brown's Park was immediate, his bond with her absolute. And now, there was that ranch to build.

Chapter XVII

HEARTBREAKS AND HEARTACHES

A new life with new friends was beginning for the Taylors. Charlie Crouse helped C.M. and Nina find a private, shady spot to make camp. It was down river from Bridgeport in a grove of cottonwoods. First thing the next morning C.M. went to work for Charlie. He hooked his gray team to a Mormon scraper to help hired men Gus Beard and Bill Aines clean river trash from the big irrigation ditch.[1]

Bill Aines was a happy-natured cowboy and C.M. liked him right off. It didn't take long for C.M. to see that the nice looking fellow was in love with Minnie Crouse. Whenever the daintily built girl appeared, Bill's face reddened a little and his eyes brightened.

Minnie Crouse was delightful. She was friendly, kind, and exceptionally pretty. She had received a fine education from the private tutor her father brought to the Park Live Ranch, from Mrs. Blair at the school on Beaver Creek, and from teachers in the east when she stayed with her Uncle Billy and Aunt Jean Tittsworth at their new home in Iowa.

Bill Aines wasn't alone in the way he felt about Minnie. She was the belle of upper Brown's Park and just about every eligible bachelor in the area found her irresistible. They competed constantly and sometimes heatedly for the chance to sport her around. Minnie never took any of it too seriously, but the men certainly did. Bill had his hands full trying to hold them off.

Once, a young man from Vernal showed up on the other side of the river with a load of freight for Bridgeport. Bill Aines recognized him and remembered that the man had paid just a little too much attention to Minnie the last time they were in Vernal.

Bill saw the man wave and over the roar of the river he heard, "Hello there. I say hello there Bill. Would you please direct me as to where I should cross?"

Bill started to point out the shallow fording place above the riffles, then stopped. Grinning, he motioned the wagon to come straight forward. Once the team and wagon were in the water, Bill began waving at them to turn down river. The inexperienced driver fell for the prank and turned directly into the swift river current.

Suddenly the current grabbed the wagon causing the horses to flounder. Just as the wagon toppled over, the young man screeched in a panic and jumped from the seat. He made it to the other side and struggled up the grassy bank. Seconds later the horses managed to drag the overturned wagon to shore. Some of the spilled freight sank immediately; the rest littered the river and bobbed around the bend and out of sight. All the while Bill was acting innocent and trying his best not to laugh out loud. The young would-be suiter was gasping and cussing.

"Damn your dirty rotten hide, you nearly got me drowned."

Bill didn't say anything. He knew the river wasn't all that deep and the only real casualties were the young fellow's dampened ego and his spilled goods.

Ben Kelly's son Roy from up in Little Hole was a much more serious rival for Bill. Roy Kelly was a tall, lanky cowboy. He occasionally worked for Charlie Crouse and he, too, wanted Minnie. On several occasions she consented to ride to Little Hole with Roy for delicious suppers of his father's fried grouse. During one trip they stopped to sit under a tree.

The young couple laughed and laughed when Minnie jumped to her feet and said, "Oh, my! A bird has spit on my lap!"[2]

One chilly moonlit evening at Bridgeport, Roy took Minnie for a walk along the riverbank. Poor Bill Aines sat in the large one-room bunkhouse and felt miserable. Then he eyed the stack of warm blankets on Roy's bed and his face perked up.

After Minnie had said a sweet good night to Roy, the young man sauntered happily into the bunkhouse, a large unheated room that was sometimes used for dances. The only light that night was a pale moonbeam shining in the window. Roy undressed and hurried to get under the warmth of his blankets.

Abruptly Roy spun around holding one threadbare quilt and said, "Why hell Bill, where's all the rest of my beddin'?"

Bill pulled his own single blanket up to his neck and answered in a hoarse whisper, "This was all I could find."

Roy was puzzled but he had no choice but to climb into bed with his one thin cover. Even though Bill had to keep his tent pole legs bent and his knees tucked under his chin to keep from freezing, he had the satisfaction of knowing that Roy was bound to be uncomfortable, too.

However, first thing the next morning Roy made a point of asking Minnie to accompany him to Little Hole. She consented and Bill Aines felt miserable once again.

C.M. sympathized with Bill. It seemed the harder the cowboy tried, the less Minnie noticed him. Bill did keep a happy spirit though, making him especially loved by children. He, in turn, liked kids and always kept a few pieces of candy in his pocket for the little ones. Jesse and Nancy knew that whenever Bill Aines came around, they were in for a treat.

Minnie Crouse, taken in 1908

One day when he ran out of sweets, he gave Jesse some money and pointed him in the direction of John Jarvie's store. Dreaming of the sack of candy he was going to buy, the little boy started hurrying up Bake Oven flat. Suddenly he realized he was alone and the flat was covered with cattle. He wanted the candy badly, but when two bulls began bellowing, throwing dirt, and knocking each other around, Jesse spun and ran back as fast as he could.

Bill was understanding and said, "I don't blame you a bit kid. We'll go to the store together when I get my work done here."

For a while the Taylor family continued to make the covered wagon their home. They got used to hearing Brown's Park's coyotes yelp and her wolves howl. They also got used to seeing Indians camped along the river near Bridgeport. They discovered Brown's Park was a much used stopping point for the Indians when they traveled between reservations.

One evening as C.M. walked to Bridgeport, he topped a knoll and saw that the big corral by the river was full of pinto, sorrel, black, dun, and palomino Indian ponies. There were tepees and camps of all kinds along the river, all the way to Bridgeport. There was a lot of activity with children running and giggling and gray smoke curling skyward from many small fires.

As C.M. walked by Charlie's dugout saloon, he heard laughter and mutterings of drunken Indians. Several bucks were gambling and were setting cross-legged on bright yellow, red, and blue blankets spread out on the dirt floor. Toward the back of the saloon, scattered here and there, other Indians slept. Earlier the Utes had skinned and eaten a big bull snake. The hide was draped over the fence to dry and would later be put to some use.

C.M. saw Charlie Crouse come out of his house with his rifle. He told one of his cowboys to take his horse and cut out a fat steer from the herd on the flat. As the roan steer trotted by, Charlie fired. Immediately the Indians began to chatter. Then they ran to the downed steer and gutted it out. As he always did, Charlie took the best meat and gave the Indians the rest. The Utes took their share, including the entrails, to the river to wash it all off, then they stoked the fire built behind the saloon to a huge orange blaze. There they cooked the beef and had a feast.

That night Charlie Crouse told C.M. many Indian stories. He talked of his fight with the half-breed when he lived at the Park Live. He talked about Indian fights on the plains and about shooting Indians for their horses.

Charlie took a few swallows of whiskey and laughed, "One time, Taylor, I lay and wait as a buck on a big sorrel gelding started to cross the river. I shot and shot, but I never could hit that Indian."

After listening for hours C.M. said, "My goodness, Charlie, you should write a book."

Charlie Crouse looked sober and said, "No Taylor, I wouldn't dare tell it all. And if I can't write it all, I won't write anything."

After many years of turbulent friendship, Charlie Crouse and Albert Williams respected each other, liked to drink together, and feared one another. Charlie often drove his team and buggy to get Albert at the Park Live where Albert was working. The two men would spend the day at Bridgeport, drinking, gambling, and playfully sparring.

One Sunday the two had been drinking most of the afternoon. C.M. Taylor and a couple of other men were nearby when Albert said, "Crouse, I has got to go home now 'cause I has chores to do."

"Oh, I'll take you after while," Charlie answered.

A few minutes later the Negro said, "Crouse, I has got to get goin'. If you don't take me pretty soon, I's goin' a foot."

Charlie Crouse frowned and said, "You black s.b., if you start down the road, I'll go in the house and get my .30-.30 and I'll kill ya!"

Albert started down the ditch bank and said, "Well, I is goin'!"

Charlie turned and ran around the side of the house. He dashed in the door and into the bedroom where he kept his rifle.

A few minutes passed. Charlie stuck his head out the door and saw Albert peeking around the corner of the house. Neither man had a gun. They both started to laugh. Before long the two drunk men rode merrily off together in the buggy.

After the two were out of sight, Minnie told C.M. and the other men that her dad had not been able to find his rifle. With relief in her voice she said, "I had it hid."

Shortly thereafter C.M. made a deal with Charlie on the Joe Tolliver place. At last the family could move from the covered wagon. Nina and C.M. were excited about moving to such a pretty place, in spite of the fact that the Jarvie boys insisted the three-room house was haunted.

The boys told the Taylors, "We got spooked when we was staying there a while back. There's some mighty strange noises in that place at night."

Within a few days the Taylors had the Tolliver house scrubbed clean and filled with family belongings. Later that night the house was very dark and quiet. The family started to fall asleep. A soft "clickety-thump, clickety-thump" caused Nina and C.M. to open their eyes. C.M. struck a match but could see nothing out of place.

Nina said, "It sounded just like a big dog walking cross the floor didn't it?"

"It surely did, but I don't see a thing," C.M. answered.

Events occurred in much the same way for the next few nights. Finally when C.M. struck the match, he caught the barest glimpse of something behind a box in the corner. A closer look revealed the unmistakable white and black spotted tip of a civit cat's tail. Nina held a candle as C.M. took aim.

C.M. whispered, "He won't stink if I can blow him in two."

Following the gunshot there was a mess to be cleaned, but there was no skunk smell! The next day everyone, including the Jarvie boys, had a good laugh about the identity of the "ghost" of the Joe Tolliver place.

Charlie Crouse often visited the Taylors at their new home. Whenever young Jesse saw him coming, he ran up to him and asked to see his pocket knife. Charlie always grinned and pulled the pretty pearl-handled knife from his pants pocket.

"Run and get a stick, boy. Then you can do some whittlin'," he'd say.

One afternoon C.M. and Jesse stopped at Jack Geishow's sheep camp in a draw near the Parsons cabin. Jack was herding sheep for the King brothers. Jesse couldn't believe it when Jack showed an interest in C.M.'s pearl handled forty-four six-shooter and his dad handed the gun to the sheepherder for a five dollar bill.

On the way home Jesse asked, "Dad, why'd you turn loose of your six-shooter?"

C.M. looked thoughtful and said, "Son, I'm in a new country now. I'm better off without that gun."

As time passed, C.M. used his gray team to haul freight for both Charlie Crouse and John Jarvie. Whenever he went on a trip he left so early that the stars were still dusted brightly in the pre-dawn sky. He learned a lesson the first time he tried to travel during a late fall afternoon.

It had been a wet autumn and the gumbo mud stuck and froze between the spokes until the big wheels were almost filled solid. C.M. knocked big chunks of mud loose every little bit, but more gobs of mud soon took their place. The weight for the horses was terrible. He stopped the team and chopped four piles of brush. He placed a pile in front of each wheel. C.M. had the horses pull the wagon forward until the wheels rested on top of the brush. Once the temperature dropped that evening, the team was able to pull the wagon off the brush piles easily and make good time across the frozen ground.

As was the common practice of the freighters, C.M. always carried a wooden keg of whiskey with a twist spout. He purchased a .25-.35 rifle and carried it in a scabbard tied on one of the team horses.

On one particular freighting trip to Rock Springs, Charlie Crouse accompanied C.M. with another supply wagon. The two men made night camp outside of Rock Springs, near the stockyards. Just before dark a Pinkerton detective rode up and got off his horse. Ignoring C.M., the detective walked straight to where Charlie was sitting by the fire.

Arrogantly the man said, "Well, hello again Mr. Crouse."

Charlie answered with a slight nod.

Immediately the detective began questioning him. He demanded to know the whereabouts of some certain men who were wanted in connection with a recent robbery. Charlie merely shrugged his shoulders and several times quietly said he didn't know. The detective was overbearing and threatening.

"Are you aware, sir, that I have the authority to put you in jail if . . . ."

Suddenly Charlie's eyes flashed and he jumped to his feet. Directly into the detective's face he said, "Listen here you son of a bitch, I said I didn't know where those men are! Even if I did, you don't need to think I'd tell you! Now get the hell out of here right now!"

126

The Pinkerton agent apparently knew he had pushed the older man too far. Without another word he mounted his horse and left.

A part of Charlie was still the bold youngster who had endured the rigors of a civil war, the great plains, and the settling of a young frontier all in his own way. However, a greater part of him had become a heavyhearted and sorrowful man. He talked to C.M. about his half brother's suicide in Vernal.

"I always accused Joe of having no nerve. You know, I believe he had more nerve than any of us. I've tried to kill myself a dozen times."[4]

More and more often when he went to see the Taylors, he would sit on the fireplace hearth, liquor jug at his side, and talk about his life. He had never imagined anything would happen to his wife, Mary. For so many years he had taken her loyalty and her comforting presence for granted.

"My goodness, Taylor," he'd say, "I had a good woman and I treated her bad."

Then he would drink deeply from the whiskey jug until he passed out across the hearth. Sometimes during his troubled sleep he would appear to stop breathing. Then with a whimper, he would start breathing once again. C.M. stayed close by and wished there was something he could do to ease Charlie's torment.

Minnie left Brown's Park and filed on a homestead on Spring Creek. Although Charlie gave up Bridgeport and went with her, he and Minnie still came back to visit the Taylors. The last time he was in Brown's Park, Charlie handed Jesse his pocket knife then sat down next to him. For a while he watched the youngster whittle on a tree branch. Then he slowly nodded his head.

"Kid, I'm going to give you that knife," he said.

Not long after that Charlie was traveling alone to Rock Springs in his buggy when he took ill. A man Charlie knew named Pete Dorrence found him slumped across the seat. Pete took Charlie to his place and tried to save him, but Charlie soon passed away. His funeral and burial was in Rock Springs. It would undoubtedly have pleased Charlie that Mary was moved from her grave by the Farm Ford in Brown's Park and placed at his side.

Brown's Park missed them both.

By their third fall at the Tolliver place, Nina had planted asparagus next to the creek and lilacs by the garden. She had a wood-burning stove to cook on now and coal oil lamps to brighten the night. She got well acquainted with many of the Brown's Park women and their families.

There was Maude Smith who moved with her husband from

127

Red Creek to Bridgeport, and then to Willow Creek. Later, when the Smiths moved to Fossil, Wyoming, Jesse went along to drive their herd of horses.

Nina also enjoyed visiting with Mrs. Pete Lowe on Beaver Creek. Mrs. Lowe was a large Danish woman with a happy disposition. She had fluffy feather mattresses and extra large

The Dishners

128

feather pillows. She had two children, a boy named Holga, and a girl, Elga. Elga was prone to sunstroke so she had to stop helping in the hay fields and stayed in the house to help her mother. Mrs. Lowe cooked for a lot of hay hands and sometimes fed them big pots of stewed nectarines from the George Kelvington place. She took good care of Harry Hindle in his old age, always seeing to it that he had plenty to eat and a clean hanky on his lap. Her generous husband, Pete, was "a breeder of body lice" and had stomach trouble. He often took a package of soda a day.5 He was hard of hearing and narrowly escaped a flash flood that roared down Willow Creek one day. He jumped from the wagon in time, but his wagon and team were swept away. One horse was never found, the other was found a long way down the creek. The horse had been rolled and tumbled until there was no hair left on his body.

Elmer Bradshaw and his family had a place at the mouth of Red Creek Canyon. He let Jesse ride his buckskin horse, Buck, to push Two-Bar cattle out of the area.

Nina cupped her hand over her nose and mouth and laughed when Mrs. James Greenhow talked about Elmer's daughter. After the girl married, her name was Gertie Dishner. Mrs. Greenhow called her "Dirty Dishes" because she piled all the used plates, silverware, skillets, and pots in a tub under the kitchen table until there were no more in the cupboard.

Nina had special friends in neighbors Amelia Teters and Leigh Myers. She also got close to Dave Tolliver's wife, Retta Green Tolliver. Retta was Charlie Green's sister. Dave was the son of Joe Tolliver. Retta and Dave lived for a while in the draw next to the Taylors while Dave did a little mining. Retta was a sweet person. Dave was a dandy by nature and tried to make a living by gambling. He was vain about his appearance and always dressed in "just so" clothes with a pistol holstered on his hip. When they eventually left their place in the Dave Tolliver Draw, they moved to Vernal.6

Nina's children loved their home at Joe Tolliver's old homestead. It was a playground for Nancy and Jesse. In the winter snow they made angel prints, snowballs, and happy-faced snowmen. Sometimes they scooped up a panful of clean snow and took it in the kitchen where fresh cream, vanilla, and sugar were added to make "ice cream." They learned from their father to stay away from the frozen river when the ice made a dull thudding sound when stepped upon. They learned they could trust the sharp cracking noises of "singing ice" which zinged in several directions announcing that it was solid.

In the summer, Nancy and Jesse ran and hid among the cedars and cliffs and picked yellow puffed dandelions and white buttercups in the meadows. They fished off the riverbank hoping to catch whitefish. One whitefish, baked whole in the oven, was enough to feed the entire family. The children also looked at pictures in the Montgomery Ward and Sears and Roebuck catalogs, played with the dog and the old tomcat, and made noise with rocks in tin cans. Sometimes they took turns churning butter until their arms ached.

The churn was a two gallon crock with a wooden lid that had a hole in it where a broom stick handle stuck through. The two children pumped the stick up and down, making the dasher on the end of the stick sloosh through the cream until chunks of butter began to form.

Nancy and Jesse also helped their folks by getting the milk cow in at night, gathering the eggs, feeding the chickens, and packing kitchen vegetable scraps to the pig. They often burst through the door together with stories about discovering a new animal track or some other excitement such as a hawk being after the chickens.

C.M. barely had time to react before the steel-blue hawks made their dives to snatch up the pullets from the chicken flock. Even with the weight in their claws the hawks sailed easily through the air and disappeared into the treetops. Although nature could be tough at times, Brown's Park had been very good to the Taylors. No one expected things to change.

Tom King

130

After Charlie Crouse left Brown's Park, the Harold King family moved into the Bridgeport house. Harold was one of five brothers in Brown's Park. The others included William, Charles, Fred, and Tom. Tom, like Bill Aines, was a frustrated admirer of Minnie Crouse. The King men came from England and arrived in the valley in the late 1890's. They built a homestead cabin on the north side of the river at the head of Swallow Canyon. It sat at the base of a mountain peak which came to be known as King's Point. Harold and his wife were about the same age as Nina and C.M. and they had two little boys. It was nice for the Taylors to have them close by.

When their other neighbor, John Jarvie, left his store to stop by for a visit, Nancy and Jesse ran happily to greet him. His handsome white beard and hair flowed in the breeze as the old fellow heartily welcomed the children's hugs. John always had some sweet treat from the store to hand out. Many times he would challenge Jesse to a foot race and the two would sail off across the meadow. Having had no girls of his own, he was especially fond of Nancy. He listened with great interest when she told him a story from her perch upon his knee.

Nancy was special to everyone. Her reddish hair bounced in long ringlets around her chubby face. Her bright blue eyes were curious and she was always busy. She was Jesse's shadow and rarely let her brother out of her sight.

The Taylors were at the Bridgeport house when first Harold King, then his two boys and Jesse started feeling sick. They each complained of having sore throats and some nausea. It looked as though they were in for a bout with something, so Nina and Mrs. King got busy making up sick beds. To soothe the inflamed throats, the women brewed some ginger tea and sweetened it with a dab of honey. When Harold and the boys developed fevers, some bitter quinine-filled sagebrush leaves were gathered. The leaves were steeped in the teapot to make a drink that would lower the fevers. Under the watchful care of the two women, the mildly ill patients were all doing fine.

Although Nancy had seemed well at first, Nina wasn't very surprised when she found her sitting quietly against the wall behind the warm wood stove. But when the little girl looked up, Nina was startled. Nancy's teeth were chattering and her eyes were droopy and hollow.

Barely above a whisper Nancy said, "I'm cold, Momma. My head hurts and oh, my throat stings so bad."

Then she began to cry and said her stomach hurt. Before Nina could get her from behind the stove, Nancy began to vomit. Nina held her daughter and put one hand under her forehead as Nancy violently threw up in a milk bucket. When Nancy calmed, Nina picked her up and carried her to bed. As Nina wiped Nancy's fevered skin with a damp rag she could feel the little girl's heart pounding in her small chest. When Nancy turned her head away from an offer of ginger tea, Nina looked in her throat. She saw that it was red, swollen, and pussy. Her tongue was covered with a grayish coat.

The next morning, reddish pink pin points started to form on Nancy's neck and chest. The rash rapidly spread to her abdomen, then to her legs and arms. A red flush spread to her temples and forehead and over the bridge of her tiny nose. The scarlet red was absent around her mouth and a distinct pallor surrounded her dry lips.

The following day, while her head and throat still throbbed, Nancy pulled at her now severely burning and aching ears. The gray disappeared around the edges of her tongue but left it raw and swollen. It began to look something like a strawberry.

By afternoon Nina began to feel sick. She and C.M. were exhausted and desperate. Everything they tried failed. Riding to town and returning with a doctor would take, at the very least, four days.

Nancy's symptoms intensified. Her temperature shot to around 108 degrees. Her throat was obstructed and she could barely breathe. Her blue eyes were glazed with pain. She tried to fight but the strep bacteria invading her blood was virulent. Nancy convulsed, then died.

With a November chill in the air, C.M. worked on a little pine coffin. Nancy was buried in it, beneath the trees at the Tolliver place. That evening when the sunset spread a golden glow over Brown's Park, a dirt mound barely showed above the blanket of russet and yellow leaves.

"It was scarlet fever, I'm certain," the doctor in Rock Springs told C.M. "It sounds as though you did everything you could have. I seriously doubt if I could have done more."

The despair and emptiness left by Nancy's death was severe. C.M. grieved deeply but found comfort in the mountains, wooded streams, and wildlife of his valley. In time he was able to square his shoulders and go on with his life.

Nina recovered from her own bout with scarlet fever, but when she grieved for Nancy she felt a tiny seed of bitterness toward Brown's Park take root.

Jesse grieved and discovered his and Nancy's hiding places and the shadows among the cedars were frightening to him now. He found no joy in walking beside the creek or in smelling his mothers' baking coffee cakes. He felt so alone. It was a feeling he could not quite shake - not for the rest of his life.

L to R: Jesse Taylor, Nancy Taylor, and King children
Sitting on plank across Charlie Crouse ditch in front of cellar at Bridgeport

133

Chapter XVIII
UNAVENGED MURDER

From the time C.M. Taylor first became friends with John Jarvie, he knew John was a wise and special man. But one evening C.M. discovered someone who felt differently about the old storekeeper.

The Taylors were staying overnight with the Kings at Bridgeport. Jesse was playing on the woodpile and C.M. was chopping a stack of wood. It was after sundown when George Hood rode up, figuring on spending the night.

"I'm sorry but we sure don't have any room here tonight," C.M. said. "Why don't you go on up to Mr. Jarvie's, I'm sure he'd have a bed for you."

George looked perturbed and answered, "Well, I guess I don't have much choice. But I don't know if the old son of a bitch will let me stay there or not."

Without another word the man roughly jerked his horse around and rode in the direction of the Jarvie place. C.M. watched him leave and said, "I don't much like the looks of that fellow."

Jesse agreed. George Hood had mean eyes.1

A few months after Nancy's death, C.M. had pretty much stopped freighting for John Jarvie and had gone to work for Martin Whalen at the Park Livestock Ranch. In the spring of 1909, C.M., Jesse, and an old man named Patty herded three thousand head of yearling black-faced sheep. The job was done mostly on foot and without the help of a dog. Nina helped out as camp tender and mover.

On the afternoon of July 6th, C.M. was sweating in the Park Livestock hayfields. Nina, in her sixth month of pregnancy, was taking care of things at the Tolliver place. Down at the Jarvie place, Jimmy Jarvie was climbing out of his saddle. The youngest Jarvie boy tied his horse to the hitching rail and expected to see his father step out the door any second. When John didn't appear, Jimmy walked in the house. It jolted him when he went through the door, to see that his father's home and store were a mess. A meal, prepared earlier, had never been cleaned up and on the table lay three used plates and an open jug of whiskey.

Jimmy hurried outside to look for his dad. He saw drag marks and dark stains of dried blood puddles in the dirt. With a sickness growing inside him, Jimmy called for his father. He followed the marks along the trail that led toward the river. Then

John Jarvie

he saw a patch of long, white hair snagged on a bush beside the path.

As the sun went down behind King's Point, Jesse and Walter Hanks, Jr. were hunting rabbits. C.M. and Gordon Wilson were still busy in the Park Live hayfields. The men were fighting more mosquitoes since it had cooled off, but were thankful to be rid of the heat. Both stopped working when they saw another ranch hand, "Luckin" Bill, riding hard toward them.

"It's old man Jarvie fellas. Somethin' bad has happened. I just saw Nina. She said Jimmy Jarvie was at the house wanting a gun. Nina said he was in an awful state and she was afraid to give him one. She said Jimmy told her he thinks somebody has robbed and killed his dad!"

Word spread from the Park Livestock and by morning most of the Jarvie boys and a sizable crowd of ranchers and ranch hands had gathered. Almost all of them had their guns but were confounded that they had very little ammunition between them. Nonetheless, they were determined and rode in a group toward John Jarvie's. Eight-year-old Jesse followed along on an old mare loaned to him by Adam Davenport.

136

When the group arrived at the Jarvie place the men began piecing things together. They learned that the day before Harold King and his wife had seen two men walk out of Jesse Ewing Canyon and head toward Jarvie's. They were undoubtedly the two who had eaten from John's plates, drank from his jug, assaulted him, robbed him, and apparently threw him in the river.

The group of ranchers thought the two were still in the area. It was surmised that they might be planning to do some horse stealing since they had taken several ropes and pairs of hobbles.

Emotions were sharp among the men. "To hell with the law!" they said. "After we capture those two birds we'll strip 'em and put 'em naked in the willows at the Park Live. We'll leave the buggers there for the mosquitoes to eat on until they confess. And when they do admit to it, by damn, we'll hang 'em from the ferry cable post!"

The group tracked the two men and discovered the hobbles and ropes in a pile part way up a draw just below Bridgeport. The tracks showed that the two had not stayed in Brown's Park but instead had left through Jesse Ewing Canyon. The group of ranchers halted at the red mouth of the steep canyon. They realized the opportunities for being caught in an ambush through the roadless climb were endless. That fact, coupled with the shortage of ammunition, made pursuit into the canyon foolhardy. Instead John, Jr. decided to go alone to notify the sheriff in Rock Springs, traveling through Red Creek Canyon rather than Jesse Ewing. The rest of the men rode back to John Jarvie's and hurriedly built a raft. They dragged the river, but found nothing.

The next day, July 8th, Harold King's brother, Bill, returned from a freighting trip to Rock Springs. When he heard what had happened he said, "Well, hell, I saw them. Both when I was headed to town and then again when I was on my way back. I never saw the one fellow's face because he never came near. But I talked to the other man both times. When I saw him the first time, he said they were headed down here to look for jobs. Then yesterday he said they had both changed their minds and were going to Rock Springs to find work on the railroad. I think most of you know him, it was George Hood."

George Hood's partner was his brother-in-law. When the two reached Rock Springs, it was about one o'clock in the morning. They both checked into the Park Hotel. On July 23, 1909, the Vernal newspaper said:

> One of them left a call for seven o'clock in the
> morning; the other was heard to get up about

10 o'clock. The latter had inquired about the first train east and had been told it would pass through about 11 o'clock. John Jarvie, Jr. had reached Rock Springs at about 10 o'clock that morning to give the alarm; but it took an hour or so before he could get hold of the officers, and in the meantime, the two fellows had gotten away.2

With the law alerted and looking for Hood and his partner, the Brown's Parkers continued their search for John Jarvie. They hunted for a week without finding a sign. Only because Brown's Park refused to turn loose of her long-time friend was he finally found. Eight days after the murder and over twenty miles downstream, Archie Jarvie discovered his father's swollen body. John was still tied in his overturned rowboat and had one arm tangled in some willows. He was buried nearby in the Lodore Cemetery.

Having found the body the full picture of what had happened could pretty much be seen. Intent on robbery the two apparently struck John on the head. As the old man ran outside, one of the men shot and the bullet struck John between the shoulders. Then at close range the wounded old man was shot through the temple. He was then dragged by his heels along the path around the house, across the west step, out the west gate and past the front of the dugout cellar where he and Nell had made their first home. John's lifeless body was then dumped into the rowboat. Once the body was tied in, the attached rope was cut and the boat set adrift on the river. The two then robbed the safe and took what they wanted from the Jarvie home and store.

John had recently been to Rock Springs to make his deposits and a one hundred dollar bill was all that the safe contained. In their haste, Hood and his partner missed a cigar box full of change on the shelf. They didn't miss the trunk where John kept many things, including his pearl-handled pistol.

It was later learned that George Hood had gotten off the train for a short stop at Point of Rocks east of Rock Springs. There he pawned a new pair of shoes and a pearl handled .44 six-shooter. He also was heard to ask if anyone could change a one hundred dollar bill.

In Brown's Park, John's friends sadly worked together to put his plundered home back in some sort of order. It was then that they discovered Nell's undisturbed possessions on the dresser top; her clothes hanging in the closet.

Brown's Park was sad, but the valley did not grieve alone.

On July 30th the front page of the **Vernal Express** read:

> It is hard to imagine John Jarvie dead. Harder
> still to think of him murdered. He was the sage
> of the Uintas, the genius of Brown's Park. He
> could almost be called the wizard of the hills
> and river. He was not only a man among men
> but he was a friend among men . . .
>
> He kept a ferry; but he was more than a ferry-
> man; he kept a store, but he was not cir-
> cumscribed by the small scope of a store-
> keeper.
>
> He was as broad and generous as far reaching
> in his good deeds as the stream which he knew
> and loved as a brother and over whose tur-
> bulent waters he had helped so many travelers
> and upon whose unwilling bosom he was set
> adrift to seek an unknown grave . . .[3]

Two five hundred dollar rewards for the killers were established. One was from the people of Rock Springs, the other
from Governor Cutler of Utah. Regardless, George Hood and
his brother-in-law had vanished. The posse was forced to give
up their search by the middle of August.

Jimmy and Archie weren't ready to give up. They made a vow
to bring their father's murderers to justice. They tried. But
Archie was killed in a suspicious coal mining accident in Idaho.
Jimmy followed the killers' trail to the eastern United States,
then back to Jackson Hole, Wyoming, and then to Pocatello,
Idaho. It was in Idaho where Jimmy "got too close" and was
pushed from his second floor hotel window. His neck was
broken; he died instantly.

Tom Jarvie eventually took all of his dad's cattle into the
Dutch John area where he wintered and summered them for
several years. He married Alice Finch, then bought a ranch near
Linwood.

John, Jr. stayed in Brown's Park. For a while he took over the
responsibilities of the home place. He didn't want the store and
tried to sell it. Elmer Bradshaw almost bought it, then decided
against it.

A light-haired young man named Charlie "Whitey" Roller
lived there for a while and was considering buying the place
and reopening the store. He was a likable sort and was said to
always take two steps backward to spit. He was "gone on"
Elmer Bradshaw's daughter, Bessie, and she seemed to like him
fine, but they never spent much time together. While Whitey

was staying at Jarvie's, he started to ride his favorite horse, Pap, across the river on the ice that winter. The ice was too weak and Pap broke through and fell into the bitter cold water. Whitey was able to save himself, but Pap was caught under the ice and killed. For the remainder of the winter, Pap was held in the same place, his head remaining visible above the ice.

One day Whitey was examining the guns in the Jarvie store. One of them misfired, blinding him in one eye. He left the place soon after but worked around Brown's Park for several more years. He married a Templeton girl from Maybell and ended up living in Vernal with his wife and a houseful of kids.

John Jarvie, Jr. eventually tore down the store and the home where he was raised. With the help of his retarded uncle "Crazy" Jarvie, he replaced the old home with a five-room whipsawed log house. However, he and his wife, Ollie Mae, spent most of their time at the "Little" Jarvie place on lower Beaver Creek. John, Jr. held on to his dad's property until 1924 when he sold it to Charlie Sparks.

Chapter XIX
THE FLYNNS

At first C.M. was friends with Mike Flynn. A time or two Mike's sons, Tim and Riley, stayed with the Taylors. Tim was older than Jesse but he was good to the youngster and the two were pals.

One evening the Taylors were making a trip to Vernal and stopped to spend the night at Mike Flynn's summer camp on Diamond Mountain at Pot Creek. Jesse was so proud of having Charlie Crouse's pearl-handled knife he had to show it off.

Tim pulled out his old broken-bladed knife and said, "Trade me."

Jesse looked up at him and said, "No I won't!"

Tim shrugged his shoulders and said, "Well, you might as well trade with me 'cause I'm gonna have that knife."

"Well you're not!" Jesse said.

That ended the conversation about the Charlie Crouse knife and Jesse had forgotten their dispute by the time they turned in for the night. It wasn't until the Taylors were well on their way to Vernal the next day that Jesse remembered what Tim had said. He hurriedly felt for his knife. It was gone. He never saw it again.

As C.M. became better acquainted with Mike Flynn, he grew aware of the man's true nature. Although Mike was personable, he was, without a doubt, a thief. It was hard for C.M. to imagine when Mike boasted that he had gone to Rock Springs banker Augustine Kendall and told him, "Yes, Mr. Kendall, I'm taking some of your calves and colts now and then 'cause I figure you got plenty. So, I'm brandin' a few of them once in a while."

That soured C.M. against Mike. Not long after Mike rode in with an admittedly stolen hind quarter of beef slung over his saddle and offered it to the Taylors.

C. M. shook his head and said, "You can just keep right on ridin', Mike. I have no taste for rustled beef, nor braggy rustlers."

After Mike rode away, C.M. told Nina, "That man's headed for trouble. I know it as well as I'm standing here. He's pushing things too far."

On October 7, 1909, with Mrs. King in attendance, Nina gave birth to Bessie Ethel at the Tolliver place. When Bess was only about a month old, C.M. received a letter from his mother in Nebraska saying that his father was very ill with asthma. "I need you here son," she wrote. In a short while C.M., Nina, Jesse, and baby Bess were in Rock Springs climbing aboard a Nebraska-bound train.

While they were away, the Taylors stayed in touch with Brown's Park through postcards and letters. One letter jarred and saddened them when it revealed that Mike Flynn's wife, Mercy, had shot and killed C.M.'s friend Gordon Wilson.

Mercy claimed that one afternoon while Mike was away trailing cattle to Pot Creek, Gordon had come, uninvited, into her home. Her story continued that when she realized the older bachelor's intent was to have his way with her, she was forced to shoot him to protect herself. The law ruled in Mercy's favor. But C.M. and many in Brown's Park kept strong suspicions that Mike and Mercy had carried out a plan. If they did, it worked. The Flynn's acquired Gordon Wilson's small herd of cattle, his fine bunch of saddle horses, and all of his personal possessions.

As the days went by in Nebraska, baby Bessie's parents feared something was wrong. When they were in her vision her eyes brightened and she smiled happily. However, she never reacted to the sounds around her, no matter how loud they were. When Nina and C.M. took her to the doctor it was confirmed - Bessie was deaf.

By the time Bess Taylor turned two, her grandfather, Samuel Taylor, had died and her father had returned his family, along with his mother and his nephew Ben, to Brown's Park. They had all learned to cope with the responsibilities of a deaf toddler. Loving Bessie was easy. The sweet nature of the little girl overshadowed her handicap until it was barely noticed. They found little ways to communicate with her. But they had already made up their minds that one day they would send her to a special school so she would have the benefit of the best education they could give her.

Because the beaver were so numerous and had shut off most of the water flowing to the Tolliver place, the Taylors didn't stay there when they returned. Instead they leased the place below Bridgeport from Augustine Kendall. C.M. and Jesse completed a partially constructed building and topped it with a dirt roof. Then they moved Charlie Crouse's meat house from Bridgeport and used it for a post office and small store for a while. C.M. had returned from Nebraska with several new saddle horses and two or three good teams. He used them to do a lot of freighting.

The little Brown's Park school on the flat above Beaver Creek had been replaced by one near Lodore Canyon on Vermillion Creek. Jesse's grandmother Taylor stayed with the boy in a dugout nearby so he could go to school. He attended school with several other children, including the Sterling, Miles, and large family of Chew kids. Jesse often smiled to himself as he watched the Chew kids arrive for school. They "looked like an army" as they skated along the ice on Vermillion Creek.

One day, when school was out for the noon recess, the children spread noisily across the school yard and ran down by the corral and horse barn. They all looked up and stopped playing when Tim Flynn rode in on a flashy white horse. The young teenager, with his long hair hanging in a single braid down his back, slipped easily off the horse. Mike Flynn had not allowed his boys to attend school and therefore only a few of the children knew Tim. Since there is often bravery in numbers, several of the older boys moved together to form a group. They began pointing and snickering at the newcomer. Together they started moving toward Tim.

One boy said, "We'll just cut that pigtail of yours."

Tim quickly reached into his pocket and pulled out his knife. With his face set, he opened the blade and backed into a corner against the corral.

"Come ahead," he said. "Come and cut my hair off."

In the meantime, one of the little kids dashed toward the school building screaming, "Miss Denny! Miss Denny, hurry!"

In an instant the teacher, Miss Winford Denny, came flying out the door. Immediately she broke up the group of bullies. She gave them all a proper scolding and sent them back to class. By that time Tim had mounted his horse and ridden silently away. He never came back.

Some time later, when the summer sun was only partially up one morning, Mike Flynn left his camp on Pot Creek to bring in the saddle horses. He was on his way back with the horses when the shadows of several riders came to a stop a short distance from the Flynn camp. Sitting quietly on their horses, with their eyes watching Mike Flynn's approach, were several Browns' Park ranchers. Included in the group were Augustine Kendall's partners in the Brown's Park Livestock Ranch, brothers-in-law Ford DeJournette and Walter Hanks.

Mike rarely was without his rifle, but he was unarmed on that particular morning. The ranchers had surprised him in the way they'd hoped. They had decided that the man was way overdue for some straight talk. They were there to deliver a warning. However, the instant Mike rode up, Tim stepped out of the tent with his dad's rifle pointed at Ford DeJournette. The boy moved slowly to a log and sat down. All the while he kept a steady bead on the head of the group's leader. The nervous ranchers said only a few words to Mike before turning their horses and riding away.

143

It was a few weeks later when Tom McCarty rode in to the Park Live. The aging outlaw stayed overnight, left on his horse early the next morning, and returned about sundown. He shared supper that night with Josie's teenage son Chick McKnight, Albert Williams, and some other ranch hands. As they all visited over coffee the older man went outside for a few minutes, then returned with an old rusty .30-.30 rifle. For the next hour or so McCarty cleaned and oiled the gun. The next morning he left, but returned again that evening. When he rode out at dawn the next morning it was for the last time. He crossed the river on the ferry at the mouth of Swallow Canyon and disappeared over the ridge.

Several hours later word came to Brown's Park that the day before, Mike Flynn had been ambushed. He was dead. He had been on his way to Vernal in his buggy to pick up Mercy and a few supplies. When his unbridled team showed up at home, Tim went to look for his dad. He found him on the road to Vernal just past some big rocks - now known as Flynn Point - slumped in the buggy with bullet holes in his back.

Albert Williams was upset over Mike Flynn's murder. He was certain he knew who was behind it. He paced back and forth, shook his head, and told C.M., " 'bout a week ago I seen Ford DeJournette with George Shipp and two o' them Two-Bar foremen out in the corral with their heads together. If I'd've knowed what they was up to, why I'd've went and told old Mike!"

A short time after the killing of Mike Flynn, Chick McKnight was crossing the river on the ferry at the mouth of Swallow Canyon. As it eased along Chick looked over the side and dreamily watched the water. Suddenly something caught his eye. He stopped the ferry and used a piece of wire and fished a rifle from the water. Chick recognized it immediately as McCarty's old .30-.30. He took the rifle back to the house and cleaned it up.

When Chick went hunting with Jesse, he showed the gun to his friend and said, "This here is 'Old Flynn' and it's quite a gun. It shoots right where you hold it every time." Old Flynn was Chick's favorite gun for years after.

The discovery of the rifle convinced everyone that their suspicions about Tom McCarty had good basis. John Jarvie, Jr. wrote up a petition to have McCarty hunted down for the murder. C.M. wouldn't sign it.

"John, I am sorry Mike ended up the way he did, but I'm afraid he'd been asking for it for a long time," he said.

Almost everyone agreed. John dropped the petition. The community didn't turn its back on the Flynn boys. Given the chance to lead an honest life, Tim grew to be a fine young man. He eventually married Joe Tolliver's pretty daughter, Rosie, and became a family man.[1]

Old school on bank of Vermillion Creek
Back Row L to R: Jesse Taylor, Miss Denny (teacher), Rosilee Miles
Front Row L to R: Doug Chew, Ralph Chew, Will Rose Sterling (in white), Mary Ethel Miles (braids), Elnora Chew
(Photo taken by Jack Evers)

Chapter XX
ANN AND JOSIE

It was in the spring of 1911, when Brown's Park heard that Ann Bassett Bernard was in trouble. In March, a stock detective had pretended to be a prospector and had moved freely among the hills around Ann's ranch on Douglas Mountain. His purpose was not to examine rocks and formations, but to watch Ann and her ranch foreman and lover, Tom Yarberry.

Through the years Ann had continued to hassle the Two-Bar outfit, but she had kicked a bit too hard when she used her legal right and refused the Two-Bar any use of the water on her land. In fighting back, the Two-Bar foreman, Bill Patton, sent the detective to obtain any evidence of wrongdoing by Ann and her foreman that he could use against them.

It was only a few days later when Stock Detective Nelson reported back to Patton. He had seen a freshly slaughtered beef carried into Ann's meat house. He had strong suspicions that if they could find the hide, it would carry the Two-Bar brand. The two men hurried back to Ann's ranch and soon located the hide and entrails of the beef. Bill Patton quickly looked for a brand, but discovered a hole in the hide of the right flank where the brand should have been. To Patton, the missing brand told a story and was proof that Ann had not butchered one of her own beef. Bill Patton hurried to Craig and filed charges. Shortly after, Ann and Tom Yarberry were arrested and indicted for rustling.

Six months later, in August, Ann and her ranch manager were brought to trial in Craig, Colorado. The trouble between Ann and Ora Haley had lasted for years and their hatred for one another had never been a secret. The trial drew a large crowd to the small town of Craig. To accommodate the many spectators, the legal proceedings were moved to the local theater.

Throughout the trial Ann never disappointed the crowd. Not during the heated arguments between the prosecution and the defense, and not when her brother Eb testified that the beef actually belonged to him and insinuated that the absence of the brand proved only that his sister was being framed. Nor did Ann disappoint the crowd when several cowboys, as well as her estranged husband Hi Bernard (Hi had traveled from Denver to help Ann) took the stand in her defense. Throughout it all, Ann remained impressive in the beauty of her appearance and behavior. Her cinnamon-colored hair was pinned in soft fluffs around her face, accenting the innocence of her greenish gray eyes. Her dresses, new and of the latest style, clung appealingly to her small-waisted figure. When she took the stand in her own defense, her voice was soft but clear and her words were those of an educated woman of quality and grace. Although Ann and her lawyers were able to persuade ten members of the jury of their innocence, two other jurors believed Ann and Tom were guilty. The trial ended in a hung jury. A new trial date was set for August, 1912, but because Ann sent word that she was ill, it was postponed until the following August.

During this same time, Ann's sister Josie was entangled in troubles of her own. Josie had divorced pharmacist Charley Ranney and then married Charles Williams of Baggs, in July, 1906. She lived with her third husband for only a few months. For her fourth husband, Josie chose a man who had lived his life as a cowboy. In 1922 she returned with Emerson "Nig" Wells to Brown's Park. The couple leased the Davenport Ranch from Augustine Kendall and moved to Willow Creek.1

Brown's Park had varied feelings about Josie Bassett Mc-Knight Ranney Williams Wells. No one disputed that the coppery-haired woman was intelligent and a hard, energetic worker. Nevertheless, some saw another, unattractive side to Josie.

In the late fall of 1912, Guy Sammuels, the owner of a large sheep ranch near Vernal, started for Rock Springs with his huge herd of lambs which were to be shipped by rail. After a few days on the trail, he reached Brown's Park. He stopped his band of sheep at the river's edge at the mouth of Swallow Canyon on the Park Livestock Ranch. Then Guy Sammuels and his herders loaded the ferry with as many sheep as it would safely hold, crossed the river, and turned the sheep loose to graze on the opposite bank. Only a small bunch could be crossed each trip so the process stretched into the following day. After each bunch of sheep was crossed, they milled around and blatted a bit. Then the lambs nibbled on the grass, brush, and weeds and spread upward into the Willow Creek meadow. Once the entire herd was ferried across the river, the gathering began. Before moving on to Rock Springs, Guy Sammuels took time to count the lambs. He counted them once, then recounted them. He discovered he had been right the first time. He was missing about 250 head!

It didn't take Sammuels and his herders long to find the tracks of the missing lambs. The tracks showed that the sheep had been purposely driven away from the others. Sheepman Sammuels was stern-faced as he and his men followed the tracks to the long, railroad tie barn in the Willow Creek lane. There they discovered the missing lambs. Their brands had been freshly trimmed with sheep shears and their marked ears were cut off.

As the men walked around the corner of the shed, they met Nig Wells face to face.

Nig's color was pale and his voice shook when he said, "Mr. Sammuels, I never had anything to do with this. I want you to know that. I didn't know anything about it and had nothin' to do with it."[2]

Guy Sammuels took his lambs and reported the theft to the authorities. Word of the attempted sheep rustling spread across Brown's Park. The rumor was that, indeed, it had not been Nig who had stolen the sheep. Instead, the guilty ones were believed to be Josie and her hired man, Peter Derrick. Nevertheless, it was Nig Wells and Peter Derrick who were arrested and charged, first with removing marks from sheep, then with grand larceny. Justice Court dismissed the case against Derrick, and Nig was bound over to District Court. His trial was scheduled to take place shortly after the holidays. But Nig Wells didn't live that long.

The exact truth about what happened to Emerson Wells during the New Year's Eve party which he and Josie attended at Linwood, Wyoming, will remain a mystery. Two very different versions of his death were told, retold, and held to for many years after. Josie Wells told one story; Minnie Crouse, who had married a big Swede named Knudsen "Knud" Ronholdt and was running a boarding house in Linwood, told a very different story.

JOSIE'S STORY
In Her Own Words:

He was a good man, a good farmer and a good man as ever lived. And he got on those whiskey drunks and went like foolish people. I didn't want to go - but some people - Rifes came, Guy Rife and his people came to our house - and his new wife and his - and another Rife boy, Will Rife's boy, and his wife, and they wanted to go to Linwood . . . And Minnie Crouse had the hotel there, and we was going to go to Linwood to a dance. I didn't want to go. I thought now if we go there they'll all get drunk. Well I should have "knowed" it. They'd drink it, and so would the people in Linwood. They were all half-breeds - French and Mexicans and Indians. All those mean people were at that time . . .

149

We danced the first night. And I went to the dance and tried to stand it all I could. I couldn't do anything else. I went with Minnie and a whole crowd of women and went to the dance. It was just across the road from the hotel in one of the old log houses... And that was New Years Eve, the dance. Danced all night till sunup. I didn't. I went home and went to bed. The next night they danced again. I went for a little while and went back and went to bed. And the next morning there was a man from Kansas City, was a horse buyer, I forgot his name. He was a very nice man, he was nice to me. And he come to see me and he said, "I think your husband is ready to quit drinking." He said he hadn't had a thing to eat, not a thing but whiskey. And he said, "He's down in the living room." It was just a kind of a bunk room - living room. Oh, there's a cot over here and a cot over here and a big stove in the middle. Just a kind of like a bunkhouse. They didn't have room enough for the people that was there. And I went and he was there. And I said, - I said, "Wells I brought you a cup of coffee, do you think you can drink it?" He said, "I'll try." Said, "I feel like hell this morning." And I said, "Well don't tell me." And I said, "You did it yourself, I didn't." And now I said, "As soon as it comes sunup, and time, we'll start for home." I said, "I can drive the team." We had a team; it wasn't very safe. It was kind of a tricky outfit. And I thought, I can drive anything to get out of here. So he drank a little of the coffee and he didn't drink anymore, and I helped him get his shoes on and - he had his shoes off and was laying down on that cot - and I helped him get his sweater on, then I got a basin of warm water for him to wash his face, and I said, "Now if you can eat some breakfast, I'll bring it over here." I said, "I haven't had breakfast yet," I said, "I'll bring our breakfast over and eat breakfast right here." He said, "All right, I don't want no breakfast." Said, "I feel like hell." Kept saying that to me. And I said, "I'm awful sorry, but I can't help, you did it yourself." And he kept like he was sick to his stomach, and I said, "Are you going to throw that whiskey up? I wish you would." So I got a slop bucket and set there by him on the bed, and I saw that he was wrong - something was wrong... And while I was fooling around there in the house, getting coffee for Wells and washing his face and those things, Ford DeJournette fell over the stove - drunk, oh, and I found five bottles of whiskey - Red Top Rye . . . And I thought, What'll I do with them, what'll I do with them. So there was a pair of rubber boots hanging on the wall, and I put the bottles down in those rubber boots. Well, it got breakfast time pretty soon, and this horse buyer said to me, he said, "If I was in your place I'd give him a drink of whiskey, he needs it." And I said, "I think he needs anything but a drink of whiskey, but if you think that's alright, I will get it." So I opened one of those . . . pint bottles. And I said to those fellows (Ford DeJournette, Bill Garrett, and the horse buyer), "Won't you boys have a drink too?" And they all took a drink out of that bottle. And I gave Wells a drink out of it, and he took a drink too. And then I combed his hair and put the bottle back - I didn't put it in the rubber boot. I put it over back of the lounge in the window. And there was about that much left in it. Well, he kept turning - kind of twisting around like he was in misery somehow, I don't know what. But I knew he was wrong. And finally he just straightened right back and died. And he threw up a little kind of foam. Right from his lungs of course. And I said to this horse buyer, "He was full of gas . . . He said, "Nothing else, nothing else, but you can't help it."

Well I laid him down and I didn't know what to do, I was stranded. I was just - I might as well have been drunk. I didn't know what in the world to do. There I was clear up in Linwood thirty miles from home, and I - oh I knew a lot of people - most everybody there, and everybody was willing to do something. And I didn't know what in the world - what turn to make. So I - there was a fellow there that had been a cowboy in Brown's Park and he had worked for my brother George. His name was Charley Olmey. And I said, "What am I going to do, Charley?" He said, "Well I tell you what I'd do. I'd send to Green River City for a casket right now." "All right," I said, "I will. Who will I send?" He said, "I'll go." So he went to Green River . . . Well he got a team and buggy and went - team and old buckboard. My own team and buckboard, and went and got the coffin. And I stayed there. There was no undertaker, there was nothing . . .

So, we laid him out and straightened him out and did the best we could. And I waited till the next day noon, till the coffin got there. They just put him in the coffin and Charley Olmey took him home to Brown's Park . . . the next day I took him down and buried him by Uncle Sam, down in that cemetery. It was on the - he died on the third day of the month of January, and was buried on the seventh. And the whole country was there. There were lots of people in Brown's Park then. Lots of people . . .3

MINNIE'S STORY
In Her Own Words:

Oren Rife, son of Billy Rife, and Leora came up with Josie and Nig. They came up in a two-wheeled cart to the dance at Linwood and rented a cabin at the boarding house early in the afternoon. They stopped at Spring Creek Gap (Minnie's homestead) and had lunch. They made themselves thoroughly at home, I guess, because Josie went through all my stuff and helped herself to jewelry; some onyx pieces that some people had made in the "pen," and Matt Warner sent to me and my people. She took some cotton embroidery from a baby shirt and my shoe and glove button hook.

By the time the dance was on, Nig was well lit. Then they went down to the dance. Nig was drunk, and they go put him to bed, then Bill Garrett shows up and they give him more drink. They gave him poison! We don't know of course, but Josie wouldn't let Leora give her baby a drink out of that glass. After midnight Garrett and Josie went to my room in the hotel and locked my door! We hammered and ham-

152

mered until they had to give in. Then I went in and kicked them out of there. I grabbed up her suitcase and it wasn't latched so it fell all open. That's when I saw my jewelry and a bottle of strychnine! I was so silly, I didn't even say anything about my things, but I grabbed the bottle and kept it. Later I gave it to George Stephens for his private museum in Green River.

The only law around was Justice of the Peace Ed Tolton, a middle-aged man. Josie told him that Nig had fits and seizures and just wrapped Ed around her finger. Everything was in her favor, so she brought Nig back to Brown's Park and said she buried him in the Lodore Cemetery. But many said the casket was empty, and so, no one knows where he's buried . . .4

Bill Garrett was a cowboy who worked for the Two-Bar and other area ranches. Brown's Park knew him to be a "wonderful roper" who preferred to do his cowboying from the back of a small horse. He sat his horses well and looked comfortable in the saddle. When he rode past the school house which sat on the bank of Vermillion Creek, young Rosilee Miles would run to the window and say, "Billy Garrett! There's Billy Garrett!" Then she would sigh and watch him until he rode out of sight. It was said, though, that Bill Garrett only had eyes for Josie. It was known that he was her lover.

Minnie Crouse Ronholdt was joined by others in her belief that Josie was capable of poisoning her husband. C.M. Taylor strongly believed Josie was capable of it. He never changed his mind, even though Josie came to him and asked for his help in convincing her neighbors that she had not done the "awful" things of which they were accusing her.

After studying her actions and her words, C.M. said, "Mrs. Wells, why in the world didn't you have an examination of the body to prove you were innocent?"

Josie looked down at her hands, folded in her lap, and said, "I didn't know about doing such things."

C.M. felt that "something was wrong someplace," for he knew Josie to be a much more independent and intelligent woman than she was acting.

A couple of days later, Sheriff Richard Pope of Vernal stopped at the Taylor home. He ate supper with the family and stayed the night. When he left first thing the next morning, he was going to Willow Creek, to speak to Josie. On his way back to Vernal that afternoon, he stopped to talk to C.M. again.

153

The sheriff met C.M. by the corral gate and said, "Taylor, I surely do believe that woman is innocent."

C.M.'s only answer was to raise his eye-brows.

All legal inquiries about the death of Nig Wells were halted that day. Not long after, C.M. and Nina saw Bill Garrett ride along the Bridgeport fence line on his little roan gelding.

As the cowboy disappeared into Jesse Ewing Canyon, C.M. commented, more to himself than to Nina, "He's getting out before she poisons him, too!"[5]

The Taylors later heard that Bill Garrett was living in Nevada, working as a ranch foreman. He never returned to Brown's Park.

In the fall of the same year that Nig Wells died, Josie left Brown's Park and moved to Jensen, Utah. A few weeks later she married Ben Morris, her hired man from Brown's Park. Josie and Ben stayed one winter in Jensen, then Josie filed on a homestead ten miles from town. The first summer they lived there in a dwelling made with board sides and a tent top. They then moved into a small cabin which Ben had built.

Once again, Josie's marriage didn't last long. She said, "I'd rather live with a coyote than a drunken man!" Then, with a skillet in her hand, Josie told her fifth husband to get out. Ben Morris later said, "Josie gave me fifteen minutes to leave. When I cleared the gate, I still had ten of them!"

As for Ann Bassett Bernard, with August of that year of 1913 came her second trial for the rustling of the Two-Bar beef. She was standing trial alone because Tom Yarberry had jumped bail and disappeared. Like the first time, the town of Craig was overflowing with spectators. Most of them strongly supported the lovely cowgirl who had taken on the rich and powerful Ora Haley.

The courtroom was packed with onlookers when Ann's lawyer smoothly turned things against Ora Haley. On the stand he duped Haley into admitting that he had almost double the amount of cattle on the range than were registered with the Moffat County Assessor. Ora Haley was discredited. After eight hours of deliberation, the jury returned with a verdict of "not guilty." Whoops, cheers, and applause roared from within the courtroom. "HURRAY FOR VICTORY" flashed across the Craig movie screen. Guns were fired into the air and a brass band paraded down the street. The large crowd lit several bonfires and danced on Main Street with Ann all night.

A Denver reporter who had had words with Ann during the trial, gave her a title in his newspaper article. He called her "Queen of the Cattle Rustlers." The title seemed so colorfully suited to her that she was known as Queen Ann from that day on.

Not long after the trial, after Ora Haley ceased his cattle operation in Brown's Park, Ann and her father, Herbert, lived for a while at the old Two-Bar site on the bank of the river. The original Brown's Park Two-Bar buildings sat at the mouth of the draw, between the J.S. Hoy and Harry Hoy bottoms. The main ranch headquarters had been moved down river to higher ground, possibly because of flooding problems at the old site.

One morning C.M. Taylor hitched the team to the wagon for Nina, while she packed a few jars of chokecherry jelly and wrapped up a couple of coffee cakes. Nina helped Jesse and Bess in the wagon, took the reins from C.M., and headed for the lower end of the Park for an overnight visit with Queen Ann. That evening, while Nina and Ann cooked the evening meal, Jesse played outside with Doug Chew.

Herbert Bassett was now about seventy years old. He wore little round spectacles and had a long gray beard. Although he was still troubled with asthma, he was spry and helped out by doing the morning and evening chores. Doug and Jesse didn't pay much attention to the older man when he turned the milk cow out of the corral so that she could go to the river and get her drink for the night. The old cow sauntered along the bank until she came to the pathway which led down a steep trail and into the water. The milk cow was in no hurry and drank the water in long, lingering gulps.

After a bit, Herbert decided the cow was taking far too long and said, "Oh, you old fool. Come outta there. Gonna drink that thing dry are you?"

The cow paid no attention, so Herbert started walking along the bank to shoo her out. Suddenly the old man lost his footing and stumbled. He fell off the bank and into the river with a loud splash! Jesse and Doug ran to where they could see, and with big eyes, watched as Herbert's head finally popped out of the water. Sputtering and wheezing, the half-drowned man pulled himself out of the river and up the bank. A trail of water trickled off him as he hobbled toward the house. After Herbert disappeared into the ranch house, the two boys began to giggle.

"Why didn't he just leave her alone and let her drink?" Doug laughed.

"Yeah, she knew how much she wanted," Jesse answered.

The boys laughed until their sides hurt. Meanwhile, in the house, Herbert Bassett changed into dry clothes and took a several minute scolding from his alarmed daughter.6

Later on Herbert Bassett moved from Brown's Park with Ann when she bought a place on South Fork, near Josie. He stayed with Josie at her place for a while. Before long he "ran off" and spent his time visiting old soldier homes in the east. He was in

155

Quincy, Illinois, the day he died on July 30, 1918. He was buried in Quincy.

By then Brown's Park had heard whispers that Ann was living up to her name of Queen of the Cattle Rustlers. It was rumored that she was involved with a band of rustlers who were using her ranch as a refuge. There, it was said, brands were altered on stolen stock brought in from the north. Some believed the talk; some did not. Brown's Park didn't much care and remained loyal to her daughter, Queen Ann.

After Josie Bassett McKnight Ranney Williams Wells Morris ran her last husband off, she decided to live her life alone. She had a little house built and continued to clear the brush on her homestead. She tended her flower and vegetable gardens along with her apricot, plum, and apple saplings. There, without electricity or telephone, she made her home for the rest of her life.

In old age, when her copper hair had turned white, Josie continued to chop wood, raise her meat and grow vegetables, flowers, and fruit. Occasionally she rode her horse the twenty mile round trip to Jensen to get her mail.

When she was questioned about being in her eighties and still sleeping outside on her porch, year round, she said, "It's covered up with vines now. I sleep there all winter and it isn't very cold. My goodness, I've got a good warm bed, and I undress in the kitchen."[7] Josie lived her life the way she wanted. She gave and received much love and enjoyment from her grandchildren and great-grandchildren who knew her as "Granny" Josie.

One winter just before Christmas, when the ground was frozen and covered with patches of snow, Josie went outside to fetch a bucket of spring water. Her horse saw the bucket and rushed to Josie, expecting grain. The mare's action caused Josie to stumble and fall to the ground. She landed wrong and painfully broke her leg. She dragged herself into the house where the next day her son Crawford and granddaughter Willda found her huddled in a blanket on the floor near the fireplace.

Josie never recovered from the trauma. The following spring, on May 1, 1964, she was staying with a granddaughter in Salt Lake City to be near her doctor, when her heart failed. On a sunny morning a few days later Brown's Park saw Josie laid to rest in the Bassett Cemetery.

In 1923 Ann Bernard married another former Ora Haley cowboy named Frank Willis. Together they ranched some, lived in California and Arizona, then settled in Leeds, Utah. About her leaving Brown's Park and her return many years later, she wrote:

I would avoid being smothered by fences, and the digging up, where every sagebrush, gulch and rock had a meaning of its own, and each blade of grass or scrubby cedar was a symphony. I could make effective my escape. If I had to be hedged in by people I would go away to the crowded cities, to mingle with the human herd and study them from the sidelines, for I had no desire to become a part of their affairs. All I asked of life was to be perpetually let alone, to go my way undisturbed. To Brown's Park and its hills and valleys (the only thing I had ever selfishly loved) I bade goodbye.

Many years went by before I returned to my "sacred cow," Brown's Park. I was lured by curiosity, as people will go back in mental morbidness to view the ravishing and despoliation by human hands. I was surprised to find so many pretty little homes tucked away in the hills. Just puncturing the landscape here and there, yielding fine dividends to their owners, a friendly folk who make up our traditional rural life in America.

Brown's Park brought back a poignant yearning to dash away and drive an avalanche of Two-Bar cattle back across the divide. Then I would awaken from my dream to discover that I had been peeping into a past that cannot return. Live Two-Bar cattle are conspicuously absent. The winds have buried all the dead ones.

Those round-up days are over. And so are most of the old knee-sprung, saddle-marked cowboys "over" - over there.[8]

Ann and Frank spent a few summers together in Brown's Park at the old Bassett Ranch where Ann spent a lot of time writing about her life. Then while in Leeds in 1953, Ann had a heart attack. Never able to regain her strength, she died on May 9, 1956. Ann had made a request to her husband that she be cremated and her ashes scattered in Brown's Park. Frank fulfilled her wish by placing her urn in the Bassett Cemetery and allowing the sweet, wild winds of Brown's Park to return Ann to the rocks, sagebrush, and cedars of her valley.

Chapter XXI

THE LODORE SCHOOL

In the fall of 1911, plans were finalized to give Brown's Park a spacious new school. In the Craig newspaper the following article about Brown's Park appeared in the November 23rd issue of the **Empire Courier**. The article first reported on the old school on Vermillion Creek, then gave a progress report on the new building.

> School commenced here November 15 with Miss Winnie Denny of Craig as teacher. The attendance is rather small at present but it is hoped more will take advantage of the school and a good teacher and attend. Miss Denny has started out right and it is hoped she will keep it up.
> Work commenced last Monday on the new school house and when it is completed Brown's Park will have one of the finest school houses in Moffat County even if it is off in one corner and not considered much by other parts of the county. The work is under the direction of Mr. Evers of the Superior Lumber Company of Rock Springs, Wyoming. It will be completed by Christmas. The building is thirty feet wide and fifty feet long.[1]

By December, Rock Springs carpenter Jack Evers and his two helpers, Charlie Hunt and Dan Hoover, from Maybell, Colorado, finished the construction on the new school house. The young building faced the red cliffs of Lodore Canyon and was a happy addition to the sagebrush ridge. Miss Denny used the Christmas break to finish moving books, maps, desks, charts, and pictures to the new building. When school resumed in January, her teaching voice pleasantly mixed with the smell of buffed oak, fresh paint, and plaster. Making a salary of sixty-five dollars per month, Miss Denny continued to teach Brown's Park children until the six month school year ended on April 15th.

On May 25, 1912, Eb Bassett was elected president of the school board for two years and Frank Myers was elected to the office of treasurer for three years. Later in the summer, there was a bit of a ruckus and an article in the Craig newspaper said:

The party or parties that cut the flag rope at the school house the night of July 4 had better return same and pay damages and avoid further trouble.[2]

It is not known whether the party, or parties, ever did as requested. When it was time for the school bell to ring the next fall, Jesse Taylor went to board with George and Ruby Bassett. Ruby McClure Bassett had originally come to Brown's Park to teach. In a short time she became George Bassett's bride and made the valley her home. She was joined by her sisters, Willa and Lucy, along with their invalid mother. The three sisters, teachers all, took good care of their mother and encouraged her in her love of gardening. They helped her work the soil, plant the seeds, water, and pull the weeds. Together they raised an abundance of vegetables and fragrant flowers.

From the first, Willa was attracted to George's gray-eyed brother, Eb. She admired him as a gentleman and a dashingly handsome cowboy. Eb began to court her and they became sweethearts.

Willa began the 1912 school year with ten-year-old Jesse as her only pupil. Together, the two walked or rode horses to school each morning. Jesse, whose hair had darkened some with age, brought in the firewood and Willa stoked the pot-bellied stove to a comfortable glow. Then they settled down to a full day of school work. When the lessons were finished for the day, teacher and pupil made their way back to George Bassett's ranch house. If the weather was favorable on Friday afternoons, Jesse usually rode to the upper end of Brown's Park to spend the weekend with his family.

On one such Friday after school, Jesse went to fetch the horses while Miss McClure finished closing up the school. When Willa took her horse's reins from Jesse, she smiled and patted the gelding on the nose, speaking words of endearment to the animal. The gelding was Eb Bassett's top cow horse. Since she adored the man, she was "crazy" about his horse. Still smiling, she put the reins over the gelding's neck and pulled her dress up a little so she could put her left foot into the stirrup. As the weight of her right foot left the ground, her skirt made a rustling sound. At that instant Eb's high-strung horse jumped sideways and roughly spilled Willa over backward. The gelding galloped in the direction of his home with the reins dragging in the dirt. Jesse ran to his teacher where she lay in a heap of petticoats and dust.

"Oh my gosh Miss McClure, are you okay? I'm so sorry, I should have held that horse 'till you got on. Are you hurt?"

Willa quickly assured the boy that she wasn't injured and that her feelings and clothing had taken the worst of it.

As Jesse helped her to her feet Willa said, "You have a long ride in front of you this afternoon, so you go ahead. I'll just walk on home. You hurry on your way to see your parents and don't worry about me."

Jesse couldn't help worrying but soon felt better when he saw his dad's good friend, "Little" Charlie Sparks trotting their way leading the runaway gelding. Jesse left then, knowing Charlie would see Miss McClure safely home. (Little Charlie Sparks homesteaded on Dry Creek, and was no relation to sheepman Charlie Sparks.)

Although he courted her for some time, Willa's romance with Eb was not meant to be. The love affair eventually faded into nothing more than memories. About seven years later, Willa became the wife of a pleasant newcomer, S.F. Ecckles, and they homesteaded just west of the Basset Ranch. Eb never married.[3]

As for schoolboy Jesse Taylor, Brown's Park watched him make many weekend trips home from school. Jesse would have enjoyed his time alone with the valley except that he was frightened. Many times he heard the low wolf howlings; he had to talk to himself to keep from taking his horse home on the run. Riding over fresh tracks left by a pack, ten or twelve in number, his fists would clench on the reins and his shoulders would tighten. If he let himself think about it, he could feel the wolves' eyes on him and imagined that they were surely nearby, watching him . . . stalking him.

When Jesse finally admitted his fears to his father, C.M. nodded his understanding. He took the boy on a trip to Rock Springs to the J.P. McDermott's Co., General Merchandise store. There C.M. picked out a polished .25-.35 rifle and paid Mr. McDermott the full price of sixteen dollars. Then he turned around and handed the gun to his son. In the days after, placing the rifle across his saddle horn made Jesse feel bold and never again afraid of the hours alone on the trail.[4]

In spite of the cold weather in December, Frank Myers and his brother Felix arrived at the Lodore school from Beaver Creek with tools, lumber, and nails. By Christmas the brothers had a cabin standing a short distance from the school. Frank had solved the problem of providing accommodations for his children so they could attend the new school. Two of his children, Fred and Julia, were welcome company for Jesse for the remainder of the year.

On September 27, 1913, the **Empire Courier** said:

Two hundred school kids playing hooky.
The superintendent's annual report shows
that many Moffat Countyians fail to grasp local
education advantages. In Brown's Park District
No. 1 where there are twenty children of school
age and where they own one of the best school
buildings in the county, only three were enrol-
led during the last year.

Frank and Felix Myers' father had died when they were still
young boys. Their mother then married a cattleman named
Anton Prestopitz. Felix had never completely recovered from
the shock of discovering Matt Rash's body on Cold Spring
Mountain. He had remained a bachelor.

Frank had married Jim and Catherine Warren's daughter,
Leigh, and had settled on Beaver Creek to raise a family. It was
"big doings" in upper Brown's Park when Felix and Frank
brought a steam engine and a thresher down Sears Canyon
from Vernal. They used their threshing machine to thresh many
fields of Brown's Park grain. They used the steam engine to set
up a sawmill operation just above the John Jarvie place. Frank
was a talented woodworker, and built many things that brought
beauty and comfort to Brown's Park homes, including dish cupboards, hutches, benches, and tables. Frank also had a contract
to be the mail carrier while C.M. and Nina had the post office at
Bridgeport. Leigh often carried the mail in the upper part of
Brown's Park. She rode horseback and almost always wore a
pretty white, starched blouse. Frank showed his desire to see
his children educated when he built the cabin near the Lodore
schoolhouse.5

A list of the Lodore schoolteachers includes:6

1911-1912 - Miss Winnie Denny
1912-1914 - Miss Willa McClure
1914-1915 - Miss Lucy McClure
1915-1917 - Willa and Lucy McClure took turns
1917-1918 - Miss Lucy McCLure
1918-1920 - No school was held at Lodore
            (Debra Sharp taught at Beaver Creek.)
1921-1922 - Miss Jones
            (Elmer Bradshaw taught for a short time.)
1923-1924 - Miss Miller
1925-1926 - Miss Florence Heartman
1926-1927 - Mr. Wilber Sullivan
1943-1944 - Gladys Bower
1944-1946 - Mrs. Jesse (Mattie) Taylor
1946-1947 - Mrs. Duward (Esther) Campbell

Student family names include: Taylor, Miles, Myers, Sterling, Vaughn, Wilson, Walker, Buffham, Hughes, Carr, Mathews, Bowen, Kemper, Burton, Roller, Fullmer, Gadds, and Grounds.

From the beginning the Lodore school was much more than a school building. It had not been finished a month before a dance date was set. The Craig newspaper carried word of the event.

> Mr. and Mrs. Ab Hughes were down from Boone Meadow and furnished the music for the dance which was held in the new school house just completed.
>
> Some of those taking part at the dance were several of the Two Bar cowboys, Clarence Brown from Red Creek, James H. Templeton, and Ebb Bassett.

Although the bachelors' dance planned for February had to be put off because of smallpox, there were hundreds of more dances to come. Ab Hughes filled the night with his hillbilly style of fiddle playing while his wife Freda chorded on the guitar. Sometimes Willa McClure or Nina Taylor chorded along on the organ. Little girls learned to dance in their daddy's arms and little boys chased each other around the dance floor. Later, beds for the sleepy children were made up in the wagon boxes, on the desks which had been pushed against the walls, or in a comfortable corner on the floor. Some of the men slipped outside for a few minutes and returned with a telltale ring around their mouths and across their noses, caused from swigging on jars of moonshine.

C.M. Taylor rarely sat out a dance. The beat of the music wouldn't let his feet be still. He would ignore the sweat trickling down his back and grab another partner for the two-step or quadrille. Listening to the sweetness of the tune he'd say: "If Brown's Park could sing, it would sound like the music from that fiddle."

At midnight the music stopped. Boxes and baskets of food were opened and spread out for all to enjoy. There was usually plenty of cold fried chicken to go along with thick-sliced buttered bread and biscuits, pickles, potato salad, and freshly brewed coffee. The ranch women never forgot to bring plenty of frosted cakes and fruit-filled pies.

After everyone had had enough to eat and rested, the dancing started up again. When the fiddle music of a waltz filled the air, the melody made emotions grow and spill over in the hearts of the young and the old. The Lodore school became a place of romance. And inevitably of some broken hearts as well.

It was not until dawn that the dancing ceased. Even then the fun was not over. The women fixed breakfast while the men watered the horses at the river and harnessed and saddled them. Then, many times, everyone was off to the nearby Two-Bar Ranch to be entertained by Charlie Crouse's son, Clarence, as he rode the toughest broncs the cowboys could find.

As more and more dances were held and the high stepping cowboys stomped the floor, whooped, and led their partners in a blur around the dance floor, the building rocked to the music. So, in the 1920s, for safety, steel support rods were imbedded in the walls, then joined in sections to crisscross the ceiling.[7]

Time passed and new faces appeared behind the fiddles and the guitars. In the twenties, there were Ab's sons, Dutch and Duke Hughes, along with fiddle player Ed Beasley. In the 1930's, Mattie Callaway Taylor played and after she taught him, Jesse Taylor drew beautiful music from the fiddle. Other musicians included Katie Buffham, Bill Dorrence, and Steve Radosevich. Jim Overy played his mouth harp as well as the guitar. Frank Budelich contributed with a string on a wash tub. Later youngsters, including Les Allen, Ginger Buffham and his cousin, Butch Buffham, played and sang some. Bill Allen was floor manager. He saw to it that the liquor stayed outside, and also used his stout voice to call the square dances.

On April 5, 1955, the responsibility for the upkeep of the Lodore school building was transferred from the school board to the Brown's Hole Home Demonstration Club, the local women's organization. Bands such as George Okano's group from Rock Springs were hired, and the dances were advertised with posters and newspaper ads to draw large crowds. From the profits of these dances and the dedication of those who cherished it, the building was maintained.

Lodore Hall, under the protection of the National Historic Register, remains standing near the weathered tombstones of the Brown's Park Cemetery. The chalkboards have cracked and aged and the school bell and desks are gone, but the solid oak floor still kicks up a dust during summer dances. The walls and surrounding sagebrush and greasewood have been soaked through with the music. The building has hosted many kinds of Brown's Park functions, including meetings, welcome and fare-well parties, baby showers, quilting bees, anniversary cele-brations, and much more. Although it has grown old and a little tired, it still serves Brown's Park well. It comes wide awake with the very first musical chord, be it from an old time fiddle or an electric steel guitar.

Lodore School

Taken by Jack Evers on the day Supt. George L. Bushyager and members of the school board inspected the building before it was used.

Lodore School, taken by builder Jack Evers in December, 1911

C.M. Taylor ferry
Dark X above C.M. Taylor

Buffalo at Taylor place

166

Chapter XXII
THE TAYLORS

Although C.M. Taylor often relied on his common sense, he had learned a lot about getting along with Brown's Park from both Charlie Crouse and John Jarvie. He drew from that knowledge often. In about 1910, when he decided to build a ferryboat, he remembered and benefitted from John Jarvie's lessons, who had ferried across the Green for many years.

It was during the winter when C.M., John Jarvie, Jr. and Little Charlie Sparks took C.M.'s big homemade sled to the mountain. The three men worked together to cut down and load several large pines onto the horse-drawn sled. Through ice and snow, the trees were hauled off the mountain to the Frank Myers sawmill where the lumber for the ferry was prepared. On a small island near the Parsons cabin, the ferry was built. Not long after the ice went off the river in the spring, the cable was set and the boat was ready to launch. A large group of Brown's Parkers were there, to help push the ferry into the water and watch as it was hooked to the cable for the first time.

The pulley on the heavy cable was under tremendous pressure when the current hit the side of the gunwales and rushed around them pushing the ferry forward. The tons of rock piled along the lower side against the railing kept the boat from dipping and taking in water. Everything held.

Charging 50 cents for a horse and rider and a $1.50 for a team and wagon, C.M., Jesse, and an old German sheepherder named John Miller, crossed many travelers. Whenever they saw that Nina had hung the white flag on the porch, they knew that they were needed at the ferry.

Men such as Pat Whalen crossed thousands of head of sheep on their way to the railroad in Rock Springs. There were also the Mormons with their sixty pound cans of honey, which they sold for five dollars a can, and their big barrels of freshly butchered pork. There were wagon loads of Indians and Indians on horseback. There were also squaws walking and leading horses with long poles on each side, where they carried their tepees and bundles of belongings.

One day when Jesse was running the ferry alone, a big, pot-bellied Indian got away with paying with washers instead of coins. Jesse was ready for him the next time, and there was no more of that.

John Roberts, who owned the Park Livestock Ranch for a while, wasn't sure he trusted the ferry. "If anything happens, I'll strip for action," he said.

Nothing did happen, until the day that Ford DeJournette and a couple of friends tried to cross the ferry themselves. They didn't know how to handle the boat and about halfway across the river it began to dip and buck. They were all alarmed but one of the men panicked and dove into the river. He was a good swimmer, but he was also hysterical. He started for one bank, turned and swam for the other, then turned and started back again. Finally, just before he got to the riffles, he managed to make it to shallow water and dragged himself to shore. Ford DeJournette and the other man stayed with the ferry and tried to get it across, but twenty feet from the bank it sank.₁ As it turned out, C.M. was ready to give up running the ferry. So Ford paid him for it, got it out of the water, and took it down the river.₂

By the time the ferry sank, C.M., Nina, Jesse, and Bessie had moved across the river into the Dr. John Parsons cabin. John Jarvie had acquired the Parsons place with a Desert Land Certificate from the government on May 12, 1902. Although the Taylors didn't move there for several years, C.M. had bought the place from John Jarvie on October 23, 1907. Bill Davenport was living in the Parsons cabin at that time, with a blanket hanging up for one of the doors. C.M. let Bill stay for as long as he wanted. About a year after he bought it, C.M. replaced the dirt roof with a shingled one, and built new doors for the cabin. When the Taylors moved in, around 1914, there was a lot of cleaning and fixing up to do.

Nina tied a rag around her head and whitewashed the walls with lime and water. With a stiff broom and lye soap and water, she scrubbed the floor of the old cabin. Soon the home that Dr. John and Daphne Parsons had built, and where outlaws like Butch Cassidy and Matt Warner had lived and hid, was home to the Taylors. C.M. carefully dug out the spring and repaired the spring house which Helena Parsons' husband, Lewis Allen, had built. (It was in that spring house where Matt Warner's wife, Rose, had fallen, sustaining a leg injury that eventually caused her death.) The cellar was fixed up, and sheds, a blacksmith shop, smoke house, corrals, and a roomy barn were built. Fruit trees, flowers, and vegetables were planted, and a rooster crowed each morning at dawn.

When August came it was time to cut the kernels off the ripened sweet corn and dry the yellow nubs in the sun. It was also time to make a trip up Sears Canyon to pick plump bittersweet clusters of purple-black elderberries and deep maroon chokecherries. The chokecherries grew so large and juicy that Nina stemmed and pitted some for pies. The rest, as was done with the elderberries, were placed in a large kettle with a few dippers of water and boiled for about fifteen minutes. The softened berries were poured into a jelly bag so the juice could be squeezed and mashed out. Sugar was boiled with the dark, steaming juice to make syrup, and a little lemon juice was added to the rest to make it jell.

Since jars were scarce, it was Jesse's job to walk along the river bank to retrieve any bottles that had floated downstream. The bottles were made into canning jars by tying a kerosene soaked string around the bottom of the neck and setting the string on fire. A little dab of cold water was poured over the hot string and the top of the bottle popped off. Jesse watched his mother fill the washed and boiled jars and seal the contents with hot wax. Although the hanging strips of tanglefoot helped some, he was amazed that not one of the always present, pesky flies ever ended up in the jelly!

Nina's tall dish cupboard, which had been made by Frank Myers, stood next to her work table where she kneaded bread and rolled out pie crusts. One afternoon Nina was busy making a couple of chokecherry pies when she heard a thump just as her dish cupboard jangled a bit. She stopped and looked up. Once again came the thump and clatter. Nina jumped backward and stood still for a moment. Again, the cupboard bumped and rattled. Nina stared at the cupboard and wiped her flour-covered hands on her apron. Slowly she took a few steps forward until she stood beside it. Ever so cautiously, she leaned forward to peek behind it. Suddenly, she was face to face with a reptile! It had been falling from log to log behind the cupboard, and was just then doing some peeking of its own. Nina let out a squeal and ran backward. She quickly recovered her breath and ran to find a big stick. She maneuvered the huge, but harmless, bull snake onto a cottonwood branch. Then she pitched the dangling snake outside and shooed it away from the house. Nina never got any flies in the jelly, but she nearly had a snake in the chokecherry pie!₃

For C.M., August meant that there was still plenty of haying to be done on the old Charlie Crouse hay meadows at Bridgeport and a little haying to be done at the Parsons place as well. The Taylors were building a cow herd, so storing feed for the livestock for the coming winter was every bit as important as preserving and storing a cellar full of food for the family.

The haying process was not an easy one. After the hay fields had been irrigated and the grass brought to maturity, the cutting began. With a hand-held scythe and a horse-drawn mower the hay was cut. After it cured in the sun for a few days, load after load was pitchforked onto the wagon and hauled to the haystack. There, using ropes and a team, the hay was rolled off the wagon into a large heap. The fields were swept clean. Every fork of hay was precious.

One morning, C.M. and Jesse were pitching hay onto the wagon when a small bunch of Indians rode out of Jesse Ewing Canyon and into the Bridgeport field.

"Dad, they're stealing the hay!" Jesse screamed.

C.M. looked up to see several of the Indians jumping off their horses, grabbing all the alfalfa they could carry under one arm and swinging back onto their ponies. In an instant, C.M. had one of the team horses unhooked and with the harness jingling, was galloping after the hay thieves. Although most of them had already reached the farm ford and were in the river, C.M. caught the last brave just after he went through the gate.

C.M. brought his horse around in front of the young Indian and said, "You owe me a dollar for that hay and you're going to pay it! And you are also going to shut that gate you left open!"

The other Indians rode back and quickly surrounded C.M. They all stood still. Without taking his eyes off the young brave, C.M. reached into his pocket for his knife and opened it. For a few moments longer, with the knife in his hand, C.M. eyed the one Indian. Finally, the Indian gave in, handed C.M. the dollar and went back to shut the gate.

That night C.M. told Nina, "I didn't feel near as brave as I acted when they all circled me. I was glad when it was over."

Later that summer when the river was running low, C.M. and Jesse built a sheep bridge across it. They bored two holes in each end of half a railroad tie and put four-inch pieces of one-inch iron rods in the holes. Then, they set the ties in the river to form a bridge. That fall, Pat Whalen bought nearly every lamb that was for sale around Vernal. He trailed the thousands of sheep over Diamond Mountain, down Sears Canyon, and into Brown's Park. The sheep crossed the river on C.M.'s sheep bridge and then were trailed on to the railroad.

After the herd left, Jesse rode and gathered fifty-two head of sheep that the herders had lost. A few days later, C.M. was working at building a road in Jesse Ewing Canyon and met the herders as they rode back. He explained that his son had found the sheep.

"Now you fellows can stop by the house and pick those lambs up. They're in the corral there. You can pay the boy for his trouble, or whatever you think is right."

Young Jesse saw the herders ride out of the canyon, cross the bridge, and head toward Sears Canyon. When his dad came home, he was tickled to hear that the sheepmen had given Jesse all fifty-two head of lambs.4

By this time, one of C.M.'s best friends was Charlie Teters. His wife, Amelia Prestopitz Teters was a happy little energetic woman and a dear friend to Nina.

Amelia had been born at the Charlie Sparks ranch and had grown up around Brown's Park. Charlie had long been a familiar face to the valley. When Charlie was thirteen he ran away from his home in Missouri. About leaving home he said: "My mother refused to cut my long blonde curls and I didn't want to run around like that anymore. Besides, I wanted to be a cowboy, so I headed west."[5]

Charlie first hired on with different outfits as a horse wrangler and cook's helper. When he got a little older he worked as a ranch hand and did a bit of drifting. He got into trouble at Powder Springs, Wyoming, and found himself in jail for refusing to tell the whereabouts of a gang of horse thieves. Later on, at the time of the Willie Strang murder, he was a young man working for Valentine Hoy at the Red Creek Ranch.

It was during one of the many drinking and gambling parties at the Park Livestock Ranch that Charlie "bristled up" at Albert Williams. The black man had drank a lot of whiskey that night. He began "running down white men" and spouted that his knife and his muscle were why he got along with them. Charlie Teters listened to him for a while, then slowly stood up. He glared at the man whom he had considered to be a friend.

In a voice as biting as twilight in mid-winter, Charlie said, "Do you think it is only out of fear that I show you respect?"

Albert, feeling the full impact of the words, dropped his head and said no more.[6]

Now, a few years later, Charlie Teters was a family man. Charlie and Amelia were married on horseback in Rock Springs. Their first two children, Bob and Rose, were born at Sweetwater, Wyoming, where Charlie worked as a teamster at the Sweetwater mine. They moved to Brown's Park to work at the Willow Creek Ranch, where their daughter, Arlie, was born. The growing Teters family then moved into a little cabin up against Cold Spring Mountain, called the Spitzie cabin. It was there that Valentine and Hazel came along. From there the family moved to the Red Creek Ranch where Charlie worked as foreman for W.H. Gottsche's Red Creek Livestock Company.

W.H. Gottsche was a big, gruff-voiced German who got his start in the livestock business by selling sacks of wool he had picked off the barbed wire fences and from dead sheep. He had an incredible passion for acquiring land and the amount of range that he and his wife, Carrie, eventually had controlling interest in was staggering. In the 1930's, Gottsche owned nearly all the land between Rock Springs and Brown's Park, excluding Clay Basin, which was owned by Charlie Sparks. In Brown's Park he owned the river bottoms, the Park Live, Willow Creek, Beaver Creek, and the Sterling place. Beyond Brown's Park, he owned land all the way to Douglas Mountain. He also owned all but a couple of small places on Diamond Mountain extending to the Crouse Reservoir.

Gottsche was good to, and depended upon, men such as foreman Charlie Teters to keep the huge operation working. He often took the family a barrel of candy with gifts packed inside. Each time he learned that Amelia was going to have another baby, he showed up at the ranch with a bolt each of flannel and material. And each fall, before school started, he took Amelia a bolt of cloth. The Teters kids happily went into the winter with new, matching clothes to wear.[7]

It was at Red Creek that Amelia and Charlie lost one of their children. Valentine, then five years old, died of spinal meningitis. He was buried on the little hill above the house near Willie Strang's grave. One Christmas, the house caught fire and burned to the ground. The family moved to the bunkhouse and before the new home was completed, Amelia gave birth to Clarice and Dorothy.

Besides being ranch foreman and continually building his cattle herd, Charlie got extra money by trapping bobcats, coyotes, and wolves. The wolves were thick, especially in the Red Creek badlands. On a moonlit night a pack could usually be seen in a certain clearing not far from the house. They often traveled along the creek and in the darkness would crawl through or leap over the corral fence and bring down colts and even cows.

One day, after a trip into the badlands, Charlie brought home a wolf pup and named him Jocko. From the beginning the pup showed friendly attention toward all the Teters children, except for Arlie. To her he showed an intense dislike. Whenever he saw her he would snarl and lunge against the chain holding him to a post. One day Hazel and Arlie went down the hill to gather the eggs from the henhouse across the creek. Jocko had now reached the size of a year-old steer. This time, when he lunged against the chain, it gave way to the force and broke. In great growling strides, the gray wolf closed in on the two little girls, his eyes intent on Arlie. Screaming, the girls dashed inside the chicken coop and jerked the door shut just before Jocko caught them. Shortly, Charlie stopped Jocko with a rifle bullet.[8]

For two winters Jesse Taylor lived at Red Creek with the Teters family. Along with the Teters, Myers, Martin, and Smith kids, he went to school in the little school house. Except for the time they spent in school, Amelia took care of all the children, five days a week, all winter long. However, each child had his or her chores to do and arguments among them were few.

Jesse Taylor and Bob Teters were about the same age and were good friends. They often rode, worked, and had fun together. Bob's dad had a lot of good horses running on the Red Creek range. One winter he hired a man to come to Red Creek and break a few. On the day he was to arrive, Bob and Jesse brought five geldings off Tepee Mountain, and had them waiting in the corral when Riney Reinhart arrived. The next morning at daylight, Jesse and Bob helped the horse breaker rope and throw the horses, put hackamores on them, and tie them to the corral fence. The boys went on to school at nine o'clock and by that night, the young cowboy had ridden all five broncs. Many times, for the next several days, when the two boys were supposed to be studying, they were looking out of the schoolhouse window at Riney Reinhart. They were fascinated by the man because he was a "real honest to goodness" horse breaker.

One afternoon they saw that Riney was having trouble getting a gelding to walk back toward the house. Riney would jerk the horse around, spur him in the ribs a bit, and slap him across the rump a time or two. Still the horse refused to walk. Riney stepped off the horse, slipped a rope around his legs, and threw him onto his side. He tied the horse's legs so the gelding could barely move, then turned and walked away. Still wearing his spurs and chaps he went into the house, sat down, and had a couple of leisurely cups of coffee. About forty-five minutes passed before he walked back to the horse. He untied his legs, and held the reins as the bronc got meekly to his feet. Riney put his foot into the stirrup and swung into the saddle. With only the slightest nudge from Riney's spurs, the gelding was ready to walk in any direction which Riney pointed him.

A young woman named Elsie Ward was the schoolteacher. She was normally a nice person, but possibly because Riney didn't pay enough attention to her, she liked to give him a hard time.

With her nose in the air she said, "I'm sure going to laugh when one of those horses throws you on your head, Mr. Reinhart."

Coiling up a rope, Riney tilted his head a bit and said, "Unless I get an arm broke or somethin' Missy, you're never gonna see it happen." She never did.9

In time Charlie Teters left Red Creek because his boss preferred sheep and Charlie preferred cattle. The Teters family then moved to the little sleepy hollow on the bank of the Green River just below the Brinegar Ranch. There, during a rainstorm that had the river running bank to bank and sloshing against the side of the house, Amelia gave birth to another baby boy. During the birth, a whooping crane flew over the house. In his misery in the storm, he croaked a low "quack" as he flew overhead.

The next morning, during the family discussion of naming the new baby, busy little Hazel said, "Let's name him Jack, that's what the stork kept calling him last night." So without further discussion, the boy was named Jack. Before long, the Teters family sold out and bought property on the edge of Rock Springs in Blairtown. There, Amelia and Thelma were born. When the youngest child was about three, Amelia and Charlie more or less separated. Amelia gathered up her brood and rented and moved into a large white boarding house in Rock Springs. There she raised her children while running the boarding house. For many years after, whenever the Taylors went to Rock Springs, they stayed in the big white house and enjoyed the Teters hospitality and scrumptious meals. Charlie Teters took over running the Valley Hotel on the other side of town. The Taylors sometimes stayed at his place as well.10

Back in Brown's Park, after the Taylors had lived at the Parsons place for a while, C.M. walked along the hillside and decided a ditch like Charlie Crouse's was what he needed. He pictured the beautiful fields he could have if he could get water to them. When he hired a surveyor from Rock Springs, however, he was told: "I'm sorry, Mr. Taylor, but there is no way in the world that you are going to get that river water to run uphill, and that's what I say you're proposing. You might as well forget putting a ditch here, it would be absolutely useless."

C.M. was not dissuaded. He had a dream of what he wanted his ranch to be - and that dream needed water. He ordered the surveying equipment from Sears and Roebuck, plotted his ditch, and went to work. He used his horses and mules to pull a slush scraper, a Mormon scraper, and other horse-drawn equipment. When he hit a cement-like conglomerate rock, he used a shovel, a pick, a crowbar, and his bare hands.

It took C.M. years and thousands of hours of work to complete the two and a half mile ditch. At last he stretched a cable across the river to hold rocks and cedar posts to divert water toward the channel. Seven years after he began work on it, C.M. opened the head of the ditch and watched. The water, acting tickled to have a new channel to discover, slid and tumbled around and along the hillside, hurrying toward the Taylor place. When it reached the outlets to the fields, it poured through them and spread happily in all directions. C.M. sat down on the ditch bank, held his face in his hands, and wept.11

During the summer of 1915, C.M., Bill Davenport, and Dave Tolliver were camped in Jesse Ewing Canyon dynamiting and working on the road. They got up one morning, had breakfast, then walked to the anvil to sharpen the drills. They noticed a folded piece of paper stuck inside the square hole in the top of the anvil. C.M. pulled the note from the anvil and read: "Mr.

Davenport, you have one week to leave Brown's Park. It will pay you to leave because you know what has happened to others who have been warned to leave here."

Word spread across Brown's Park that Eb Bassett and Chick McKnight had received the same message. It was feared that Tom McCarty was back. The only explanation of the notes that C.M. could give Nina was: "I guess some of the big outfits figure those fellows have been stealing their cattle, that's all I can figure."

Bill Davenport was frightened about the note. He said, "I'm subject to death. I'm gettin' outta here. If you see anybody strange hanging around, I want you to come and tell me."

Bill only had a pack horse, a saddle horse, his camp outfit, and a little money in the bank. He left before a week was up. Eb Bassett went to Denver and stayed through the winter. Chick McKnight went to Nevada for a while. Eb and Chick eventually returned to Brown's Park. Bill Davenport went to work herding sheep for Keith Smith at Linwood, Wyoming. He never returned.12

C.M. continued to work hard to develop a cattle ranch. To get money to build his cattle herd, C.M. hired on as foreman for the Park Live. He later took the contract with P&R Drilling to supply the company with wood for their boilers to make the steam which powered their drills. Also for P&R, with four of his horses, a Martin ditcher, a Fresno, and a tumblebug, C.M. built the roads over Clay Basin Hill and the treacherous Hoy Dugway.

Any dab of extra money he could save, and all the profits from the sale of any cattle, went back into expanding the herd. Each year the haystacks on the Taylor place grew a little larger, and after each fall gathering, the wintering pastures were speckled with more livestock carrying C.M.'s 72 brand. He fed his cattle well; he kept only the cows who were the best mothers; he protected newly weaned calves from the wolves by hanging lighted lanterns on the corral posts at night. Because of a natural cow sense and excellent management, C.M.'s dreams were beginning to come true.

Many times, upon her silken air, Brown's Park heard a now familiar "Cawwww! Cawwww!" and then the cracking report of a bull whip. Again and again these sounds carried for miles as C.M. Taylor, now one of Brown's Park's most respected cattlemen, worked his fine herd of cattle. It might be when he rode up and down the sandy banks urging his cattle to cross the river, or as he drove them toward their summer range on Cold Spring Mountain, or when he brought them off the steep mountain slopes in the fall. His bull whip was a beauty. It had a long, hickory handle attached to fifteen feet of braided rawhide with a buckskin popper on the end. C.M. was talented with the whip and when it wasn't in his hand, it was coiled around his saddle horn.

C.M. sat well in his slick, A-fork saddle on the back of his favorite horse, a dappled gray named Coon. Over his brown-checked Pendleton pants, made in Oregon, he wore black bat-wing chaps. His Blucher boots were made in Olathe, Kansas, and were high-heeled and high-topped with mule ears and plenty of stitching and inlay. On his left foot, he wore a silver-mounted G.S. Garcia spur from Elko, Nevada. When quest-ioned on why he wore only one spur, he said, "Oh, if you spur one side, the other'n'll come along." He wore a ten-gallon Stetson and laughed that "the bigger the hat, the better the hand." He also joked, "I'll never hire a man who wears a straw hat or rolls his own cigarettes. If he's not workin' on a smoke, he's chasin' his hat!"[13]

Although C.M. knew cattle, there was one tall, rangey steer with long horns that nearly got the best of him. The red and white brockle-faced steer was eight years old and "as tall as a saddle horse," weighing around sixteen hundred pounds. He belonged to the Sevens outfit in Colorado. For several years cowboys had tried to drive him away from Brown's Park and back to the Sevens Ranch near Craig. The steer would always "quit" their herd in the night and disappear. The following sum-mer he would show up again on Cold Spring Mountain.

One fall, a Sevens representative rode into the Taylor ranch. Over a cup of coffee the man said, "Mr. Taylor, I know that big steer of ours has been running with your cattle all summer again. If you'll run him in with your herd when you gather, and butcher the darn thing, we'll give you the hide, head, and half the meat."

It was late in the fall when C.M. and Jesse brought the steer off the mountain with the other cattle. When they were close to the ranch the rest of the herd walked off the bank and crossed the river on the ice without any trouble. But the big steer refused.

C.M. told Jesse, "There's no sense in fighting him, we'll go over to the house and get things ready and just butcher him here."

About an hour later, C.M. and Jesse started back across the river on foot, with the meat saw, a rifle, and two butcher knives. The steer was feeding in the sand knolls and kept jerking his head up, watching the two as they got closer.

Jesse began to feel uneasy. "That thing looks like he's gonna take after us," he said.

"Let him come!" C.M. answered.

The steer had not yet moved when C.M. raised the rifle and

fired. The bullet missed the intended spot between the eyes and hit four or five inches low in the bridge of his nose. The steer shook his massive head, snorted, and started to charge! Jesse spun and began to run.

Jesse heard his dad yell, "Don't run, you can't outrun him!"

Jesse turned back and saw his dad struggling to get the jammed cartridge shell out of the rifle. The steer, with blood trickling from the wound, was carrying his horns close to the ground and closing in with great long leaps. C.M. dropped flat on his back just as the steer reached him. The horns swept across the top of his body as the enraged animal sailed over him and landed on C.M.'s rifle, breaking the stock in two. A horn caught in one of C.M.'s gloves, skinning it from his hand and pitching it thirty feet into the air. Bellowing, the steer repeatedly jumped back and forth across C.M., bunting him with his head and trying to hook him with his horns. Desperate to help his father, Jesse screamed and ran at the animal. He grabbed him by the tail and pounded on his rump. The steer ignored him. Heaps of sand were slung in every direction as the steer kept after C.M., but because of the curve in the end of his horns the steer could not hit his mark. Finally, the intensity of the attack and the loss of blood began to weaken the animal. His eyes glazed and he fell to his knees.

C.M. took hold of the steer's front leg and yelled, "Get him by the tail and maybe we can get him down."

Jesse discovered that it was like "pulling on a house" and couldn't budge him. Jesse then grabbed his dad by the hand and pulled him free. The steer never moved when the shaken, but uninjured, father and son ran as fast as they could.

The next morning C.M. and Jesse rode horses when they went after the steer. Jesse's first rifle shot glanced off the left horn, taking a nick out of it. The next one slammed into the steer's massive neck. The battle was over. Their half of the butchered beef provided the Taylors with plenty of meat for many months to come. The steer's huge head was beautifully mounted and hung on the wall in the Taylor ranch house.[14]

Besides being active in better range interests and management, C.M. was also a conservationist. He loved all forms of wildlife and surrounded himself with them. He introduced pheasants to the valley and grinned when he heard them throughout the day. He admired the Canada geese as they flew overhead and landed in the nearby fields. He brought peacocks to his ranch and came to love the calls they made from their roosts in the tall trees. He went to Colorado and bought buffalo, six heifers and two bulls. For his little buffalo herd he built a special six-strand wire fence around a large grassy field near the house. He was not successful in getting quail to flourish and the bullfrogs he brought in never sang in the summer evenings. But the pond at Salt Springs which he kept preserved and protected was a wonderful home for whooping cranes, blue herons, ducks, and wild swans. Besides being a safe place from hunters, the pond was near a natural salt lick, which drew all sorts of wildlife from deer to badgers.

One day, a would-be hunter stopped at the Taylor place for directions to the Salt Springs pond. The man was aghast when C.M., sitting on Coon, told him that no hunting was ever allowed there.

"Mr. Taylor, I don't believe you know who you're talking to. I happen to be a church preacher from Craig, Colorado, and I insist that I be able to go duck hunting!"

C.M. looked down at the little man on the ground and slowly took his bull whip from its coiled nest around the saddle horn. Calmly he said, "I don't care if you are the Christ Jesus from Heaven, you're not hunting my pond!"

The preacher's face reddened. He spun on his heel and stomped away.[15] For many years to come, the wildlife of Brown's Park benefitted from C.M.'s protection, and from his alfalfa and grain fields. All of Brown's Park benefitted from this man in one way or another. C.M. Taylor was one of her finest. She had done well back in 1906 when she convinced him to stay.

C.M. Taylor Place with peacocks roosting in trees

178

Chapter XXIII

RATTLESNAKE JACK AND WILDCAT SAM

John Cave was known as "Rattlesnake Jack" and his corker of a son, Gus Cave, was "Wildcat Sam." They arrived in Brown's Park just after the start of World War I. They had a team of mules, two saddle horses, a hand cart, and the chassis from an old automobile for a wagon. Rattlesnake was a kind fellow, clean shaven and in his seventies. He made camp on the north side of the river, just down from the Taylors at the head of Gauge Canyon. There, with occasional help from his son, he hauled gravel and sand off the point of the hill to be washed in a sluice box and then searched for gold.

The first fall, C.M. Taylor hired Wildcat Sam to cut cedar posts to riprap the ditch to prevent the banks from washing. Wildcat never did chop many trees, though. Instead, he usually found a warm, out-of-sight spot in the cedars. There he sat, peeked through the branches, and watched for C.M. Although Wildcat Sam was surely the worst worker C.M. ever had, he was certainly the most comical.

Wildcat Sam was tall and in his late thirties. He was a sight like no other Brown's Park had ever seen. He could have been good looking if not for the scraggly, long, black whiskers he had most of the time; or for the juicy wad of Horseshoe tobacco he kept stuffed into his left cheek. He rarely shaved and claimed he hadn't had a bath in seven years. He usually had his knees poking out of a layer of three or four pairs of Levis, and, believe it or not, he wore iron shoes, size twelve! The tops of the shoes were leather but the sides and soles were made of iron.

One day Wildcat was at Beaver Creek helping Frank Myers load a rowboat into the back of a wagon. Wildcat rammed his foot under the boat for a brace and the weight cracked his shoe. Frank took the broken shoe into his blacksmith shop and repaired it with rivets and a couple of strips of iron, so all was well.

Frank Myers traded four horses for the first Model T Ford in Brown's Park. Frank didn't know how to drive, so Wildcat said he would teach him.

"Frank, you give it the gas and I'll steer," he said.

Then they were off, the two tall men sitting in the seat close together, going around and around in circles in the yard. The car would almost stop and Wildcat would yell, "More gas, Frank! Give it more gas!"

The car would spit and buck as Frank nearly "choked it down" with too much gas. Teenager Jesse Taylor stood on the sidelines

179

and laughed until tears ran from his eyes. Wildcat finally did teach Frank to drive, but the old car was broke down so often that Frank didn't get much practice.

Although Wildcat used a six-shooter, he always carried a rifle with just one shell, which he said he was "savin' for the recruitin' officer." He told that he got his nickname in Colorado.

"I was agoin' to ride a bad horse that mornin', and when I stepped out of the livery barn, I seen me a cat. Well, I grabbed him by the tail and swung up on the bronc and I used him for a quirt. First that yeowlin' bugger dug that horse in the flank and then I swung him around in a big circle and he dug him in the front shoulders. With that cat a scratchin' and that bronc a kickin' I had a helluva ride! Ever'body called me Wildcat Sam after that."

Wildcat bought an old Montana saddle from C.M. and used it on his little iron-gray mare that he called Jyperina. The saddle was odd-shaped, having a tall horn, no swell, and extra big stirrups. Wildcat carried his bedroll on the front of his saddle and called it his bucking roll.

One day he had a white mare in the Taylor's round corral and told Jesse he'd show him how to ride a bronc. He climbed on her, iron shoes and all. Although she couldn't buck hard, she bucked a little and Wildcat did ride her fine. When he got off he turned around to look at Jesse and said, "By gosh, I been aridin' without my spurs. It's a wonder I hadn't've got throwed!"

Wildcat was not much of a worker, but he was entertaining. There was a big old jackrabbit that lived in the sand knolls across the river from the Taylor house. It was usually about sundown when the rabbit would whiz across the countryside with Wildcat and Jyperina hot on his trail. Wildcat would jerk out his big six-shooter and be firing repeatedly as they all flew over the knolls, through the brush, and across the swells and gullies. Then, the old rabbit would circle, pick up speed, and they would all run back again. Night after night the Taylors laughed and watched from across the river as the old jackrabbit got the best of Wildcat Sam.

One fall afternoon Wildcat and Jesse each took a chunk of Horseshoe tobacco and went together to run a few wild horses in Clay Basin. They had found a herd of flashy colored Indian ponies and were soon in the middle of them on a dead run, jumping over sagebrush and dodging cedars. Coming down off a ridge, Wildcat made it to the lead, running Jyperina at full speed. Then all at once, the mare stepped in a hole and flipped end over end, throwing Wildcat head first. Jesse reined in his horse and hurried to see if Wildcat was hurt. By then the older man was already on his feet and gathering up Jyperina's reins.

He looked up at Jesse and said, "If it hadn't've been for that tarpaulin, I'd've felt the effects of that saddle!"

Although Wildcat's commotion had turned the horse herd, he and Jesse decided not to chase them any more that day. Instead, they made camp at Mountain Home Spring and prepared to spend the night. Just at nightfall, Jesse and Wildcat spotted the flickering light of two small fires in the distance. There had been several small campfires spotted around Brown's Park lately and C.M. had warned his son to stay clear of any he saw.

"They are more than likely slackers," he said, "men who don't want to go to the army."

All of a sudden, Wildcat jumped up and grabbed his rifle. He laid it on the ground then stuck his ear on the barrel. "By hell, I can hear a woman screaming," he said. "I think somebody's fell into one of them old mine shafts."

Jesse was leery but when he listened into the barrel he said, "It seems like maybe I do hear something."

Then Wildcat jerked up the gun and swung it around toward a dark patch of quaking aspens. "Is that a pair of legs up there by that tree?" he whispered.

"I don't think so," Jesse answered.

"Well," he said, still whispering, "If I knowed it was, I'd just guess at the rest of him."

Although Jesse was nervous the rest of the night, nothing else happened. The next morning, Wildcat said he was mighty glad that he didn't have to fire his rifle and waste his one shell.

Wildcat and his dad, Rattlesnake Jack, had been staying in Charlie Crouse's cellar at Bridgeport. That evening, as Jesse and Wildcat neared the cellar, they saw Rattlesnake peek his head out the door and strain his neck to see who was approaching.

As Jyperina stepped through the sagebrush Wildcat spoke out, "Did yuh see yer shadder, Paw?"

The next spring, John Roberts, who along with his wife, Bessie, had purchased the Park Live in 1917, bought a big batch of Hereford cattle from Kansas and was trailing them home from the stockyards in Rock Springs. Wildcat met up with them and John hired him on. After being on the trail with Wildcat for a while, a few of the drovers put their heads together and decided Wildcat needed a bath.

"Now don't let on," they told their boss, "but when we get to the river, we're going to give him a dunking." After the plan was made, nothing more was said about it.

On the flat above the river, Wildcat surprised everyone and said, "I think I'll go on to camp." He spun Jyperina around and loped off.

As he rode away one of the men said, "He must have got wind that he was gonna get wet."

Later that summer Wildcat was working for Albert Willams at Bridgeport. The aging black man was leasing Bridgeport from C.M. Taylor for half the crop of hay. Wildcat usually slept outside in his bedroll.

Early one morning, when Albert walked passed him, one of Wildcat's legs was partially uncovered.

"Why, man," Albert later told C.M., "I believes that man HASN'T had no bath in seven years! I seen his bare leg stickin' out from under the blankets this mornin' and it was a regular elephant pelt."

Wildcat and Rattlesnake only stayed around Brown's Park for about four years. Although she didn't make them rich, she did offer them the best showing of gold that she had. Before he left Brown's Park, Wildcat did meet up with the recruiting officer. It was on horseback in the middle of the Green River. He didn't have to use his one bullet, though. He found out, to his dismay, that the army didn't want him anyway.[1]

Chapter XXIV
MARIE TAYLOR

In August, 1915, C.M. carefully drove his team and wagon down Sears Canyon. Nina sat beside him, holding the newest member of their family in her arms. Baby Nina Marie had been born in Dave and Retta Tolliver's home in Vernal and was now two weeks old. In time, Brown's Park would count on Marie to be a preserver of her history. For now, this lucky girl's adventures of growing up a Taylor in Brown's Park were just beginning.

From the time the little girl with brown hair and large blue eyes first started to chatter like a chipmunk and hang onto her dad's pant leg, C.M. adored her. Although everyone else called her Marie, he always called her "Babe." He sometimes ate foods he didn't like because he saw that she watched his plate and refused to eat anything he didn't. If she misbehaved, his slightest look of disapproval instantly melted her to tears.

The three Taylor children were very different from one another. C.M. would shake his head, laugh, and say, "I've got the darndest family. I've got one kid who can talk and won't; one kid who would talk if she could; and one kid who talks ALL the time."

Ever since Nancy's death from scarlet fever, Jesse's relationship with his father had been strained. Although the boy had grown tall and extremely good looking, he had often been withdrawn and moody since that day so long ago when he lost his sister to scarlet fever. Nina's over-protectiveness of her son through the years had not helped Jesse to build his self-confidence, nor had it allowed C.M. and Jesse to grow any closer. Even though he usually gave in to their wants, Jesse would not allow himself to become very involved with his two sisters. At nineteen, he married the schoolteacher, Debra Sharp, and left home. Although father and son always loved each other, they remained worlds apart in the way they looked at life.

Bessie was like a fragile piece of porcelain to her folks. She had grown into a sweet, tiny-built girl, adored by all who knew her. She spent each winter in Ogden, Utah, where she attended a school for the deaf. She could speak just a few words out loud. However, her little hands fluttered like butterfly wings as she spoke in sign language. Bessie was fun-loving, but shy. She was also never very physically strong, due to a liver condition.

Marie was not like her brother or her sister. She was very much like her father. C.M. and Marie smelled the same wonderful things in the country air and saw the same excitement in the golden dawn. They got the same satisfaction from watching a newborn calf suck and worked the same way over a sick one. It was natural to them both to have fun, no matter whether they were dancing at Lodore, or trying to trail cattle in a blizzard.

Although Marie enjoyed learning how to cook, clean, and do embroidery stitching, she preferred the outdoors. Always fearful that she would get hung up in a stirrup, C.M. insisted Marie ride bareback until she was older. By the time his "Babe" was eight years old, C.M. could count on her to help him brand, ride after cattle, or chop hay with her little scythe. He also knew he could count on her to climb on her light gray mare, Polly, and with a shovel lying across the mare's withers, go do the irrigating wherever it needed to be done. Although Marie rarely hit a note on key, she loved music and often sang cowboy ballads as she went. She never had Bessie's delicate loveliness, but her unique features and happy, energetic personality made her charmingly beautiful. She loved her life. It was a pioneer lifestyle; one which suited both C.M. and his daughter perfectly.

C.M. often told Marie the stories about the valley which Charlie Crouse and John Jarvie had told him. She absorbed the tales with big eyes and strongly felt a part of it all. Each time she rode by the Jarvie place she thought about the white-bearded old gentleman and his pretty little Nell.

She often rode with the ghosts of Butch Cassidy and the Wild Bunch along hidden trails and watched for phantom lawmen from the edge of red sandstone cliffs.

Whenever she was near the crumbling rock saloon on the old military road, she thought about Jesse Ewing, and the way he had killed Charlie Roberts on the river ice. She felt a special sorrow for the young cowboy. Many times she slid off her horse and picked a fistful of Indian paintbrush, daisies, or whatever pretty blossoms she could find. Then she slowly rode toward the ruins of the outpost to Charlie Roberts' grave. Once there, feeling frightened but determined, she jumped off her horse, quickly placed the wild flowers on the rocky grave, jumped back on her horse, and hurried away.

Marie loved the times when the Indians made camp nearby with their pointed tepees and their bonfires smelling of cedar smoke. One evening, she watched a camp of Utes through the fence as the women prepared to cook the evening meal. While the women cooked, the kids ran around playing, and the bucks slept on their bellies on blankets on the ground. All of a sudden, one of the dark-skinned little kids stepped in a big iron skillet of hot grease. The child shrieked in pain and the squaws scurried and shrieked along with him. The men, however, barely raised their heads to look at the commotion. They merely grunted and

C.M. Taylor family (Marie holding rifle)

Marie Taylor on Polly

went back to sleep. The men's reaction amused Marie and made her giggle.

Before Marie started to school, the Indian children were usually her only playmates. One of her little friends gave her a comb and Marie happily ran home to show it off. She was all smiles when she rushed into the house.

"Mother, lookie what I got!" she shouted. But instead of being happy, Nina grabbed the comb out of her daughter's hand.

"Did you comb your hair with this, Marie?" Nina demanded.

"Huh-uh, I didn't," Marie answered weakly. Nevertheless, Nina grabbed her little girl and stuck her head in the wash basin and began scrubbing it with lye soap and water.

"You'll have lice for sure," Nina mumbled.

Marie felt dreadful that she couldn't have her Indian comb, but she knew how "picky" her mother could be and accepted it. She did hurry back to play with her friends as quickly as she could manage, though.

Marie developed a great fondness for the Indians and their culture. She listened carefully when her dad told her it was against the Indian belief to bother the arrowheads which lay scattered everywhere on the hills and among the cedars. Once, when she rode down a sandy draw near home, her horse's hoof kicked up a glistening blackness which caught her eye. She looked down and saw that it was an obsidian spearhead, seven or eight inches long.

"Oh, how pretty!" she said aloud. However, she didn't question the belief of the Utes and rode on.

Each evening, Marie enjoyed going to fetch the tame, boney-hipped, big-bellied milk cows. She watched the evening sky being painted with a sunset, and breathed in the air that was heavy with evening aromas. If Marie happened to see a daddy longlegs spider, she would pick it up and gently hold it from crawling away.

"Which way are those two ole girls tonight?" she'd ask.

The spider would always reach out a free leg as if to point. In a moment or two, Marie would be happily on her way to get Shorty and Jersey, and the spider would be safely back on the fence post or in the grass.

Marie usually did the milking. She would give a cow some hay or grain, then push against her right hip and say, "Heist, girl. Heist now." That would cause the cow to step back with her right hind leg, giving Marie room to reach her udder. Then Marie would sit on a short, wobbly milk stool, hold the milk bucket between her knees, lean her forehead into the cow's flank, and begin to squeeze the milk from the teats. "Give down

Bessie and Marie Taylor taken in early 1920's

Jesse, Marie, and Bessie Taylor

C.M. Taylor Place

188

C.M. Taylor haying the Joe Tolliver Place in 1922

Frank and Leigh Myers

189

Dorothy Teters and Charlie Teters on Peanuts and Star in Rock Springs, Wyoming

Amelia Teters

C.M. and Nina Taylor (Courtesy Hazel Overy)

Crossing the river on the ice

Bertha Worley   Della Worley

Felix Myers

Wilson Garrison and Marie Taylor putting cattle across river

193

Hazel Teters Overy   **Jim Overy**

now, ole girl," she'd say. It was rare that Marie got through a
milking without receiving a couple of stinging swipes in the face
from the cow's tail.

After the wrist and hand tiring job was done, Marie took the
milk to the kitchen to be strained through cheesecloth into
eight-pound lard pails. Then Marie was off, packing the milk
down the pathway through the wild roses to the springhouse.
There, the pails of milk were placed on submerged rock shelves
so that the cold water almost reached their tops. The milk, along
with the butter, and three gallon crockery jars of cream, was
kept deliciously cold. Other foods were kept fresh in the springhouse as well. There was the fifty-gallon barrel of salted-down
cucumbers from which Nina made sweet pickles all winter
long, and the big crockery jars filled with layers of sausage
patties and waxy grease.

Marie loved the springhouse. The sweet-smelling wild roses,
with their candy-pink, lemon-centered blossoms, completely
covered and surrounded the little log building. Inside, the icy
water came up from the ground in tiny, constant bubbles. The
water "tasted funny" though, and was rarely used for drinking
water.

Once she was old enough, Marie attended school at Lodore
during the winter. Sometimes she boarded with other families
and sometimes she stayed with her mother in a sheepwagon
near the school. One winter she boarded with the Earl Gadds
family at the Two-Bar Ranch. Every day Mrs. Gadds cheerfully
sent Marie off to school. When noontime arrived, Marie happily nibbled on the lunch which Mrs. Gadds had packed for her

194

that morning. It tasted good to the youngster, even though it almost always was simply a boiled potato and a raw onion.

When Christmas vacation came along, it was time for C.M. to put on his long horse-hide coat with the wooden buttons and make a trip to Rock Springs. There he would pick up Bessie at the train station, and little Hazel Teters from her mother's boarding house. He would keep the girls cozy during their December wagon ride by tucking them under a huge buffalo robe. For their feet, he heated several round riverbank rocks and either wrapped the hot rocks in horse blankets or first in paper and then in gunnysacks. He then placed the rocks on the wagon floor and the girls rode with their feet on top.[1]

Hazel, a pretty little girl with auburn hair and hazel eyes, looked forward to spending her Christmas and summer vacations with the Taylors. She was made to feel very much a part of the family. She called C.M., "Daddy" Taylor, and Nina, "Momma" Taylor, and thought of Bess and Marie as her sisters. She enjoyed the gentleness and the way that no one ever raised their voice in anger in the Taylor house.

However, Marie's "fearless" ways worried Hazel and she often said, "Oh, Marie, you're gonna get killed doing that!" Then she'd peek through her fingers and watch her younger friend perform some "daredevil" stunt. Many times she watched as Marie rode her horse at a gallop, sometimes with a saddle, sometimes bareback, and reached down to swoop up her hat from the brush. Hazel was amazed at how her friend crossed the river alone in the trolley or in the rowboat. She admired how Daddy Taylor asked for, and respected, Marie's opinion. She could see that he trusted his daughter to always complete a job and knew she would do it well. During playtime, Hazel, Bessie, and Marie often rode Polly together. Although Marie was the youngest, there was never any doubt that she would sit in front and have the reins in her hands to guide the mare. Marie always was, unquestionably, "the boss."[2]

When Marie was about nine years old, she was very happy to learn that her Grandmother Taylor was moving back to Brown's Park. Her grandmother and cousin, Ben, had lived a few years on Mike Flynn's old place on Diamond and then had bought ten acres in Vernal and moved there. Ben was now married and living in Vernal. C.M., with Jesse's help, moved the King homestead cabin which sat behind King's Point, to the Taylor place. The family worked together to make it a cozy home for C.M.'s mother. It was Marie's job to keep a washtub filled with cow and buffalo chips for her grandmother's fire.

One day Marie's good friend, Ethel Beasley, was visiting and the girls were supposed to fill the tub with chips. The girls had a lot of exciting things planned, but picking up chips wasn't one of them. The two hurried and just scooped up handfuls of broken and mashed pieces of dry manure to fill the tub. Then, to make it look good, they spread a layer of big chips on the top. Soon the girls were off playing on the roof of the shed and climbing the big tree behind it. It wasn't long before Marie's conscience began biting at her. She soon felt terribly guilty. She knew there was bound to be trouble because of her thoughtlessness, when her grandmother told what she had done. Marie waited, but her grandmother never mentioned the incident to anyone. Every time Marie looked at her chubby grandmother, smoking her pipe and busily going about her day, Marie's heart ached. It was a lesson that branded the little girl very deeply.

In 1926 Marie experienced the sweetness of her first crush. At the last dance at Lodore, Marie had danced often with a wonderfully handsome young Brown's Park cowboy named "Little" Joe Carr. She could hardly wait until the next dance so that she could see him again.

Joe's father, William J. Carr, was born in Boulder, Colorado. His mother, Ella, was born in the south. The couple arrived in Brown's Park in 1921 and settled on the old Gordon Wilson place at Chokecherry. On that exquisite mountain meadow they planted fruit trees and yellow rose bushes and worked to make a home for their large family. Their children, Frank, Bill, Guy, Fred, Gene, Sam, Joe, Jim, Harry, Emily, Lilyen, Lida, Nellie, Doris, and Hazel, did their many chores, played on the big rock near the house, and sprouted toward adulthood.

Only a few days after Marie and Little Joe had eaten the midnight supper together at the dance, she received word that he was missing and feared drowned.

A search of the river was organized when his saddle horse and two broncs with ropes tangled around their legs were found near the Two-Bar Ranch. Jesse went to help. With boats and hooks the men dragged the river and Jesse Hughes and Bob Teters set off some dynamite charges hoping to bring the body up. Finally, not far from where the horse tracks had gone into the river, a hook caught in Little Joe's chaps and he was brought to the surface. No one knew what happened. It was guessed that the two broncs he apparently had tied to his saddle horn had spooked while crossing the river, and jerked Joe's horse over on top of him. The water wasn't very deep.

"He never was in swimming water," Jesse said.₃

At first Marie didn't think she could bear the news that Jesse brought back with him. Of course, she did bear it. She "took it on the chin" as she would so many other things in the years to come.

A few months later, construction work on the new Taylor

home began. C.M. hauled the lumber for the new house from Ruple Sawmill on Diamond Mountain. On the days that he was going, Marie hopped out of her bed at the first sound of movement, so that she would be ready to leave by four o'clock. The trip to the sawmill took them up the Old Place Draw, then up Sears Canyon, and on to Pot Creek. The constant rhythm of the wagon wheels, the harness, and the horses' hooves always lulled Marie to sleep.

In 1927 the new home was nearly ready to move into, when Grandmother Taylor became very ill. She was diagnosed as having stomach cancer. Marie often stayed at her grandmother's bedside to comfort and help her.

"Now, Marie," the old heavyset woman said, "if I get so's I can't light my pipe, I want you to light it for me."

In the weeks to come, Marie lit the corncob pipe for her grandmother many times, until the old woman finally turned her head away from the offer. Not long after, with C.M. at her bedside, Nancy Taylor died. Marie was deeply saddened by this, the second real unhappiness she had ever known.

Life continued on in Brown's Park. When the new Taylor home was completed, it was a beauty. It had hardwood floors, three bedrooms, a kitchen, dining room, living room, and a bathroom with a pretty legged bathtub and a kerosene water heater. The walls of the house were painted in various pastel shades. Nina made attractive designs on some of them by dipping large rags in paint, wringing the excess out, and then rolling them along the walls to form patterns. Several large, oval-framed family pictures were hung up as soon as the paint was dry.

There was a large, black cookstove in the kitchen, plenty of cupboards, a coffee grinder hooked to a work table, and a roomy pantry with lots of shelves. The meals were always eaten in the dining room where a buffet and china closet gleamed with wood polish and tableware. C.M.'s mother's long, oak dining table sat along one wall and was always covered with a cloth. A long, wood and brass clock hung on the wall and swung its pendulum in a pleasant rhythm. The large bay window was filled with geraniums. They thrived on the thick rays of sunlight and were soon covered with clusters of red and pink blossoms.

In the living room was a brick fireplace with an intricately carved antique clock that chimed on the hour as it ticked away on the mantle. Comfortably arranged in the room were a couch, an easy chair, and an oak rocker. In the corner was a tall oak bookcase with upward lifting glass doors showing off the multicolored rows of books behind them.

Sometimes in the evenings, by the light of wall mounted glass kerosene lamps, the girls embroidered or did tatting while C.M. read from his collection of Zane Grey books, including **Riders of the Purple Sage** and **Thundering Herd**. Occasionally, Nina played her silver harmonica or chorded on the black and tan striped oak piano.

Off the kitchen and dining room was a large, screened-in porch. There was a rack on the porch wall for C.M.'s guns and a work table for Nina. On the table, Nina kept a crock of clabbered milk covered with a piece of cheesecloth. She used the sour milk for baking and also enjoyed eating the curds and whey.

Outside, a pie cherry tree that was usually full of robins, spread shade across the porch and kitchen. Along with a variety of apple trees and a row of crab apples, there were pear, black cherry, peach, and plum trees. And there were apricot trees that produced fruit the size of hen's eggs. In the spring, the fragrant lilac and fruit blossoms perfumed the air. The iris plants grew tall and flowered in elegant colors. Columbine, transplanted from the mountain, bloomed beneath the kitchen window. There was a bonanza of flowering bushes and plants that increased in beauty as the season progressed. They were irresistible to many nectar-loving creatures, including a large family of hummingbirds.4

The yard fence had pretty wire gates with vine-covered arches above them. The entire front area sweeping away from the house was in lawn. C.M. kept the grass short and groomed with a horse-drawn mower. The Taylors had transformed the old Dr. Parsons home site into Brown's Park's loveliest ranch.

Whenever C.M. announced that he was going to have one of his oyster stew and cracker suppers, many of the neighbors showed up to join the fun. C.M. did the cooking and kept dipping in and filling bowls with the steaming soup, made of milk, oysters, butter, salt, and pepper, until everyone was full. Then the men usually headed to the corrals to visit and the kids ran to play while the women chatted and cleaned up the dishes.

One winter Marie stayed with the Garrison family and went to school at Beaver Creek. The Garrison home - which would later burn - was the house built by John Jarvie, Jr. and his uncle following John Jarvie's murder. Rancher Charlie Sparks had purchased the Jarvie place and had moved the house to the old Myers place on Beaver Creek near the graves of Jim and Catherine Warren. The house was positioned so that one side was next to a spring which came out of the side of a bank. With cement and rock work, it was fixed so that the sparkling water continually ran through that portion of the house.

All together there were seven Garrison kids. Elsie, Shirley, and Laura were much younger than Edna, Edith, Wilson, and

Lester, who were full of laughter and fun. The older ones were close to Marie and Bessie's ages. Marie never made it a secret that cowboys were her favorite heroes, with her dad heading the list. Because of her personality and the fancy way she rode and roped, the Garrison kids nicknamed her "Tex Taylor." They playfully called Bessie, "Shorty." The Taylors and the Garrisons soon became close friends. From the beginning, Bessie and Wilson were attracted to each other.

Wilson Garrison was born in Bells, Texas, on May 26, 1909. His family moved to Kentucky where Wilson did most of his growing up. His family went back to Texas, then in July, 1925, moved to Brown's Park. During the winter, when a lot of other young men were out of work, Wilson was happy to feed sheep for Charlie Sparks.5

As time passed, Marie had many beaus, including Lige Worley, Otho Callaway, and Hays Hughes, but she danced with all the young cowboys. Once Bessie got acquainted with Wilson, she signed to her sister and to Hazel Teters and said, "How come you need so many boyfriends?" Then she smiled brightly, held up one finger, and said, "I only need just one." Everyone knew that "just one" was Wilson Garrison. Even though Bessie couldn't hear the music, she could feel the beat of it. With Wilson she danced everything from the schottische to the two-step.

The dances at the Lodore school continued to be enjoyed by almost everyone in Brown's Park. On the afternoon of the dance, Nina and the girls bathed with perfumed toilet soap and put on their pretty dresses. Although Nina curled her hair with the curling iron heated in a lamp chimney, Hazel, Bess, and Marie wore their straight hair in dutch bobs until they later began to get permanent waves. Once they had made the wagon trip to the dance, they met up with many friends. Besides the Garrisons, some of them included: the Callaways, Wilsons, Carrs, Hugheses, Myerses, Beasleys, and the Worleys.

Ab and Freda Hughes were from the backwoods of the south and in the late teens or early twenties they moved to a spring located just east of Brown's Park in Boone Draw. Ab's sister, Mattie Hughes, moved to Brown's Park and became Eb Bassett's girlfriend and much later his fiancee.

Ab and Freda had a few goats and a houseful of children. Ab was a wild horse chasing, live-off-the-land sort of a fellow. His wife and twelve or thirteen kids usually sustained on a plate full of corn bread and deer meat or sow belly and boiled beans. Ab was the mail carrier for Brown's Park for many years. After he got his Model T, he always took two or three of the kids along to push him up the hills.

199

Ab's folk style fiddle music added a lot of enjoyment to the dances. He was a heavy drinker and it was common for him to fall asleep while playing, and yet continue to play for a half hour or so before waking up. Dutch, Duke, and Hays Hughes learned from their dad and played the fiddle too. Hays Hughes was a fairly good cowhand and always wore black leather cuffs decorated with red gemstones. He danced many dances with Marie Taylor. He fell in love with her early on. It was later said that it was because Marie couldn't love him back that he remained a bachelor throughout his life.[6]

William C. "Teto" Wilson was a miner from the Winton coal mining camp near Rock Springs. In the mid-twenties, he and his wife, Florence Belle, moved to Beaver Basin on Cold Spring Mountain. They had three children, Archie, W.D., and Marybeth.[7] Apple-cheeked Marybeth eventually married shyly handsome Harry Carr.

In the spring of 1917, Boone Callaway - who was a descendant of Daniel Boone - his wife, Fannie, and their children Mattie, Otho, and E.K., traveled by train from Texaco and Farwell, New Mexico, to Craig, Colorado. There they made camp until the mud dried up enough for them to move to Spring Creek near the town of Great Divide. In 1925 they moved to Brown's Park. At first they lived in the Spitzie cabin, then they homesteaded near Isom Dart's cabin on Cold Spring Mountain. There they ran beautiful roan Durham and Hereford cross cattle.[8]

Ed Beasley, his wife, and children, Margaret, Fred, Neil, and Ethel, lived at Willow Creek from 1924 through 1926. Ethel and Marie were close friends.

A very special friend of Marie's was Bertha Worley. Bertha's mother, Della, had moved with her husband from Virginia to Akron, Colorado, in December, 1916. Della left her husband in Merino, Colorado, and took her children, James, Amos, Zula, Pete, Doug, Lydia, Elijah, Bertha, and Lona, to live in a one-room log cabin near the Lodore School in Brown's Park. Her oldest, Amos, married and moved to a homestead on Cold Spring Mountain. Amos was killed there, dragged to death by a pair of mules he was trying to break to work.

In 1921 Della and the rest of the children moved to the Amos Worley homestead cabin. There Della acquired land of her own and she and her children survived the summers with love, the barest of necessities, and a lot of hard work. Each winter, usually about November, Della took her children to Rock Springs so they could attend school. A few years later the pioneer spirited woman moved her family to Brown's Park when she homesteaded in Bull Canyon.

Bertha and Marie were both strong, energetic teenage girls. Each had a love for the cowboy life and rode a lot of miles, often singing loudly, and had years of fun times together. Bertha spent many nights and ate many meals with the Taylors. Nina's homebaked bread was one of her favorites. C.M. always called Bertha "Dorothy" in fun. When they went to town and Marie bought anything new, C.M. would say, "Don't you think you ought to get Dorothy one of those, too?" Marie was "all for that" and got a lot of pleasure from sharing with her friend. Many years later, Bertha would describe Marie as "the joy of my childhood."₉

In the fall of 1928, when it came time for Bessie to return to Ogden for her senior year, her mother and Marie made plans to go with her. Nina and C.M. felt that it would be a good opportunity for Marie to finish her education in the city. It was decided that C.M. would stay alone at the ranch, and Nina would take care of the girls in Ogden.

By then C.M. had purchased a Dodge touring car. It was a handsome automobile with curtains that could be rolled up or down, to either let in the sunshine or to keep out the snow and rain. C.M. started the car one morning, and the family climbed in for a comfortable ride to the train station in Rock Springs. Marie felt a terrible lump in her throat as she watched the cedars, sagebrush, and blue mountains of her valley move by the window and disappear behind her. The aching lump would remain for some time to come.

For the first time in Marie Taylor's life she felt insignificant, embarrassed, and lost. In Brown's Park she was Tex Taylor! In the modern apartment and the bustling city school, she didn't know who she was. Every day, she was late for every class and each time the laughter brought stinging tears to her eyes and made her stomach hurt. She had never complained to her parents in her life. It never occurred to her to do so now. Instead she swallowed hard, ducked her head, and tried to find her way through this world where she was such an outsider.

The school year and the following summer finally passed. It was time to be thinking about getting Marie ready for another winter in Ogden. On his way to bed, C.M. passed Marie's closed door and heard several muffled sobs. He stopped, opened the door and softy asked, "Babe, are you alright?"

In a tiny voice she answered, "Yes, I'm okay."

C.M. stepped across the room, sat down on the edge of the bed, and touched her on the shoulder. "What is it, Babe?"

Marie could hold back the tears no longer. "Oh, Dad, I'm already so homesick I can hardly stand it! I don't want to disappoint you and mother, but I don't want to go back there."

C.M.'s heart gave in as his daughter's misery poured out. He hugged her tight and made up his mind how it was going to be.

"You don't have to go, Babe. You can stay home if that's what you really want."

It was most definitely what she wanted. She helped take care of the house and when there was outside work to be done she was, as always, her dad's best right hand.

Marie hadn't seen Hazel Teters very much since Hazel's sister, Rose, married Bill Logan. Instead of going to Brown's Park, Hazel spent most of the summers at her sister's ranch. Marie was happy for her though, when Hazel told her she was going to marry Jim Overy. Jim was a big man with jet black hair and eyes so deep brown that they were nearly black. Hazel and Jim had met a year earlier at a rodeo in Rock Springs. To get Hazel's attention, Jim had teased her by taking her "tie down" and refusing to give it back. Hazel snubbed him for a while, but Jim's persistent grin soon won her over. They were married on September 28, 1929.10

The following spring, while living in an apartment in Rock Springs, Hazel and Jim had a baby girl. Because of the bond between Hazel and the Taylor girls, the baby was named Bessie Marie. Bessie Marie was beautiful, with lashes so long that when her eyes were open they curled over her eyebrows. When she slept, the lashes brushed softly against the top of her cheeks.

When Bessie Marie was eight months old, one of the neighbor kids inadvertently exposed her to whooping cough. Hazel was terrified, and fearfully watched over her baby. As hard as she wished them away, the signs of the illness began to show. Bessie Marie was soon in a battle with the devastating disease, giving in to the relentless tickle that lead to the convulsive spasmodic cough. After every string of coughs came the sickening crowing sound that Bessie Marie made as she fought to get air back into her body.

There was little the doctor could do. In spite of Hazel's constant care, her daughter only got sicker. Then pneumonia developed.

During the afternoon when Jim's mother Sarah and his aunt Mary McDonald were there helping out, a glowing light came through the window and spread across the sick baby.

"Oh, Hazel," Aunt Mary said, "God has come for her."

Hazel was weary from the suffering she had watched her daughter endure, and devastated with the thought of losing her child. She walked to the cradle and slowly put her hand into the light. She was awed that her hand made no shadow on the baby. Within a short time, Bessie Marie took her final breath.11

Marie hurt so badly for her friends. She longed for words that would bring Hazel and Jim some comfort. There were none. Her arms were what Hazel needed most, anyway. Although Jim and Hazel would eventually be blessed with three healthy daughters, the pain of the loss of Bessie Marie would remain with them always.

One afternoon during the spring of 1931, Nina and Marie were returning home from getting the mail at the post office at Callaways. Nina drove the Dodge touring car over a hill and noticed a couple of men working on two cars parked off the side of the road in the Beaver Creek lane. When the older man turned around, they recognized the familiar face of Charlie Green.

They visited with him for a few minutes, then Charlie said, "I want to introduce you to my nephew from Vernal." He turned and called out, "Bill, come on over here, there's somebody I want you to meet."

A young man crawled from the innards of the Model T Ford and walked toward them. He was a messy sight, covered from head to toe with smudgy automobile grease. He started to reach out a grimy hand, then jerked it back. By then, he had gotten close enough for Marie to see his face, the blackness of his hair, and the blueness of his eyes. She forgot about the grease. When he smiled and nodded to her, she forgot everything, except that his name was Bill Allen.[12]

Chapter XXV

BILL ALLEN

William Edward Allen was born on July 10, 1913, with his father's full eyebrows, dark hair, and good looks. Twenty-four years earlier his mother, Elnora Green Allen - sister to Charlie and Retta Green - had been born on September 13, 1889. Elnora's grandparents had been Mormon converts who had arrived in Utah in 1852 with the Pioneer Hand Cart Company. When the town of Cedarview, Utah, was just getting started, her parents, Ephraim and Sidney Thayne Green, purchased a lot near the edge of their farm and built a general store.

On December 23, 1906, Elnora married the son of a Union Pacific railroad engineer, Warren Leslie Allen, Jr. In 1910 when Elnora and Leslie bought a coal mine just north of White Rocks, they already had a daughter, Lela, and a baby boy, Delphas. In a couple of years, Leslie and Elnora sold their mine and spent the winter on Elnora's brother's farm at Cedarview. There Elnora had a baby girl and named her Zora. That spring the couple bought two adjoining lots in Cedarview. They built a cabin next door to the general store so they would be nearby to help Elnora's folks. In the heat of the summer on July 10, 1913, William "Bill" was born. Two weeks later, Elnora's mother died from typhoid fever. After losing his wife, Elnora's father no longer wanted the store and went to Manti to work in the temple. Leslie and Elnora purchased the merchandise, rented the building, and carried on with the store.

During the winter of 1914, Leslie and Elnora bought two one-acre lots in the new town of Neola, Utah, and started its first store. The store caught fire and burned to the ground, but the young couple was not discouraged and quickly rebuilt. On December 6, 1915, their fifth child, Verda Marie, was born.

Of all the Allen children, Bill's best pal was his pretty sister, Zora. They had hours of fun playing in the hay manger behind the store and riding their fat old horse, Roany. The brother and sister were so little, they had to tie a rope onto the stirrup so that they could hoist the saddle onto Roany's back. They thought nothing of it and went through the process almost every day. They also enjoyed watching the busy farmers with their work horses as the big-hoofed team went around and around on the horse-powered threshing machines. Bill was fascinated and anxious to see just how everything worked the day he saw Neola's first steam-powered thresher go to work.

For a week or two each summer, Bill went with his family up Uintah Canyon along with aunts, uncles, and cousins. They made camp in a soft meadow and soon the boys hurried off to fish. The rest of the family picked wild raspberries and used them to make wild berry pie. The kids played hide-and-seek in the trees and bent quaking aspen saplings down and rode them for bucking horses. If Bill got bucked off, the toddler would scramble to his feet and jump back in the middle of the sapling, determined to get the best of the "bronc" and be the best rider.

Each holiday meant a house full of relatives and a big meal of stuffed turkey, pumpkin pies, and suet pudding. The Allen children, although they had their chores to do, were all happy and carefree. In the evenings they buttered their hands and pulled molasses flavored taffy or made honey candy, and often played kick-the-can. Bill always had enough to eat, a warm bed to snuggle into, and plenty of clean clothes. The Allen children had parents they could count on to provide a comfortable and steady way of life.

One rainy night in September, 1916, three-year-old Bill was roughly awakened by a turmoil in the house. He could hear his father moaning in pain and his mother frantically hurrying to get him to the hospital. That night, the lives of Bill and the other four Allen children were forever altered. At the hospital, during that dark rainstorm, their thirty-two year old father died from a ruptured appendix.

By the winter of 1918, things were getting rough. Elnora had not managed the store well and had given out so much credit that only a small amount of money dribbled in. It had been an early winter and it stayed bitterly cold day after day. The price of hay rose as the temperatures fell. By midwinter, Elnora could no longer afford to feed the milk cow, and was forced to sell her. Bill and the rest of the family learned how to get along without the milk, cream, and butter which the cow had so generously provided. They were quickly learning how to get along without a lot of things.

The next summer, Elnora put the store up for lease. His mother sent Bill and his brother and sisters to Roosevelt to live with relatives and she went alone to the Stores Mining Camp to take work as a cook. Bill felt his stomach ache with missing her and his home.

At Stores, Elnora met Joseph Emanuel Christensen, a widower with two children named Don and Edna. In December, she married the gentle small-built miner. Joseph was a kind man, but because he was an epileptic, and by nature a vagabond, he never found steady work. From the time of the marriage, life for Bill, his step brother Don, and the other four Allen children, was a whirlwind of different homes, new schools and short-lived friendships. Life became a struggle. Young Bill

206

Allen learned that work and survival had the same definition.

Shortly after Joseph and Elnora were married they went to Roosevelt to pick up the children. The youngsters rode in the canvas-covered back of the truck with the December air whispering around their necks and ears and seeping through their clothes. By the time they reached the Stores Mining Camp, Bill was very sick. When morning arrived, so did his measle dots. Within a short time, he had passed them around to the other children and most of the family stayed sick through the holidays. Bill and the others did have fun later on, riding sleighs down the snowy slopes near the mine.

The family left the mining camp and moved to Elnora's little house next to the store in Neola. From there they moved to Price for half a school year, then they moved to Bicknell. There Bill helped his stepfather haul gasoline for Brinkerhoff's store in a tank which sat in the back of a wagon.

One time they got a load at Salina and were driving over the summit when a wheel broke. Joseph became ill and luckily soon caught a ride to town. Bill waited overnight with the wagon. With big eyes, he watched as the evening shadows turned black and listened to strange scratching and bumping noises around him. He huddled in a corner of the wagon, slept a few minutes at a time, and waited for dawn. From the first hint of light until sunup, he slept hard and unafraid. When the sun began to warm the top of his head, he woke up. The little boy dug through the supplies for some breakfast and discovered that the night noises had been pack rats making off with all the eating utensils.

Not long after that ordeal, Bill's family moved back to Neola. Joseph sold the store and used the money to lease a little place and buy a herd of milk cows. However, it wasn't long before the cow herd, along with everything that Elnora and her first husband, Leslie Allen, had accumulated, had substantially dwindled. Bill watched as one by one the cows, along with the other belongings, were sold or bartered. Although the family usually raised a big garden each summer and canned many jars of plums, apples, cherries, and peaches, there was very little money. As Elnora began having more children, there was even less.

One fall Bill decided to make some money by gleaning alfalfa seed from plants along ditch banks and from small patches left by the threshers. He let Zora in on his plan. The youngsters talked about making enough money to buy new winter coats by the time the snow began to fall. They worked hard, day after day, stripping the seed heads by hand and piling them in neat heaps along the way. Their hands got sore but they were proud of their work, and of the clean gathering of top quality seed.

However, when the seed was sold, Bill and Zora didn't get new coats. They felt terrible when their folks took the money, which turned out to be more than Joseph and Elnora had made all summer.

The next spring, Joseph and the children planted their thirty-acre field with seed alfalfa. About the time the crop reached its prime and was nearing harvest, Joseph sold the cows and got a Model T Ford. The day they went to pick up the car, Bill and his big brother, Del, were to bring the team and wagon home with a load of fruit. The boys were not far from Neola when they saw a heavy white sheet that reached from the ground high into the sky, sweep down at them. The hail began small, but as the force of the storm increased, so did the size of the ice balls. The horses went wild and began to run. Screaming at each other over the roar of the storm, the young boys decided to head the horses toward a grove of trees. Del turned the horses so that one went to the left and one to the right of a sturdy cottonwood. Bill jumped from the wagon and ran around in front of the horses and grabbed one by the bit. Del secured the brake and hurried to grab the bit of the other. There they held the horses as the leaves and branches were torn from the trees and until the freezing, pounding storm had passed. While the air calmed and the sun found its way through the clouds, Del and Bill backed the team away from the tree and started for home. As they passed their alfalfa field, Bill felt his eyes get watery when he saw nothing but stems and stubs, which the hail had left after stripping the seed crop. The boys soon discovered that it had also taken the entire roof off their house.

In October, Joseph and Elnora loaded the small Model T with clothes, food, and their seven children and started for California. They left Neola and made it to Miton where the transmission went out. A week later they pushed the car up Indian Canyon and rode down through American Fork. The Model T was equipped with small wooden rim tires which had difficulty carrying the weight of nine passengers and their belongings. One day, pushing the car up the hills and riding down, they made it twenty-five miles, with a frustrating seventeen flat tires. When they reached Price, they stayed overnight with relatives. There they got better tires before going on. By the time they reached Filmore, the weather had turned colder and the car had to be jacked up until its front tires were off the ground before it could be cranked to a start.

On the desert between Filmore and Beaver, something went wrong with the car and it refused to run. Everyone caught a ride into town, except Joseph and ten-year-old Bill. They stayed behind with the car. The two were stranded for several days and had been left with only two canteens of water. Each night, two or three little gray fox found their way to the grub box. Bill stayed up a couple of nights trying to catch one, but was never quick enough. Time went by and the water dwindled. At last Bill sucked on the metal openings of the canteens, but there was not a drop of water left to moisten his tongue.

When no one returned for them, Bill and his stepfather drained the water from the car's radiator and made both coffee and tea. Bill's throat stung with thirst, but the radiator water was so bitter with iron they couldn't drink it. Luckily, a lone car happened by and Joseph caught a ride. Bill stayed alone then, until his brother Del finally came for him the next day.

The car was repaired in Beaver, but by the time the family reached St. George the food supply, consisting mostly of flour, lard, sugar, and salt for making bread and gravy, and mush-like "lumpy-dick," was nearly gone. The kids had a little camera they had earned by selling salve. Joseph and Elnora traded it for flour. They stayed in St. George for a while where they all worked picking fruit in the orchards until they could afford to go on.

When the family reached Las Vegas, they had very little left. Joseph traded the Model T to a card-playing gambler for a little house. Bill and the others stepped inside and looked around at their new home. It was nothing more than a single room board shack, with a dirt floor. As soon as their belongings were moved in, Joseph and the children went to look for ways to earn money. Bill and some of the other children bent over and picked through the smelly dump for brass and aluminum or anything else they could sell for a few pennies.

In January the family left Las Vegas and headed for California. Joseph had traded the shack for a Buick pickup, which had good tires, but no top. It was merely a windshield, a seat, and a box in the back. The cold wind tangled their hair and often kept the travelers huddled up, but good luck pushed them forward. They made it to Elnora's sister Sadie's house between Whittier and Home Gardens in California without many problems.

At Home Gardens, Bill lived with and worked for a good-hearted bachelor dairyman named Frenchie. Each morning Bill and Frenchie were up by four o'clock and were soon milking the dairy herd by hand. When each had finished his half of the herd, the milk was put through a cooler and bottled in quart bottles. The filled bottles were then put in baskets and loaded onto the wagon. By eight o'clock they began their deliveries. An hour later, Frenchie would drop Bill off at school. When school got out at three, Bill would walk back to the dairy. It was his job to get out the steamer and wash the bottles and the rest of the equipment until everything sparkled. At five or six that evening, Frenchie and Bill started the milking process again. Frenchie was very kind to Bill and he made the boy feel comfortable and at home at the dairy.

Bill continued to work for Frenchie seven days a week for a dollar a day. Occasionally, Frenchie gave him a Sunday afternoon off. On those days, since he knew that Bill turned all of his wages over to his parents, the older man would slip the boy an extra quarter or fifty cents. The youngster used the money to take his sister Zora to the show or to buy some watermelon or a candy bar for them to share. If any money was left over, Bill put it in a can and carefully buried it.

After a little more than a year had passed, and Bill had completed the sixth grade, he sadly said goodbye to Frenchie. Del, working at a dairy in Chino, and Lela, living with relatives, stayed in California. But Bill and the rest of the family drove back to Utah in a four-door, canvas-topped auto. It was a bumpy ride. Although a new highway was under construction, the one they traveled was filled with broken asphalt chunks and pot holes.

That early spring, at twelve years of age, Bill went to work for sheepman T.A. Gardner. It seemed that wherever Bill went, he found work easily. Often the farmers and ranchers sought him out because he had proven himself to be honest and a hard and dependable worker. When he went to work for Mr. Gardner, he began by helping shear the yearlings and doing the irrigating.

The Gardner place was located across the river from where Bill's folks lived. In June the river got so high that Bill couldn't safely take a horse across it and he didn't get to see his family for a while. As soon as the river dropped, he borrowed a horse and forded the river to visit his folks. When he got to their place, he was dumbfounded to discover they were gone and no one seemed to know where. The desertion painfully nagged at Bill, making him feel a little sick for the first few days. But he kept his pride and never let on to anyone how he felt. His thirteenth birthday, on July tenth, came and went with still no word from his family. When T.A. Gardner's herder quit, he hired Bill full time. For two weeks at a time, Bill stayed on the desert south of Miton with two-thousand yearling sheep, his horse, Slim, and a dog.

The only water supply for the sheep was in the bottom of a creek. The sun was so hot that the animals laid around the water panting all through the day, until it began to cool off at six or seven in the evening. Then, with a blanket and a can of pork and beans tied on his horse, Bill drove the yearlings to fresh feed. The sheep hurriedly nibbled and munched until dark, then bedded down. When the herd was quiet, Bill hobbled his horse and spread his blanket on the ground. When he took his hat off, his pale forehead clashed in the moonlight with his brown face, and his black hair stayed wadded in a thick clump on the top of his head. Before long, the youngster stretched out on the blanket and slept. If the sheep moved in the night, Bill sleepily got up and followed along. At first light he hurried to gather the herd and push them back to water because by nine o'clock the sheep would refuse to move in the intense heat. At camp in the sheepwagon during the day, Bill passed the time reading, sleeping, and making donuts. After his two weeks were up, Mr. Gardner came to relieve him and Bill went to the Gardner ranch to milk, irrigate, and take care of things. After a while, Mr. Gardner sent a boy with Bill when he went out on the desert, so that he wouldn't have to be alone so much.

When school started in September, Bill had saved three hundred dollars. He found a place with the Glines family where he could live, work, and go to school. He heard that his family was living in Park City, Utah, but had received no word from them. Then in October they drove up in a Model T roadster. As they drove him to Park City, they told him they needed 250 dollars to pay for the car.

"It'll be your car, Bill," they said. Bill gave them the money, knowing that they knew he was too young to drive.

At Park City, Bill worked digging six foot deep trenches for sewer and water lines in the rocky soil. He knew he was being paid fifty cents a foot, but he never knew how much he made because he never saw any of it. That was the way it was, and always had been. It was his nature to show his parents the utmost respect and he would not let them down even though he, at times, felt very let down.

At Christmas time, the family went to Roosevelt and moved into a two-room house. Whenever Bill wasn't attending school that winter, he hauled wood to sell. When summer came, he went back to work for T.A. Gardner. The next fall, he moved to Vernal with his family and went to work putting up hay on the Rasmussen place. After finishing that job, he fed cows on the Perry place. He was always a busy young man.

Bill was very saddened the day he learned that T.A. Gardner had been killed. Mr. Gardner and his daughter, Thelma, had gone to check on the sheep one afternoon and were driving back to Miton in their Buick sedan. It was raining hard as they drove up Nine Mile Canyon. Driving around a bend they were terrified by the sight of a wall of water heading toward them. Thelma heard her dad yell, "Jump, Thelma!" Father and daughter both threw their doors open. The force immediately slammed the door shut on T.A., but it grabbed Thelma and threw her into a bank where she caught hold of a cedar. Three or four days later, T.A. was found at the bottom of the canyon, where the rushing waters of the flash flood had left him.

Bill continued to work feeding cows on Ashley Creek while he finished the eighth grade in Vernal. He got a summer job irrigating for Don B. Colton, and then for John L. Sidaway. At the same time, he put up hay on the place that his stepfather had leased in Davis ward.

It was during this time that Bill got a gelding and broke him to ride. One Sunday afternoon he was riding with some friends when they decided to have a race. They all took off toward the church, urging their horses to run as fast as they could. From the beginning, he and his gelding held the lead. Not far from the church, they raced over a little rise. It was as they came off a small ridge that his horse, three lengths in the lead, stumbled a little. As soon as Bill could get him stopped, he jumped from his limping horse. He gently led the crippled gelding home. His fear that the gelding's leg had been broken was realized when he heard a jarring gunshot put the young horse out of its misery.

Later, Bill got a fancy looking, tall thoroughbred. He was pretty, but hard to keep and hard to handle. One day, he was riding him when a horse trader named Orsen Hall came by.

"Wanna sell your horse?" he asked.

"Nope," Bill anwered.

"Well, how about tradin'?"

"I might trade, but I don't want to be without a horse."

"Well," the horse trader said, "come on up one of these days. I've got a little sorrel horse I'm just getting broke. I'll make you a good deal on him."

The next day, Bill traded the thoroughbred for the nice looking gelding. He also got the hackamore the sorrel was wearing and ten dollars "to boot." The whip-broke bronc was touchy and tried to run away with him on the way home, but Bill still didn't doubt that the sorrel was special. Whenever Bill had spare time, he worked with his new horse. With the kindness the gelding was shown, he soon began to trust the teenager. Bill only had to slap his thigh and say, "Come on." The horse would hurry to him and would follow him wherever he went. Bill was more attached to the horse than he had ever been to anything.

The next fall after finishing the eighth grade, Bill tried to feed cows and attend high school at the same time. In all his years of school, he had never been in the same school two years in a row. Many times he had been in three or four different ones. Still, Bill managed to make a grade each year. But now, he had grown tired of the battle and decided to quit school. He worked for Nels Weeks in the coal mine, hauling the filled cars from the mine with a mule named Tiny, and dumping the load outside. Then his folks got a coal mine not far from Vernal. Bill worked there, digging coal, filling the cars, then pushing the heavy loads outside to dump by hand. Eventually, they got a Model T ton truck and he used it to deliver coal on the weekends.

By now, because of the years of constant hard physical work, Bill's body had developed into one similar to a boxer's. At a distance he didn't seem overly large, but a closer look revealed stout thighs, shoulders, arms, and hands with thick, strong fingers. He demanded a lot of himself, and sometimes did things by hand that were normally done with a team of horses, such as tripping a hay stacker. He stayed sun and wind-tanned all year around, causing his eyes to seem a deeper blue. When he went with his good friends Mel Burke and Ralph Southam to "argue" with the girls or swipe some chickens for a "chickeree" feast, he laughed often and his eyes had a happy twinkle.

Bill Allen on his sorrel

213

When the weather was getting warm the first of April, Bill's red-headed Uncle Charlie Green drove in, in his old Model T Ford. Uncle Charlie said, "Bill, how would you like to head over the mountain to Brown's Hole with me? I've been thinking about taking my boat so we could float down Lodore Canyon and trap beaver."

The sixteen-year-old was very anxious to go with his uncle, who was fun and always ready to tell a comical story. Later that day, Uncle Charlie discovered that someone had taken his boat so they wouldn't be able to trap beaver.

"Oh, well," the older man said, "you can go over there with me anyway, Bill, and we'll do a little prospecting."

Several days later, after Bill had stopped the car from spitting water and spewing steam in Vernal, and then repaired the timing gear on top of Diamond Mountain, the two drove down Crouse Canyon and pulled to a stop in front of the Brown's Park Live Stock ranch house. The ranch was now owned by W.H. Gottsche and Stanley Crouse, son of Charlie Crouse. Stanley, who ran the ranch, wasn't home, but two of his hired men, old Albert Williams and Husky Muir, welcomed their old friend Charlie Green and his nephew.

After spending the night, Uncle Charlie and Bill drove down the road a couple of miles to cross the river on Stanley Crouse's ferry at the Colorado-Utah state line. The ferry was the same one C.M. Taylor had built years earlier and was still in pretty good shape. It was located just up from where the swinging bridge had blown down. Although they noticed the river was low, they pulled the car onto the ferry and started crossing. They were only part way across the Green River when Bill and his uncle felt the ferry hit a sandbar and heard it grind to a halt. The two looked at each other, shrugged, and got out the fishing gear.

A while later, Stanley Crouse showed up on the opposite bank. "Whatchu doin'?" he drawled.

Uncle Charlie hollered back, "Oh, just sittin' here, waitin' for the river to come up."

Stanley began to laugh. "That river ain't comin' up this year, it's too damn dry!" Then they all laughed at the predicament.

Then Stanley hollered, "You two want a job?"

"Sure."

"Well, go on back to the house and tell Husky Muir to get a tent and some grub and bring it down. We'll get the car off the ferry and then we'll start fixing the bridge."

After the men got the ferryboat off the sandbar, they let it float down the river to the site where the bridge had blown down. There the car was driven safely onto the bank. The men then used the ferry to load the bridge parts, which were strewn across the river, and float them to the bank. Then they began to work repairing the bridge.

About three weeks later, when Uncle Charlie and Bill left the Park Live, the swinging bridge of cable and boards and no side rails, which Stanley Crouse had built in 1927, was repaired. They were on their way to do a little prospecting but left with the promise that they would return in June to help Stanley Crouse hay. Uncle Charlie's car wasn't running very well when they drove it across the bridge and started up the hill. It was barely running when they met up with Gene and Sam Carr.

Afer visiting for a while, one of the Carr boys said, "Our brother, Little Joe, was drowned a while back. He had a roadster that's in pretty fair shape if you want to buy it."

Bill bought the car, and he and Uncle Charlie pulled the two cars off the road in the Beaver Creek lane to work them over. Bill was busy tearing the old Model T engine down to get parts for the new car when he noticed a fancy Dodge touring car pull up. Then he heard his uncle call to him. Bill walked toward the car and saw an older woman and a young girl inside. He suddenly became self-conscious that he was covered with grease. He started to, then realized he didn't dare offer to shake hands.

He heard Nina Taylor say, "Come on up to the house for supper and spend the night if you like."

Later on, when Marie took Bill across the river in the trolley, he put his hand in the wrong place, causing his finger to get pinched in the pulley. That incident became the playful joke that Marie Taylor "caught" Bill Allen in the trolley.

Through the summer, Bill and his uncle did a little prospecting, built fence for C.M. Taylor, and hayed for Stanley Crouse. At the end of July, Uncle Charlie and Bill took a short trip to Vernal with plans of soon returning to Brown's Park. C.M. offered Uncle Charlie a homestead he was relinquishing at the head of Galloway Draw on Cold Spring Mountain and offered Bill a full time job. Both Charlie and Bill took C.M. up on the offers.

As soon as Bill got to Vernal, he gave his folks most of his summer wages. He was anxious to see his sorrel gelding and mentioned that he intended to take him to Brown's Park when he went back. His folks looked at him, shook their heads, and told him that his horse was no longer there. Bill dropped his head, tightened his jaw, and silently endured the injustice when they said, "We sold him."

A short time later Brown's Park saw Bill come out of Sears Canyon with his few belongings under his arm. She watched as he followed the little clear creek which led to the Taylor ranch.

Young Bill Allen looked straight ahead; unaware that a new world had opened for him, and that this blue-tinted valley was about to determine the rest of his life.[1]

Chapter XXVI
ROMANCES AND FAREWELLS

The weather was pleasantly warm the day Marie Taylor and her friend Bertha Worley rode their horses off Cold Spring Mountain. Marie's face was tanned to a peachy gold and her slightly dusty, straight hair hung a few inches below her Stetson. She wore a scarf loosely around her neck, and a long-sleeved shirt under a light vest. Her buff colored bat-wing chaps showed they had been well used and were "properly broke in." They protectively fit over her Levis and reached down to her spurs. Marie had been on the mountain helping her family ride after cattle. The Taylors had gathered over one hundred head of C.M.'s huge three and four-year-old steers. They would soon be leaving the mountain with the chuck wagon and the steers, trailing to Bitter Creek to the stockyards. Today, Bertha and Marie were on their way to the Taylor Ranch to see if the new hired man, Bill Allen, had arrived to take care of the chores.

As the girls came through the saddle from Little Beaver to Birch Creek, Marie patted her tall black gelding, Speed, on the neck and said, "I sure hope Bill's there, 'cause I'm winning a bet with Edith Garrison if he is. Edith really thought he was cute and bet me that he'd come to see her before me."

Now sixteen, Marie had grown into a tall, strapping young cowgirl. Her blue eyes were trained to spot deer, elk, or cattle that were camouflaged by the countryside, from an incredible distance. The way she never held back, but spurred her horse into a lope and roped a horse or a calf that the men had not been able to catch, could have been viewed as cockiness. However, Marie was not conceited, she just had a strong sense of her own abilities. She was considered a top hand.

When Marie laughed, her nose crinkled to reveal a broad grin. Although she wouldn't admit it as she rode beside Bertha, something in her stomach fluttered at the thought of seeing the young man from Vernal.

When the girls arrived at the ranch, they discovered Bill had been there for several days. He had busied himself finding chores to do and had spent a lot of time splitting and stacking firewood. He was glad to see the girls and the three teenagers spent a pleasant afternoon visiting. As the girls rode back to the mountain, for some reason which Marie couldn't explain to herself, she felt proud that Bill was obviously a hard worker.

During the autumn and winter months, Bill helped hay the old Tolliver place; he cut cedars and hewed them to build a new chicken house; he worked on the windmill's water storage tank;

217

he burned brush; he ran (rounded up) wild horses and broke one of the mares, Montan, for Marie; and he rode after cattle.

While the weather was still warm that fall, Bill spent time with the Taylors on Cold Spring Mountain building a cabin and corrals. In the unfinished cabin at night, since there were no beds, they spread quilts on the floor and made one long bed where everyone slept including Hays Hughes, Bill, C.M., Nina, Bessie, and Marie.₁

During the coldest part of the winter, Bill helped haul logs and boulders and piled them on the ice on the river at an upward angle at the head of C.M.'s big ditch. When the ice thawed in the spring, the "wing" settled into the river and diverted a good share of water into the ditch.

Marie spent quite a bit of time riding with Bill teaching him the names of the canyons, creeks, and mountain peaks. One chilly afternoon, Marie was on Speed, and Bill was on a smaller, roan-colored gelding named Frosty, a touchy young horse, known to buck now and then. Bill and Marie were on their way home after looking for cattle tracks in the snow on the Bradshaw place. They were on the flat above the Jarvie place when Bill's horse began to step around and bob his head.

With a note of warning in her voice, Marie said, "Better look out, he'll throw you off!"

With a smirk Bill answered, "Aw, he can't do that."

Then he leaned back in the saddle and hooked Frosty in the shoulders with his spurs. Instantly, Frosty's head dropped between his knees and Bill flipped out of the saddle. He flew over Frosty's head and landed in the snow on his head and shoulders. Hiding a smile, Marie touched her spurs to the black's sides and hurried to catch Frosty. She gathered up the reins and led him back. Then she saw that Bill had his head down, with his chin on his chest, and was intent on something.

"What's the matter, did it hurt you?" she asked.

Still looking down, slowly Bill said, "Naw . . . it broke my zipper." Then he looked up and they both began to laugh.₂

Bill had not been in Brown's Park very long when a man showed up riding the sorrel gelding that Bill had owned and his folks had sold.

The man said, "I heard that you might be interested in this horse. I've come to make you a deal on him."

His "deal" turned out to be a high price that Bill found impossible to meet. Although he wanted the horse with all his heart, he shook his head and said, "You might as well take him back over the mountain, because I can't afford him."

Bill watched the man ride away on the horse, with the hope

that one day he would get him back. However, he later heard that after the man left that day, he stopped for the night at a cabin on Diamond Mountain. He fed the sorrel grain from a sack he found inside the building, unaware that the oats had been laced with poison to kill prairie dogs. Within minutes the sorrel was dead.[3]

Marie Taylor on Speed   **Bill Allen on Frosty**

Marie Taylor   Bill Allen

An evening walk on the Taylor Place

Bill Allen

Marie Taylor

L to R: Bessie, Marie, and Jesse Taylor

At Christmas time, Bill and Marie rode to Rock Springs in the back of C.M.'s 1930 Chevy truck with quilts tucked around them for warmth. In Rock Springs, Bill bought a new saddle with an Association tree, and a new bridle to match. They were the first he had owned and he was very proud of them.

By the time the new year of 1932 arrived, Brown's Park knew that Marie Taylor was in love. In the soft light of the coal oil lamp beside her bed, she wrote about her "sweet kisses from Billie dear." However, because young love doesn't follow the smoothest road, her diary also held a page now and then with hurt in the words. But the bad times were few, and as springtime grew closer, so did Bill and Marie.

It had been a rough winter for Bess. She had always had bouts of illness, but when she got sick the first part of January, she stayed sick. On the eleventh of January, C.M., Nina, and Marie took her to Rock Springs to the doctor. He said he did not believe that she was in a "dangerous condition," but he wanted her to remain in town for a while. Nina stayed with Bess in Rock Springs, and C.M. and Marie, who was now "chief cook and bottle washer," returned to the ranch. For the next two months, C.M. and Marie made many hurried trips through snow and mud after receiving word that Bess was gravely ill. Usually a few days later, she would show signs of recovery and would be released from the hospital. C.M. and Marie would return to the ranch. Before long, though, Bess would be sick again.

During one particularly bad episode, Marie hurried to town with her dad. She wrote these words in her diary:

> March 22, 1932
> Got Dr. Arbogast and took Bess to hospital. Am staying all night with her. A lot of nurses up here. I sure wish you were here Bill.

> March 23, 1932
> Stayed with Bess last night. Got up early. Went to x-ray room two times with Bess and they took four x-rays. Dr. Arbogast and Dr. Chambers examined her then we brought her home.

> March 24, 1932
> Dad and Stanley Crouse went home this morning. I didn't do much. I sure wish I could see you Billie dear. Stormy today.

March 24, 1932

Went down town and got Bessie's Easter rabbit. While I was gone to the P.O., Mother talked to Bess and when I came back Mother told me. I couldn't keep from crying.[4]

Wilson and Bessie Garrison wedding with Bill Allen and Marie Taylor in back

Marie and Bill Allen wedding with Bess and Wilson

Before long, Bessie was able to return to Brown's Park. She could not feel saddened by the news of her pregnancy. Because of it, the wedding that she and Wilson Garrison had dreamed about was no longer rejected by her mother. Instead, there was happy talk about a mint green wedding dress and how the bright spray of silk flowers would look in her hair. In Vernal, on May fourth, Wilson and Bess were married. It would

224

be one of the happiest marriages Brown's Park would ever see.

After the wedding, Bill took some time off and stayed in Vernal. Marie worried that he would never come back, but he did. On July thirty-first, she could hardly believe it when he asked her dad's permission to give her an engagement ring. Marie was seventeen and Bill nineteen when they were married in Salt Lake City on September 22, 1932. They made their home on the ranch in the little house where Grandmother Taylor had lived. They worked for C.M. for forty dollars a month and boarded themselves with their own milk cow and flock of chickens. Uncle Charlie Green relinquished the homestead at the head of Galloway to Bill. Although he was only nineteen, Bill was able to file on the land because he was now married.

The young couple spent the 1933-34 winter in Vernal working in the coal mine. Marie cooked for the miners and ran the scales while Bill worked in the mine. They traded the coal for groceries, mining fuses, and powder. They also traded coal for wheat. They took the wheat to the mill to have it ground into flour, then traded the flour for cattle. When they trailed thirteen head of cattle to Brown's Park the last of April, they had the beginning of their herd. That summer, Marie stayed alone on Cold Spring Mountain to look after her dad's cattle. She made twenty-five dollars a month, while Bill made forty dollars a month working in the hay fields for Stanley Crouse.

Brown's Park, as well as most of the west, had grown dusty from a several year drought. Times were especially tough for stockmen because they had no feed for their cattle and there was no market for the cattle. The government started a program to help. Through the subsidy program, cows were bought for twelve dollars a head, yearlings for fourteen dollars, and two-year-olds for sixteen dollars. The beef was then butchered and given away to anyone in need. Finding it tough to feed their growing herd, Bill and Marie sold a few head of their cattle on the program.

The next spring, Bill, Marie, and their little dog, Fannie, rode the bus to Bill's sister Lela, and her husband Truman's home in California. Through the summer, Bill drove an ice truck and sold refrigerators while Marie worked in a peach cannery. By fall, they were able to purchase a new Model A sedan and a two-wheel trailer. They loaded the trailer with home-canned fruit and returned to Brown's Park. They bought hay from George Bassett, who had sold all of his cattle, to feed their herd during the coming winter. For a few months that fall, Bill lived in Rock Springs and worked dumping coal at a mine in Blairtown, then returned to the ranch to work for C.M. When they were in California, Marie had miscarried three months into her first

225

pregnancy. It had been a deep loss to the young woman. Now Marie was very happy to discover that she was expecting again.[5]

Bessie and Wilson had named their little boy Melvin. Although Wilson and Bess had worked at a few other jobs, most of the last three years had been spent working on the Taylor place in the winter, and living on Cold Spring Mountain in the summer. Bessie, with little Melvin on a pillow on the front of her saddle, often went along and helped Wilson when he was working cattle. She was a good cook and made Wilson's favorite stew with everything in it "except the dishrag." When they held each other at the dances, their obvious happiness made the onlookers nod their heads and smile. C.M. had recently sold them some land across the river. In his spare time, Wilson cut down pine trees and hauled the logs off the mountain. He soon had a good start on a cabin where his little family planned to make their home.

In May, 1936, Loren Bowen and his sister, from Little Hole, were staying with Bob Teters at Bridgeport. The Taylors got word that Loren was sick and needed a ride to the doctor. Bill decided to take him to Vernal, and Marie, who was nearing the end of her pregnancy, went along. It was discovered that Loren had scarlet fever. A couple of weeks later, Marie began to feel ill. Bill decided to take her to Rock Springs to stay with Mrs. Teters until the baby came.

In the meantime, Wilson and Bess had been packing things up to move to Cold Spring for the summer. They were nearly ready to go when Bess began to feel a little sick. It was decided that Wilson would take their things to the mountain and Bess would rest at her mother's. When Wilson returned a few days later, Bess hadn't gotten any better. He stayed to take care of her and the place while everyone else went to Rock Springs to see the live performance of cowboy Tom Mix.

Wilson took Bessie's lunch to her bedroom, then sat down at the table near the bay window to eat his own. Suddenly a little bird flew to the window and fluttered in a strange manner in front of it for several seconds. It flew away, then returned and once again fluttered for over a minute. C.M.'s hound dog began to howl in long, doleful calls. Wilson had never heard the dog make such sounds before. He felt uneasy, but shook it off and went about the day caring for his wife and doing the chores.

When C.M., Nina, and Melvin returned from Rock Springs, Wilson decided he had better go back to the mountain to take care of the cattle. The doctor in Rock Springs had been consulted and he said simply to give Bess plenty of liquids but not much food. Everyone was certain that Bess would recover soon.

226

Bessie, Wilson, and Melvin Garrison

227

Wilson Garrison crossing on the trolley

Wilson planned to come back in a few days to get her and their son.

It was the first day of June and the mountain air was just beginning to warm as the morning sun gained strength. Wilson was tightening the cinch on Peanuts, his little black cow horse. He was getting ready to drive the cattle out of the timber and away from the poisonous purple larkspur, as he did each morning. Then he saw a rider loping toward him and soon recognized Bob Teters.

Bob's sweating horse came to a stop a few feet away and Wilson heard him say, "Charlie Taylor sent me to get you, Wilson. Bessie's taken a turn for the worse. You better hurry."

A few minutes later, the two men on horseback raced over the brush and new sprouts of grass. Before long, Bob pulled back on his reins and yelled, "My horse is wore out, Wilson, you go on ahead and I'll be along later."

Without a change of expression, Wilson waved a gloved hand and spurred Peanuts into a gallop. His horse's hooves crunched in a repeated pattern on the lacelike ice that had formed overnight on the meadow.

Moving swiftly down the steep grade of Birch Canyon, Peanuts stumbled, then caught himself. His hooves ground in the shale. Rocks and dirt flipped backward, then lay silent as the horse and rider hurried on.

The gelding's nostrils were flared, and his neck and shoulders were curly with sweat when they made the final descent out of the canyon. They crossed Willow Creek then loped the miles across the flats and draws and down the hillsides. The gelding's sides heaved; flecks of foam from his bridled mouth landed along the side of the trail as they strained on. Wilson knew that he was pushing the horse too hard, but he had no choice. Finally, the young man saw the river in the near distance, with the Taylor Ranch spreading out quietly on the other side. His anxiety deepened.

The river was high, as it always was this time of year. Wilson jerked the saddle and bridle off the black and threw them into the waiting rowboat. He shooed the horse into the river and jumped into the boat. Peanuts was waiting for him on the other side when Wilson's boat scraped against the bank. In seconds he had Peanuts saddled and was galloping to the house. Wilson could hear the air wheezing in and out of the horse's winded lungs, but the house was so close and he was almost to Bess. Wilson rode into the yard, jumped off his horse and ran.

Just before he got to the yard gate, he saw Dr. Arbogast step out of the porch. Wilson stopped. A tingling sensation spread across his shoulders, down into his stomach and rushed in a wave down his legs, leaving them numb.

The doctor's voice was soft. "She's gone," he said.

As the day wore on, Wilson learned that Bess had died before the doctor arrived. The tall man said, "She had scarlet fever, Wilson. The glands in her throat were so swollen that they closed it off. It wouldn't have mattered if there'd been a dozen doctors here. There is nothing that could have been done."

Nina sat in the rocking chair and clung to little Melvin. With eyes filled with tears she quietly spoke about the morning. She explained that she had been giving Bessie a sponge bath when she had pulled back the covers and saw black spots on Bessie's legs. She knew Bessie wasn't breathing right. Nina was alarmed and ran to the corral where C.M. was hitching up the team. C.M. immediately sent Bob Teters to the mountain while he hurried to Beaver Creek to call the doctor. Nina rushed back to Bessie. She felt very alone and helpless while her sweet daughter struggled harder and harder to breathe. As she had with Nancy, Nina tried everything she could think of to help, but her daughter's agony only increased. The familiar sounds of the battle tore at Nina. She saw Bessie weakly raise her hand and sign, "Take care of the baby." Then she closed her eyes and was still.

From those first moments without Bessie, Wilson was lost. His very being was altered. His jolly nature was gone. He would never again be the same man. At least a thousand times through the years, Wilson would remember the little bird at the window and hear the sad howls of the dog. He had never before believed in omens - he would never doubt their existence again.[6]

In accordance with the state laws, Bessie's casket was sealed with solder before it was transported to Rock Springs for burial. During her funeral on the third of June, her sister Marie lay covered with a scarlet rash, and in the agony of hard labor. When tiny Lucille Marie Allen finally struggled her way into the world, her skin was fiery red, but her lungs and heart were strong. Although life had drastically changed for so many, it seemed determined to go on.

Bill consoled Wilson and the Taylors as best he could. When he was sure that Marie and his baby were alright, he left for the mountain. He spent most of that summer on Cold Spring. It took him a long time to recover from the sadness he'd seen, and from the ether pneumonia he had developed while helping administer to Marie while she was having their baby. He worked at building a cabin on his homestead at Galloway and at taking care of his own, and George Radosevich's cattle.

Bill knew Mr. Radosevich as a pleasant and easygoing fellow. The small, moustached man stood only a little over five and a half feet tall. For many years he ran a store and meat market in Blairtown and in 1933 had purchased the Willow Creek Ranch in Brown's Park from Charlie Sparks' widow. George's wife, Mary, was a proud and patient woman who loved children. The Radosevich's had lost four of their own, Emelija, Fanny, Olga, and Danica, in an epidemic in 1915. Still living were John, Steve, Angelia, and George. Although the ranch passed back and forth between the sons, it was Steve and his wife, Arlie Teters Radosevich, who finally took over running it.[7]

In the fall after Bessie died, C.M. asked Wilson and Bill if they would help him move Nancy from her grave at the Joe Tolliver place to the Rock Springs cemetery. The beaver had diverted the creek and water had started to run over the grave.

"I want to take her to be with Bess," he said. But when the job of digging up the grave was half completed, C.M. became overwhelmed with grief. Bill and Wilson took the man, who had come to mean so much to them, to a nearby log to rest. The two young men completed the job, gently speaking to C.M. all the while.[8]

230

As time passed, C.M. counted more and more on Bill and Marie to run the ranch. Wilson stayed in Brown's Park for a few years, then moved to Rock Springs and went to work for the Cream O' Weber dairy. Before long he married a young woman named Ann, who was the mother of a little girl named Lois.

C.M. and Nina kept Melvin with them. They leased the ranch to Bill and Marie but continued living in the main house. C.M. spent his time working around the home place, experimenting with different kinds of seeds and potatoes, contributing his knowledge to the livestock boards, traveling a little, and delighting in his growing number of grandchildren. Although he didn't ride horseback on the cattle drives much anymore, he always went along with a wagon or a truck to take the camp and to cook the grub.

Cabin at Galloway

C.M. Taylor and Bill Allen preparing for the cattle drive to Rock Springs

Shipping the cattle from the Willow Creek Ranch (Courtesy Hazel Overy)

232

One year, C.M., Bill, Wilson, Charlie Green, and several other cowboys left Brown's Park for Rock Springs with a large herd of cattle in the month of October. Not far from Rock Springs, near the top of Quaking Aspen Mountain, they were hit with a strong, cold wind, and fine snow. The wind howled and the snow flew sideways like billions of ice arrows. In the blizzard, C.M. managed to tie a canvas to the back of the truck and anchor it to the ground to form a small tent. There he built a fire and had stew bubbling, potatoes frying, and coffee steaming for the cowboys as they shivered in, one by one. Even that day C.M. managed to find some fun in what he was doing and greeted each of the men with a hearty smile. Although he had slowed some, he was still as rugged as he had been when Brown's Park first got acquainted with him.

Later that day the cattle reached the summit. The relief that the horsebackers and their herd felt was immediate when they started off the other side of the mountain. The wind and the snow disappeared and warmer air took their place. The cattle trotted and loped down the descending draw. Before long the herd and the cowboys were at the Chicken Ranch, a few miles from Rock Springs, where they stopped for the night.

It was about four o'clock the next morning when Bill was awakened by a noise. He heard his Uncle Charlie saying, "Charlie? Are you okay Charlie? Bill, there's something the matter with Charlie Taylor!"

A lamp was lit and Bill saw his father-in-law on the floor on his hands and knees looking pained and dazed. C.M. seemed unaware of his surroundings. Bill sat down on the floor behind him, took hold of him and gently leaned C.M.'s back against his chest. C.M. was unresponsive to the men, as Bill talked to him and Wilson rubbed his legs and arms. Suddenly his eyes focused and he struggled loose.

A little perturbed, he said, "What's the matter with you fellas? Of course I'm alright!"

C.M. had no recollection of what had happened to him that early morning. He remembered only that he had gotten out of bed to look out the door to see if it was still raining. Apparently, he had blacked out and toppled over, falling head first into a metal bucket. That racket was what awakened the others. He did seem fine then, but, sadly, it was a prelude of what lay ahead for C.M. Taylor.9

In the fall of 1939 Brown's Park watched as several trucks - one was a semi with a fifth wheel underneath, the others were eighteen to twenty foot bobtails - from the Isles Truck Company of Craig, Colorado, pulled into the accessible corrals at Willow Creek Ranch. Bill Allen was waiting there with his calves that were to be shipped. They were about to gain the distinc-

233

tion of being the very first cattle ever trucked from the valley. From then on, more and more of the Brown's Park ranchers followed Bill's example and used Beaver Brother's trucks, Gray Truck Lines, and other stock trucking companies, instead of trailing the several day trip to the stockyards.10

Bill and Marie continued to lease the Taylor Ranch until 1942, when they bought the Jarvie place from Frank Jenkins and moved across the river. In addition to Lucille, they now had a boy named Charles, born December 2, 1937; a daughter, Billie Dee, born on January 3, 1939; and another son, William Leslie, born on November 23, 1941. Barbara Lee died at birth on March 30, 1943.

Although Nina, who had hardened considerably, showed blatant partiality to Melvin, C.M. treasured all of the grandchildren Jesse, Bessie, and Marie had given him. He strongly

One of the first BLM meetings in area
Summer of 1939

Front row L to R: Louie Wiggins, C.M. Taylor, Arlie Radosevich, Georgann Radosevich, Nina Taylor, Steve Radosevich

Back row: Colorado Grazier Johnson, Mrs. Charlie Sparks, Kenneth Buckley, Mandy Wiggins (in front of Kenneth), Leigh Myers, Frank Myers, Mary Myers, Marie Allen holding Billie Dee, Lucille Allen, Bill Allen and Charlie Allen

admired ambition, and not only had big plans for Marie in the ranching business, but also for any of his grandsons who showed the desire to work hard.

One afternoon in 1943, C.M. was telling stories to young Lucille and Melvin while he worked near the river bank. He was busy building a footbridge that would connect the north side of the river with the south and would be a way for his grand-children to safely cross the river when they wanted to come for a visit. It was then, while he listened to the soft roar of the river, and to the giggles of the playing children, that apoplexy collap-sed the big man to the ground. The damaging stroke would be joined by another and gradually carry C.M. off to a crippling world. The one place he had said he could never bear to be.

Not long after the stroke, C.M. knew that he had to leave the valley and move to town. He sold his little buffalo herd and watched as they were slaughtered for meat. He tried to decide what to take and what to leave and ached with saying goodbye to his strong-limbed fruit trees and the saddle horses that had served him so well. He leaned against a corral post and looked over his pretty place, at the lovely home and all the buildings he had built when his hands were strong. Then he lifted his eyes to the mountains, the ones that had called to him so long ago. To them and to his old love, Brown's Park, he bid farewell.

Shortly after Nina and C.M. moved to Rock Springs, Bill and Marie bought a home a couple of blocks away so that Marie could be near her dad as much as possible. While Marie stayed in Rock Springs with the kids on school days, Bill ran their place in Brown's Park alone.

By the time the new year arrived in 1946, C.M. Taylor lay in a hospital bed, barely recognizable. His condition and suffering had steadily grown worse. The only part of his body that he had been able to move for a long time was his eyes. He had been allergic to nearly all of the medication that the doctors had tried to give him since the stroke and only got sicker when they tried something new. Finally, with Nina and Marie, who had dili-gently cared for him at his bedside, the life of the Brown's Park cattleman came to an end.

Marie's world was never the same without her dad. But he had given her his character, so she continued to work hard and enjoy life the way he had taught her to do. Although Marie had always been most comfortable in the saddle loping through the brush, she now had a large family to care for, and did it proudly. By spring, with little Winona "Nonie," who had been born on November 23, 1944, still in diapers, Marie discovered that she was expecting once again.

The deep-rooted love between Marie and Bill was still there, but theirs had not been an easy marriage. The differences in their background grew more and more evident. Where Marie was lighthearted, Bill could be harsh. Where she saw her father's logical way to accomplish something, Bill insisted on his own way. Where she found the joy in a day's work, he found the task to be merely one more job to do before soberly moving to the next one. The way her husband distanced himself from her and so much of the family life puzzled and hurt her. Every day the strain drove them a little farther apart.

It was tough for Bill, who had the responsibility of bossing men his own age and older. C.M. Taylor had been like a father to him. Now, once again, there was no one to ask, "Am I doing all right? Am I heading down the right path?" Bill's own mother and stepfather always seemed to need guidance rather than give it, and they and most of their children were a constant financial drain. As it had for so much of his life, work meant survival. No one understood the burden that Bill carried, and he wouldn't let Marie get close enough to find out.

All three of Bill and Marie's daughters were lovely, but the one named for her father was exceptionally pretty. Billie Dee had long brown hair and soft almond-shaped eyes. She was so gentle and happy that she could brighten a room just by hurrying through it. From the time she was tiny, she was her mother's willing helper, but she loved the outdoors as well. Whenever she sang, even her father stopped to listen. The pureness of the sound made him smile.

It was June 4, 1946, when the Bill Allen and Steve Radosevich children giggled and teased each other in the back of Bill and

Lucille, Billie Dee, Marie, Charlie, Bill Allen

236

Marie's truck. Bill drove up the side of Cold Spring Mountain, while Marie sat beside him holding Nonie on her lap. Lucille, their oldest, had turned ten the day before, but the birthday picnic had been put off a day because of rain. Marie had Lucille's favorite banana cake tucked safely in a box along with the fried chicken, potato salad, buns, and other goodies to satisfy the tummies of the children.

The mountain breeze was strong with the scent of wild flowers, pine, and sage. As the truck moved along, the breeze found its way through the protective stock rack and tousled and whipped the hair of the excited group of children. They were all having fun and no one noticed when seven-year-old Billie Dee started climbing up the fifty-gallon gas barrel that stood in the corner next to the truck cab. No one noticed that her new seat was flush with the top of the rack. No one noticed that Billie Dee had no place to hang on. And no one paid much attention to the truck as it slowed, then dropped into a rut, causing it to jolt sideways.

But the children saw the jerking motion fling Billie Dee from her seat on the barrel. They watched as she flew outward and downward. They screamed as she hit a fence post, then a four-foot bank, and was tossed beneath the dual tires of her father's truck.

In the blur of the next few moments, Bill slammed on the brakes as Marie tossed Nonie from her lap. Bill reached his little girl first. He saw the tire marks across her chest and the blood gush from her mouth as he tried to lift her. Then Marie was there, kneeling over her child and feeling herself going . . . shattering . . . . . Then she looked up and saw the terrified little faces behind the rack. She knew that she couldn't give in; not yet. Instead, she sat in the back of the truck as it sped toward Rock Springs and held herself steady, while she cradled Billie Dee's lifeless body close to her own.

As she always had when Marie needed her, Hazel Teters Overy quickly arrived and became Marie's cushion. She was there to cook, clean, and care for the many people who arrived for the funeral. Although Hazel carried much of the burden, Marie stayed busy and seemed strong throughout the arrangement making, and through the day of the funeral.

Bill was devastated. Marie knew that. She looked at him from across the room and saw the guilt and the anguish in his face. He was standing in the corner of the crowded house, alone, when Marie walked toward him with Nonie in her arms. She stopped in front of him and looked into his pained eyes with all the love that she felt for him. Then she gently placed their youngest child in his arms. Bill's body and face went limp. In that instant, the differences between them fell away because they had no significance. The tattered bond between them was on the mend.

It wasn't until later that evening, after everyone left, that Marie's private time with Billie Dee came. It was then that she gave in to the grieving torment that turned loose and engulfed her.[11]

Chapter XXVII

JESSE TAYLOR

As soon as Jesse Taylor got married in 1919, he and his wife, Debra, went to work through the summer for Hi Bernard, foreman for Charlie Sparks at Willow Creek. There were a lot of cowboys there then; big plans for building up the Willow Creek Ranch were in the making. Jesse helped put up fence and work the stock while Deb cooked for the hired men.1

In 1919 Hi Bernard was aging, but he was still highly respected for his keen management skills, and for being the "fine old gentleman" that he was. Charlie Sparks had not forgotten that Hi Bernard had helped him years ago when he protested against the big Colorado cattlemen and their plans to be rid of all the sheepmen. It pleased Charlie Sparks to have work for Hi Bernard, and it pleased Hi Bernard to have work to do.

Although Jesse enjoyed working at the Willow Creek Ranch, he and Deb left Brown's Park when a friend got him a job in the gilsonite mine at Rainbow, on the other side of Vernal. The couple stayed there through the winter, then returned home to Brown's Park. It turned out to be an extremely hard winter. It devastated the King brothers' sheep herd. "We're done," they told Jesse, just before they pulled out of the area. Only their name at King's Point remained in Brown's Park.

Jesse worked for his father, taking care of the place across the river for half the hay. He sold the hay to Charlie Shipp, who was living at Beaver Creek, for 150 dollars total. Jesse then went to work helping his dad dig the big ditch. Deb went to the Red Creek Ranch, where the George Shipp family was living, to teach school. Every Friday night Jesse would ride his horse to Red Creek to spend a day or so with her.

Later, they bought the Spitzie place in lower Brown's Park. By then they had a little girl, Margaret, and a boy, Jesse, Jr. but they had little left of their marriage.

When at eighteen, Jesse Taylor had married Debra Sharp, she was a nineteen-year-old schoolteacher from Missouri. Debra was a big woman with a coarse voice that Jesse discovered went along with a bossy manner. She had chosen the quiet, good-looking cowboy, grabbed him by the hand and dragged him into a life with her before he thought of protesting. The two brought out the worst in each other. The neighbors could usually tell "which way the wind was blowing" between the two. If they were having trouble, Deb was ready to "bite your head off at the shoulders." But, if the young couple was getting along okay, Deb could be "almost" pleasant. Jesse didn't ever say much and he smiled less. It wasn't long before Deb went her way and Jesse went his. She went to Denver to divorce him, and it was there that little Margaret became ill and died. Those were sad days for Jesse Taylor.

After a while, Jesse's good friend, Bob Teters, came to stay with him. They did some trapping and a little cowboying. One afternoon they were riding up the river when they spotted a wild pig. There were quite a few hogs along the river. Years earlier, just as Jimmy Goodson had done, the Two-Bar had turned a bunch of them loose to fend for themselves in the plentiful roots and sprouts of the marshes. When the Two-Bar cowboys wanted fresh pork, they caught two or three, penned them up, and fed them grain until they were prime for slaughter. Usually at the first sight or smell of a man, the wild pigs shot into the tules or willows to hide. The lone boar that Jesse and Bob spotted that day sniffed and watched, but stood his ground.

"Let's have a little fun and see if we can catch that ole boy," Jesse said.

In seconds, Bob had his rope in his hand and was loping toward the hog from one direction while Jesse was swinging his rope from the other. The boar whirled just as Jesse's loop closed around his neck. Instantly the hog was screaming, but instead of fighting the rope, he started climbing up it, with his huge mouth frothing and his long teeth snapping. Jesse's hand, which seconds before had dallied the rope around the saddle horn in one direction, was frantically undoing the dally in the other. He spurred his horse around to run and his end of the rope zinged through the air as he let it go. The freed boar loped away causing the loop to slacken around his neck. The rope was jerked off by the willows as he crashed into the thicket and disappeared.

As Jesse stepped off his horse to pick up his rope he began to laugh, "I've never been so damn glad to turn loose of my rope in my life. How do you suppose them Two-Bar fellows managed it all those years?"

It wasn't long after that when Jesse went to work haying one summer for Bill Grounds of the Two-Bar. Jesse had long admired the outfit. He could recall when he was a youngster and M. Wilson "Willis" Rankin was still foreman, that the Two-Bar had thousands of cattle on Snake River and up Spring Creek. The cattle were alert and wild and traveled in a "long keen" trot. The range they covered was vast and a fifty percent calf crop each year was all that was expected. Every fall Jesse watched five or six Two-Bar cowboys come off Mountain Home into the Park with a herd of horses. They stayed on a steady lope as they headed down country, galloping for the Two-Bar.

Store at the Sterling Place taken August 21, 1950

After Jesse finishd haying for the Two-Bar, he was hired by Ed Cox to tear down two big rooms at the old abandoned Two-Bar on the river bank, and move them to the spring at the Sterling place. Charlie Sparks now owned the Sterling place, and was setting Ed Cox up to start a store and post office. Jesse borrowed a four-horse team from Bill Grounds. With the help of William Carr and Charlie Rover, a dry land farmer from Douglas Mountain, he tore down the rooms and moved them. The men built a house and fixed up a store, then helped Ed move in.

Ed Cox was well liked and known as a good salesman. He ran a nice store for quite awhile. Then he went "haywire," and started drinking heavily. He would show up on Cold Spring Mountain, spend the night at one place, then leave early in the morning and stop at another place that night. Before long, someone "took him out of the country" and Brown's Park didn't see him again. Elmer Trevennon and his wife took over the store, ran it for two or three years, then sold out and went to Maybell.

It was about 1922 when Jesse went to work for Stanley Crouse at the place above the lane on Beaver Creek. It was there that he got acquainted with Mandy Tolliver Lombard's granddaughters, Florence and Ellie Tolliver. Florence was oldest and the most attractive. John "Shorty" Stallard wanted her, but she had eyes only for Jesse. Her younger sister, Ellie, was rather scrawny and sickly, but for some reason Jesse liked her best. Jesse was friends with them both and one Saturday evening, accompanied the two to a dance at Lodore.

241

John Jarvie, Jr. told C.M., "You tell Jesse he wants to watch that fellow or he's liable to get killed. Shorty Stallard is jealous and he rides in the washes and acts just like a coyote." Jesse was given the warning, but he never had any trouble with the other young man.

Florence and Ellie were the daughters of John Tolliver. John was Mandy's son whom she had left in Virginia. After Mandy's husband, Mike Lombard, died, she wrote often to her son, asking him to come to Brown's Park and take over her place. John finally left his job in the coal mines and brought his wife and large family to the valley.

Mandy Tolliver, a little bow-legged woman with gray hair tied in a knot at the back of her head, wore long dresses and walked with a cane. She used tobacco by dipping a small stick with a rag on the end into a can of snuff, rolling the rag end around a little, then putting that end of the stick inside her cheek. She was not a gentle person. As a matter of fact, she could be downright contrary. She was, in fact, so mean to her daughter-in-law, that John soon moved his family away from his mother's place. Stanley Crouse felt sorry for the family and gave John work so that he could make enough money to return to Virginia.

The day that the family was leaving Brown's Park, several people, including Jesse and his dad, gathered on the river bank to say goodbye. Florence desperately wanted Jesse for her husband and started begging him to go to Virginia with them.

Her father said, "Jesse, I'll guarantee you a job in the coal mines with me if you will come."

Jesse, standing among the listening crowd, looked at Florence. Her eyes were pleading and "her mouth was hanging open" as she took the conversation in. Jesse didn't know what to say. He thought Florence was a nice girl, but he had no thought of going off to Virginia, nor did he have any romantic notions about the girl.

"Oh, well, okay. I'll follow you out there," Jesse stammered.

C.M. swung around and said, "Aw, you know that ain't so."

"Yes I will," he nodded. "I'll be there inside of three months."

As the John Tolliver family left, Florence was "grinning from ear to ear" and satisfied that she had won her man. Jesse felt bad because he had no intention of following them, but he didn't have to feel guilty for long. In a short time Mandy told Jesse that she had received word Florence had married someone else.

A while after the family left, Jesse went to clean the little bunkhouse where Florence and Ellie had been sleeping. He noticed something hidden in the crack of a log and had to laugh when he reached in and pulled out two snuff "dip sticks."

The following year, George Bassett hired Jesse. He spent quite a bit of time cutting posts and building fence on the Bassett place. He worked a lot with Eb Bassett and the two became friends. One fall cattle prices were low and George held back shipping, hoping the prices would come up. By the last of November, he decided he wasn't going to have feed enough to hold them any longer, and gave Eb and Jesse the job of trailing them to Bitter Creek.

There wasn't much snow in the Park, but the surrounding country had a good foot of it. There was no storm in the air, but it was miserably cold and the cows didn't want to trail. They fought the cattle the entire day. They spent the first night with Charlie Sparks. When they left at daylight Charlie had his hired man, Guy McNurlen, a former Two-Bar cowboy, go along with food and a wagon. The air was bitter cold and the snow lay in drifts of dry sparkles that crunched and squeaked beneath the animals's hooves. It had blown into the thousands of washes. Time after time the cows left the road to search for a bite of grass, only to fall into the camouflaged crevices. After Eb's horse took a header into one, he rode by Jesse and said, "I think I'll take my stirrups off so I'll be all clear." The two men finally battled the cattle through the gate of an isolated wild horse corral at midnight.

In the blue dawn the next morning, Jesse saddled the big Bassett buckskin he had been riding. Neither Eb nor Jesse were riding with saddle blankets. The instant Jesse settled his weight into the stiff saddle, the buckskin lurched into a jarring, jamming, bucking fit through the brush. Jesse got him stopped and didn't get thrown, but it was a "fine" way to start the day!

Finally, after another eighteen freezing hours, the men could see the silhouette of the stockyards in the night's blackness. They were relieved to know that Guy McNurlen was there to have the gate open. The men thought their job was nearly done. But every time the cattle were about to go through the gate, a train or a lone engine would rumble and clank by. The frightened cattle would spin, run back, and scatter in all directions. The exhausted cowboys were hoarse from yelling and their horses were ready to give out. They eventually corralled the herd, well after midnight, after Guy borrowed a saddle horse and helped. After the train cars were spotted (the doors brought even with the loading chute) and the floors covered with sand, the cattle were loaded.

When the last boxcar door slid shut, Jesse murmured, "That was a helluva trip for fifty bucks a month."

Brown's Park got word about three months later that Hi Bernard had passed away in Rock Springs. His death left an empty

Danny Beddole   "Wash" Sparks   Bill Kennon   Eb Bassett
(Glade Ross collection)

Bill Kennon   George Bassett
(Glade Ross collection)

244

place in the valley. Hi had led the remarkable life of a true cowboy; trail bossing a herd of eight thousand Texas longhorns when he was only seventeen; working as foreman for some huge ranches in Wyoming and Colordo, including the Two-Bar and the Sevens; and surviving one of his biggest challenges, being married to "the queen of the cattle rustlers." In all his adventures, Hi Bernard had not accumulated much more than his tailored clothing, a saddle horse or two, and his gear. He had lived with Eb Bassett for a while before he went to work for Charlie Sparks at Willow Creek. Five or six years later his health failed and Charlie took him to his home in Rock Springs. On February 3, 1924, Hi Bernard died. He was buried in the Rock Springs cemetery, in a plot which had been purchased by his long-time friend, Charlie Sparks.

The following year, Brown's Park had to give up Eb Bassett. Eb had been accused of stealing and butchering a cow and had left the Park to go to Craig for a hearing. On the way, he stopped at the Frank Lawrence place west of Craig to spend the night. That evening, he told Frank that he was going out to feed his horse. When he didn't return to the house, Frank went to look for him. He discovered that Eb had committed suicide by drinking strychnine. Beside him lay a note. It read: "No one but me knew or suspected what I was going to do, no one. Eb Bassett."

When Jesse heard the news, he remembered the way Eb had dropped his head and said, "I see that man's face every night in my sleep." Jesse knew that Eb was truly haunted by the lynching of John Bennett. Jesse understood that many things in that cowboy's life had not gone right.

Eb never married, but he was engaged to widow Mattie Hughes Edwards when he died. He willed her his belongings, and the right to live in the original Bassett house for the rest of her life. Mattie had a stone put on Eb's grave with the words, "Dear Old Pal." She moved into the Bassett house, even though some of the family protested against it. Queen Ann especially wanted her out, and made threats that she would see to it that Mattie didn't stay.

One morning, Mattie went to Craig to visit her niece. Harry Carr was returning from Craig late that night when he saw the glowing flames of a fire. He hurried toward the blaze, but by the time he reached it, Mattie's home, the house that Herbert and Elizabeth Bassett had built, was nearly gone. There was nothing he could do.

The fire sparked a lot of suspicions in the minds of the Brown's Parkers. Regardless, Mattie left Brown's Park and Queen Ann and her husband built a one-room cabin at the Bassett home place, where they spent several summers.

The same year that Eb died, 1925, Jesse married Mattie Cal-

Mattie Callaway

Jesse Taylor homestead

Jesse Taylor

Mattie Taylor cleaning old Crouse ditch

Jesse Taylor haying

laway on the thirtieth of July. She too was a schoolteacher, but unlike Deb, Mattie was a pretty, sensitive, and hard-working girl. Jesse and Mattie moved to their homestead that Jesse had built with lumber he had hauled from Ruple Sawmill. He had built the one-room cabin on the flat (Taylor Flat) between the Joe Tolliver meadow and the Jarvie place.

Eventually Jesse traded his homestead for his dad's place across the river below Bridgeport and continued his little ranching operation. There Jesse and Mattie lived in the log cabin on the river bank where C.M. and Nina had lived before moving to the Parsons. There was a rocked up water well nearby that at one time had a rope and bucket on a wooden crank, but the well was not usable anymore. Jesse and Mattie used one room, that had a window overlooking the river, for a cooling room. They half-filled a large pan with water, placed their cream, milk, and other perishable items in the water, and covered it all with a damp dishcloth.

The first of Jesse and Mattie's children was named Mary, and the second, Claude. The two youngsters were inseparable and went by the collective pretend name of "Billy-Mary." One day when Charlie Green stopped by, he watched the two little kids riding double on their old horse and snickered, "That Billy-Mary is quite a cowboy, ain't he?"

During the depression, life was as rough in Brown's Park as it was in the rest of the country. Bob and Nora Teters and their family, who had been "starving" in Little Hole, moved down and ranched with Jesse and Mattie for a while. In the arrangement, Jesse gave Bob half of their big garden, a third of the hay,

248

and an opportunity to build up his cattle herd a little.

Jesse and Mattie had only thirty head of cattle but there was no market for them. Then President Franklin Roosevelt's WPA (Works Progress Administration) gave him and several others work, widening the road up Jesse Ewing Canyon. That work lasted through the fall, winter, and spring. Cattle prices came up a little, and things looked better for Jesse and Mattie.

As the years passed, Jesse and Mattie had three more sons, Allen, Roy, and Orvil. Charlie Green still came by, leading Nubbins and Rock, his two "companions." Nubbins, who had once belonged to C.M., was a long-legged sorrel. Rock was a dark, blood bay with a big roman nose. He looked more like bucking stock than a saddle or pack horse. Charlie nearly always showed up at Jesse's when there was a dance scheduled at Lodore. The Taylor boys couldn't help but smile as they watched the older man comb and comb the front of his red hair to get it perfect, while he ignored the nest of tangles and a turkey tail sticking up in the back.

One day, Charlie returned to Brown's Park after visiting the Burton's at Greendale. They had given him a gunnysack of potatoes which he packed all the way over the mountain. When he got to the edge of the river, he wasn't about to leave his "taters." Charlie always swam like a dog, paddling with his hands and keeping his head and shoulders out of the water. Determined to get his potatoes back to camp, Charlie held onto the sack and waded out into the water at the Parson ford.

Jesse Taylor family

249

Billy-Mary

When he hit deep water, he paddled while he pulled on the sack until he made it to the big rock in the middle of the river. After he caught his breath, he continued across and finally struggled out of the water with his gunnysack of potatoes safely in tow.₂ He was of a tough and hardy breed, as so many of the Brown's Park people were.

Other tough critters that Jesse called friends were Frank and Leigh Myers' cowboy sons, Fred, Frankie, and Walt. After Bessie's death, Wilson Garrison eventually sold his cabin across the river from the Taylor place, to Harry Carr. Harry and Marybeth lived there for a while, then sold it to bachelors, Walt and Frankie Myers.

One spring, Frankie rolled his tongue in his mouth and told Jesse, "The other day, Walt and I found a grave down there at the cabin. It's hidden in among them cottonwoods and dogberry bushes. You ever see it?"

"Why no, I haven't. I'll come down one of these days and take a look at it," Jesse answered.

A while later Jesse went to have Frankie show him the grave, a rather small mound with a board at each end. Jesse shook his head and said, "I have no idea who that could be."

Frankie turned around then and said, "Well, it's noon. Let's get some dinner."

Jesse knew that Frankie was a good cook and followed him back to the cabin. In a short time, Frankie had the wood

250

beginning to pop and put out heat in the stove. He grabbed a can of corn, opened it, and poured it into a saucepan. By then the stove was getting good and hot, and Frankie set the pan of corn on it. The two men heard scratching above them. They raised their eyes just in time to see a mother mouse with a baby hanging on each teat fall from the ceiling, smack into the pan of corn.

"Ohhhh! Ohhhh!" Frankie cried as he spun around and grabbed a big spoon.

The mother mouse was struggling in the corn when Frankie scooped down with the spoon and rescued her and her babies. Frankie got the family of mice outside and came back to the stove.

"Purt near ruined the corn!" he said.

Jesse just nodded his head and laughed. Then he sat down with Frankie to eat the noon meal, which included the "purt near ruined" pan of corn.

All of Jesse's children loved their granddad, C.M. Taylor. When they were little and crossed the river to visit their grandma and grandpa, Allen always grabbed C.M.'s tall mule-eared boots off the porch. For an hour or so the blonde, curly haired little boy proudly slopped around in the boots which hit him halfway up the thigh.

Every Christmas, Allen knew that he could look forward to getting a new, pretty handled pocketknife, a set of toy pistols in a tooled leather holster, or some other present a boy would cherish. He knew that his grandpa would not give him some "silly thing" like a hanky or a tie.

With the idea of having school nearby, Jesse and several men moved his homestead cabin from Taylor Flat - they crossed the river on the ice - to a spot next to the road a short distance from his ranch house. It became the Bridgeport School. The teacher was paid sixty dollars a month and Jesse and Mattie received twenty dollars a month to board her. After a couple of years, with some financial help from the county, the men cut logs on the mountain and put up a matching cabin beside it for the teacherage.

It was in the Bridgeport school that Allen sat doing his studies and heard a far off, "Cawww! Cawww!" then a cracking report. His hazel eyes brightened. He could clearly picture his adored Grandpa Taylor, who always called him son, in his big hat and chaps with his bullwhip in his hand. Allen's mind raced outside, jumped on a horse, and helped his grandpa drive the cattle across the river. He itched to go. It was torture to sit still and try to pay attention to the teacher.[3]

Allen was fourteen when his grandfather died. It was a long time before the aching hollowness left the pit of his young

Bridgeport School

Allen Taylor

252

stomach. However, the wit and charm Allen picked up from C.M. stayed with him.

Jesse had purchased a home in Rock Springs where Mattie and the kids stayed during the week while the boys went to school (Mary married Bill Baker and Claude joined the Navy). For quite a while Jesse and Mattie had not had a happy marriage; eventually they separated. Although both were miserable and lonesome after the divorce, they never reunited.

Jesse stayed at the ranch. In 1948 he and Fred Myers tore Charlie Crouse's house down at Bridgeport, marked the logs and moved them down to Jesse's place with a team and wagon. They rebuilt the logs into a two-story home. There in that handsomely rustic log ranch house, Jesse finished raising his boys. He remained a quiet man, and his boys often thought a hard man. He began to show signs of mellowing when his handsome son, Allen, married Jim and Pearl Graham's daughter, Francis, in 1950, and brought her home to the ranch. Francis was a cowgirl, raised on the Graham place east of the 4-J Basin. She was a dark-haired beauty with light eyes and the high cheekbones of her French/Canadian-Indian mother. Jesse immediately loved Francis. He was gentle to her and to his brand new baby granddaughter.

The years had bent Jesse forward a little at the hips and he combed his graying hair, that he let grow long on one side, over the top of his balding head. He still enjoyed his chewing tobacco as much as he had when he was a teenager and Wildcat Sam brought him a twelve-pound box of Horseshoe tobacco from Rock Springs. The aged man loved each of his new grandchildren. His gray eyes lit up when he played the fiddle for them. He put his hand over his mouth and snickered, or slapped his knee and chuckled when he shared his memories of growing up and living with the characters of Brown's Park.

253

Chapter XXVIII

LIFE ON THE PARK LIVE

The twentieth century was half over and Brown's Park was still content to hold to many of her old ways. Although the fires of the Indian campgrounds had been cold for a good many years, most of them were relatively undisturbed. On knolls with scenic views and within cozy growths of cedars, the presence of the tribes who had lived there in the past centuries could be strongly felt. Matedes, manos, arrowheads, pottery, and other artifacts lay where nothing but hooves, an occasional rancher, summer downpours, or melting snowdrifts moved them. Some of the original pioneer and outlaw dwellings had disappeared, but there were others, such as Dr. Parsons' cabin at the Taylor place and Charlie and Mary Crouse's log home at the Park Live that still stood stoutly against the winds.

One midafternoon, the thick row of trees shading the screened-in porch of the old Crouse ranch house stood tall, their leaves barely rustling in the breeze. Inside the porch, Marie Allen took a rare minute to rest on her cool feather tick bed and read a few pages of a western romance novel. Bill and the older kids, Lucille, Leslie, and Charlie, were on the bench working in the hay field. Her three younger children, Nonie, Bobby, and Diana, had just finished helping her in the garden and were scattered around on the bed beside her. They munched on salt-sprinkled green apples from the old Crouse orchard and made plans to catch their horse as soon as it cooled off some. Before long they finished their apples and bounced off the bed to go wading in the creek. Marie got up to start work on a batch of bread so it would be baked in time for supper. She watched through the screen and smiled as her happy youngsters ran down the little hill and hurried across the pasture that led to Crouse Creek. As always, Nonie was in the lead followed closely by a tough little towheaded cowboy, Robert "Bobby" Carl, who had been born on December 30, 1946. Trailing along behind, with her taffy-colored hair bouncing, was the youngest of the Allen children, Diana Floy, born on July 29, 1949.

Marie remembered vividly when they were living at Beaver Creek after leaving the Jarvie place. Nonie had collapsed in the garden, suddenly unable to move her left leg, and her right hand hung limply from her wrist. Marie and Bill had been afraid to move the seven-year-old for fear of a back injury. Bill had hurried to the Mountain Fuel camp at Clay Basin, where there was a phone, to call Dr. Paul Kos in Rock Springs. The diagnosis of polio had terrified Marie, but she had never revealed that to

Nonie. Instead she told her daughter, "You've got an awful big job to do, Sis. But we're going to do it together."

Marie stood over Nonie day in and day out, wrapping hot towels around the little girl's leg and arm. The relentless summer heat and the boiling water made the sweat pour from them both. There were times when the stifling steam rose around them, and their misery made them cry. But neither of them ever faltered and in time Nonie completely recovered.₁ Now, a few years later, Nonie's long slender legs carried her across the pasture and into the willows on a lope.

Marie stepped outside onto the pathway carrying two empty water buckets. She walked in front of the kitchen window that was filled with red blossoming geraniums, toward the little creek that sparkled and gurgled past the house. Marie dipped the buckets into the well, made from a wooden barrel buried in the creek, and jerked them upward when they were full. She stopped for a moment, set the buckets down and looked around at the big tree-surrounded yard. The honeysuckle bushes in front were tall and bushy. Wild roses and lilacs bordered the lawn. The poppies were bobbing their big orange heads among the arranged deer horns while the hollyhocks yawned in all sorts of colors. In back, standing among the elms, box elders, and cottonwoods, three apricot trees bowed with heavy clusters of nearly ripe fruit. Looking through the intertwined old branches, Marie could see the bunkhouse, Lucille's flower garden behind the old ice house, the chicken coop and tack shed where Minnie Crouse had been born, and the large set of corrals in the distance.

Although the house wasn't very big, having only two bedrooms, a living room, kitchen, pantry and porch, it was well built. It held the heat well during the cold winter days and the surrounding trees kept it shaded and cool in the summer. Marie liked the way the old log house with its dirt roof was filled with history. She spoke of that history often. She also liked the way it was protectively tucked near the foot of Diamond Mountain. The beauty of nearby King's Point, which towered above Swallow Canyon, was one of her favorite views. It certainly wasn't the C.M. Taylor place. But she decided it was a pretty nice substitute.

It had been a blow to Marie when her mother had sternly refused to sell Bill and her the Taylor Ranch after C.M. died. The icy words her mother spoke stung her.

"No, I won't sell you the place. I won't sell it to you and I won't sell it to anyone who will!"

Marie didn't understand. She thought perhaps her mother had grown so bitter because she had given up two of her daughters to the valley. She apparently wanted her third one

King's Point—view from Park Live Ranch

away from there. Also, Marie knew that her mother had never fully approved of any of the mates her children chose. She knew that Bill was no exception. Marie did not confront her mother about the subject again and remained a loyal, caring daughter.

In 1947, not long after W.H. Gottsche died, Stanley Crouse had been forced to sell the Park Live to Lee Watson. Four years later, Bill and Marie leased Beaver Creek and the Park Live from Watsons. The Allens moved from the Jarvie place and lived for a year or two at Beaver Creek. Then the family moved across the river and settled into a life on the pretty Brown's Park Livestock Ranch, which they bought in 1957. The ranch was operated under the name of Allen Livestock and the animals carried the quarter circle A brand.

Nina Taylor gave her son Jesse the responsibility of running her cattle along with his. No one lived at the Taylor place. In 1957 Melvin Garrison, the grandson Nina had raised and cherished, was tragically killed in a car accident a few months before he was to get out of the Army. Two years later, when Jesse said he didn't want it, Nina sold the C.M. Taylor Ranch to a man from Bountiful, Utah, named Harold Calder.

There was still no electricity or telephone service in Brown's Park. (Years earlier, Charlie Sparks had hired John Jarvie, Jr. to bring a phone line from Rock Springs to Brown's Park and put phones in at Willow Creek and Beaver Creek. Later, W.H. Gottsche brought a line from Rock Springs through Sage Creek to Maxim to then to Red Creek and on to the Park Live Ranch.

However, the lines were not kept in repair and stayed working only a few years.) The Allens did replace the wood stove at the Park Live with a huge, black, restaurant-style propane stove and the delicate mantles of brighter gas lights took the place of the flickering wicks of coal oil lamps, except in the bedrooms.

Most of the people in the ranching community were friends. They attended dances and enjoyed club meetings and other occasions and were always glad to help each other and co-operated on the range.

A trip off the steep hill into Bull Canyon would find the door of the Bob and Dorothy Simpson home. They had purchased Della Worley's holdings on Cold Spring and her homestead at Bull Canyon. Bob's dad Gene had earlier run the ranch at Pablo Springs for Steve and Georgia Simos, who had bought it from George Bassett.

In 1936 George Bassett had sold 650 acres of his ranch and his BLM privileges to Steve Simos for 10,000 dollars. He kept a few acres in the northwest corner of his place so he could retire and spend his last years.

Steve Simos came to America from Greece in 1912. He went to Salt Lake City, then to Brigham City, Utah, where he worked in a copper mine. In 1923 he and his brother George used their savings to buy a small band of sheep in Price, Utah. Two years later, they had expanded their herd a little when they moved to Colorado in search of better range and fewer problems with cattlemen. They leased summer range by Steamboat Springs and winter range on Skull Creek in the Dinosaur, Colorado, area then bought a homestead nearby.

In November, 1934, Steve returned to Greece to visit his brother and sister and to find a wife. Steve returned to Craig, Colorado, in April, 1935, with his new wife, Georgia, at his side, and anxious to help him with his ranching business.

A year later, Steve leased land from several homesteaders in the Greystone, Colorado, area in order to expand his winter range. On discovering that the weather and feed were so good, he and Georgia decided to look for property to buy in the area. That was when Steve heard from a cousin that the George Bassett place in Brown's Park was for sale. After Steve and Georgia bought George's place, they hired Sam Carr to stay there and put up the hay. When the house burned down, it was replaced with one from Greystone.

In March, 1948, when Steve Simos died from heart failure brought on by emphysema, he left Georgia alone with their two children, Connie and Jimmy. Georgia didn't want to sell the ranching business that she and Steve had worked so hard to build. Instead, in the fall of 1949, she sold the sheep and leased out the land.

A year later, Georgia returned to her village in Greece. In April of 1951, she married George Raftopoulos, a childhood acquaintance, and returned with him to America. In 1952 a son named John was born to the couple. The following year they had a second little boy named Steve.

By the time the lease on their land expired in 1953, George and Georgia had purchased enough sheep to stock their range. The sheep business was quite good through the fifties for George and Georgia. However, George was dissatisfied that in order to winter their three thousand sheep, it was necessary to use a permit in the Skull Creek area near Dinosaur for half of their ewes for part of the winter before moving them to Brown's Park. George had become quite attached to Brown's Park. He discovered that the weather was far more dependable there, and the soils were sandy. Even if the snows came, they melted off more quickly and left less mud behind than in other areas. A few years later he purchased land and BLM permits from Rick Worrick, north of Douglas Mountain, and east of the Green River. He was then able to sell his holdings at Skull Creek and have everything closer to Brown's Park.2

Tom Blevins, and his wife, Freddie, a lovely dark-haired schoolteacher with a beautiful singing voice, now owned the original S.F. Ecckles homestead near Joe Springs. The Ecckles place had passed from S.F. Ecckles to Sam Carr, then to Frank Dennison, and finally to the son of a one-time sheriff of Moffat County, Tom Blevins.

Steve and Arlie Radosevich were still at the Willow Creek Ranch. Arlie stayed busy raising her family and cooking huge meals in her ranch kitchen. Steve was now a warden with the Utah Fish and Game Commission.

Delbert and Ann Ducey settled east of Brown's Park and started the tiny town of Greystone. Greystone consisted of a gas pump, the post office which served Brown's Park, and a little store that was surrounded by flowers in the summer. Delbert, a tall, quiet man, and white-haired Ann were kind and friendly people, always ready to help in any community project.

Charlie Sparks' daughters Martha and Margaret and their husbands, Kenneth Buckley and Wright Dickinson, traveled from their places just outside the Park to enjoy any get-togethers.

A unique couple from Douglas Mountain who the Park people enjoyed was Duward Campbell and his schoolteacher wife, Esther. Duward always wore a big straw cowboy hat slightly cocked on his head. He whistled softly while he worked his palomino horses and was a true lover of nature. If a spider took up houskeeping in the corner of their kitchen, Duward gently managed to relocate her outside in a suitable place. He never killed another living creature if he could prevent it. He was a great practical joker. Eating with the Campbells was usually an event which included a series of break-away forks, flies in fake ice cubes, or rubber spiders in the sugar bowl. The three younger Allen children adored the older cowboy and listened to his drawling voice as he told stories about the early day outlaws.

Others in and around Brown's Park who joined in social gatherings in the Park were the families of Reg and Floy Buffham, Boyd and Wanda Walker, Clare Burton and his son Tom, Harry and Marybeth Carr, Chet and Warrine Solace, Minford and Chloe Vaughn, Buck and Ethel Tisdel, Joe Guttierrez, Tom and Dorothy LaFever, Bruce and Marian MacLeod, Tom and Elnora Peterson, Ed Wilson, Art and Vondell Gardner, and Pete Perusick.

When the late Mandy Tolliver Lombard was about seventy years old, she married her hired hand, Louie Wiggins, who happened to be thirty years younger than Mandy. Louie was an easy going fellow, but he needed Mandy's stern hand to control his drinking. Bill Allen thought a lot of ornery old bowlegged Mandy. He couldn't help but snicker when she came "uncorked" at her huband.

"Goddamn you Louie, I'll knock you over the head with this shovel. I'll beat your brains out. You ain't worth a damn!" she'd yell.

Louie wouldn't pay much attention, and would go quietly on with whatever he was doing. He knew what Bill knew, that Mandy wasn't near as mean as she liked people to think.

When Bill good-naturedly teased her, Mandy stomped her walking stick on the ground and said, "Damn you, Bill Allen, come over here so I can hit you with this cane."

Bill missed the old lady when she passed away in 1949 at the age of eighty-eight.

During the mid-1940's, the school houses from Beaver Creek, Greystone, and the Baker homestead on Cold Spring Mountain were moved to a new location in Brown's Park. The buildings were placed at the foot of a hill at the lower edge of the valley. There they provided adequate living facilities for the teacher as well as a school house for the Brown's Park youngsters, through the eighth grade. However, because Marie wanted to be available to her aging mother, and because Bill had made a promise long ago not to uproot his children's schooling the way his had been, the Allen children didn't go to school there. Instead, Bill and Marie continued to live apart during the school week so that their children could attend school in Rock Springs.

Marie and Nina Taylor

Every Friday afternoon, as soon as school was out, Marie loaded her children in the car and drove a couple of hours on a dirt road to Brown's Park. Then she carefully drove across the river on the old swinging bridge that Stanley Crouse had built. The bridge was not very steady; it had no side rails, and was not much more than boards laid side by side on a cable frame.

One Friday night, Brown's Park was getting a spring rainstorm that was being splattered around by a hefty wind. It was well after dark when Marie stopped the car at the edge of the bridge. In the yellow beam of the headlights, she saw that the old bridge was not only heaving sideways, but also up and down. She reached over and patted Luella Logan, a friend that was along. Then she said, "Now everybody sit real still." She put the car in gear, slowly let out on the clutch and steered the car onto the bridge. As always, the weight of the car caused the bridge to hump up and moan as it went. Suddenly Marie took her foot off the gas and abruptly brought the car to a halt.

Staring ahead at the gaping space in the bridge she kept her voice calm. "Looks like the wind has blown some of the boards off. Everybody just sit here now, I'll get out and see what I can do about it," she said.

The car was bobbing like a cork in a pond when Marie opened the door. The rain pelted her in the face as she climbed

261

Crossing thresher on old bridge

New bridge built in 1954

Stockade corral at Park Live

View of ponds around the bend from the Park Live house

out. She carefully got down on her hands and knees beside the car, then crawled behind it. In the red aura of the taillights she jerked three flat boards loose from the old bridge, dragged them to the front of the car, crawled to the hole and laid the boards across it. Quickly she crawled back and climbed into the car.

"This is going to work just fine," she gasped.

Secretly praying that the boards would stay, Marie put the car in gear. Finally, the tires left the bridge and took hold of solid ground and bumped off the bridge on the other side. Marie closed her eyes for a second, breathed deeply, then drove on. No one suspected that her legs were numb with the realization of the danger her children had been in. Through the years, she brought them through many such close calls, which were inevitable when driving dirt roads in the winter.

Because she showed no outward fear when she had to "take a run at" a muddy hill four or five times, or when the bumper of the car pushed snow to break trail, her children took such times in stride. When she gripped the wheel with both hands and giggled, "Boy, this road is slicker 'n Toby's hinder," the children never thought to ask who Toby was. They just laughed and trusted her to handle the situation. She often encouraged the children to sing. Occasionally she sang her two favorite cowboy ballads, "Little Joe the Wrangler" and "Billy Vanero."

During the spring of 1952, when the river was running high, Bill discovered two boats, built to fasten together, washed up on the Flynn Bottom. They had floated down river from the Flaming Gorge country and belonged to the Bureau of Reclamation. They considered them worthless since a large hole had been knocked in the side of one. Bill repaired the hole, tarred the boats, and constructed them into a ferry with a high railing to hold stock. He put the ferry into the water just above where Beaver Creek entered the river, in the same place Stanley Crouse had used the Taylor ferry. However, some unknown person misused it before long, and the big, sturdy ferry sank in the river, where it remains buried beneath a sandbar.

The same year that Bill built his ferry, the swinging bridge went out for the last time. For the next two winters on Friday nights, Bill met Marie and the kids at the river below Swallow Canyon. If the ice was solid, the family walked or drove across. Otherwise, they crossed in the darkness in a rowboat. Two years later, a new and sturdier bridge was constructed at the site of the old one.

Arriving at the ranch after five days in town was always a joyful time for Marie. Especially in the spring. The evening air was sweet with the smell of the greening pastures, the thawed river

264

and creeks, and the fruit blossoms. The two ponds just around the bend from the house were noisy with thousands of frogs, insects, and waterfowl. Her favorite sound was the yells of the descendants of her father's peacocks that roosted in the tall trees between the house and nearby bunkhouse. Their calls, always more numerous in the spring, made her feel content and happy.

Spring also meant that it was time to swim the cattle across the river and trail them to the summer range on Cold Spring Mountain. Bill and Marie always got up before daylight the day of the drive. Bill stirred the sour milk hotcake batter with a steady, "ploop, ploop," while Marie made the coffee and fried bacon and eggs. The boys sauntered in from the bunkhouse and the girls sat on the bench behind the table and rubbed their eyes. When breakfast was over, everyone hurried to grab a coat and hat and head for the corral to saddle and bridle their horses. If she wasn't going to be able to catch up with the herd with lunch for some reason, before the smaller kids went out the door Marie kissed them on the cheek, said "Bye, Sugar-Dugar," and stuffed a hotcake sandwich in their pockets. The fluffy hotcakes wrapped around a fried egg and dill pickle would taste mighty good when their bellies began to growl. She knew they were in for a long, hard day. They wouldn't return home before dark, and very seldom would they be out of their saddles for the next twelve to fifteen hours.

When her tired bunch dragged in that night, Marie met them at the door with the aroma of something yummy clinging to her apron, such as frying deer steaks and a cobbler filled with whole plums, baking in the oven. Her hands and cheeks were warm and pink from standing over the stove. Her blue eyes twinkled as she encouraged them to wash up and then hurried to pile the food onto platters and into big bowls.

In the summer, Bill and Marie usually had a house full of visiting relatives. They also opened their home and gave jobs to a number of teenage boys. Some of the boys just needed the work; others were having trouble at home and needed a new direction. Before long, the fresh air, ranch work, sense of family, and hearty meals at the Park Live began to give them a feeling of contentment and satisfaction at the end of the day. They soon stood taller, browner, and a lot prouder, dressed in Levis and straw hats, ready to climb on their horses at dawn.

Two of the young men who were extra special to Marie were John D. Story and Sheldon Gurr. Besides being good cowhands, they were bright and full of fun. Calling Marie "Ma" Allen, and showing his white teeth in a wide grin, John could talk her out of a quart jar of peaches from the pantry every time.

Although Bill had ridden broncs in several rodeos, he had quit doing it, knowing that with his responsibilities, he shouldn't take such chances. However, along with his oldest son Charlie and with Sheldon and John, he did his share of the horse breaking around the ranch. The three younger men often rode in the rodeos and were getting a little cocky about their abilities. When Bill and Marie arrived to watch one particular rodeo in Vernal, Bill discovered that, as a joke, the boys had entered him in the bull riding, saddle bronc, and bareback riding. Bill just raised his eyebrows and grinned a little. That evening, when the rodeo was over, Bill was laughing! He had taken first place in the bull riding, split first in the saddle bronc, and placed second in the bareback event. The three sheepish boys had all been thrown off.

The yearly roundup of the horse herd to brand the colts and pick out the best young horses to break was a favorite time of Marie's. The palominos, pintos, sorrels, roans, bays, blacks, and buckskins snorted and loped and trotted around the corral with their manes and tails flying, trying to escape the ropes. With her movie camera in hand and the younger kids perched safely around, Marie found a seat on the shed above the stockade corral and watched the boys ride the broncs. When the rodeo was about done, Marie and the girls hurried to the house to get supper on the table. Everyone washed up in the basin at the wooden stand on the porch with hot water poured from the red-trimmed, white enamel teakettle mixed with a cooling dipper of cold water from the bucket. The men usually dampened their hair down and slicked it back with a comb. By the time they began to shuffle across the kitchen linoleum and take their place at the table, Marie had the food ready. She took great pride in the meals she placed before the hungry men. It might be fresh mutton ribs, sprinkled with salt and pepper, and baked in her big black pan until they were brown and crispy, accompanied by a big skillet of fried potatoes and onions, some sweet and sour Harvard beets, creamy coleslaw with tomatoes, and hot buttered buns, along with a dessert of thick slices of her grandmother's spice cake covered with a rich vanilla sauce called "dip." There was always a big pot of hot coffee and a pitcher of fresh cold milk. If she had stopped in the canyon to pick an arm load of Brigham tea sprigs, she would have a pot of that delicious brown liquid steeping, too.

After the dishes were done, Leslie and Charlie often got out their guitars and played while they sang. Sometimes the kids made taffy or popcorn and played board games or cards. One of the smaller kids would climb up on their dad's jiggling knee and Bill would entertain everyone by singing, "Frog Went A'Courtin'," "That Gol Darned Wheel," "The Strawberry Roan," and "The Crow went Caw." Then he'd quickly say the alphabet

John Story   Sheldon Gurr

Corrals at the Park Live

backward and spout a list of tongue twisters without ever making a mistake.

It was not an easy life for Marie. She washed clothes on the scrub board until sweat soaked the front of her blouse and ran in droplets from her temples. She sprinkled down baskets full of clothes and ironed them with irons heated on the stove. Marie often did the milking and sometimes she put on her gold-colored cowboy hat and went out to the hay field to run the baler. She raised an acre of garden and canned huge kettles of a large variety of pickles, spicy chili sauce, jellies and jams, chokecherry and elderberry syrup, pears, peaches, apricots, and plums. She dried corn in the sunlight and baked bread and cookies "by the washtub full." Using a wooden paddle and a wooden bowl, she patted the water from the churned butter and made big sweet yellow squares. She let some of the milk clabber, strained it, then put the chunks in a cloth bag and hung it on the clothes line to finish draining. Then before serving the fresh cottage cheese, she added a little cream and plenty of salt and pepper. She chopped the heads off three or four chickens at a time, then scalded and cleaned them. She rolled the plump chicken pieces in flour, sprinkled them with seasoning and fried a grillful in bacon grease. In order to feed the usual ranch house full of people, Marie began planning for the next meal as soon as the dishes from the last one were washed. Her days were very busy, yet she was never too busy to join in a water fight with the kids, or to decipher their bawling from their laughter and go on the run to see what was wrong.

After Bill's half brothers and sister had left home, his mother, Elnora, and stepfather, Joseph, traveled from Salt Lake to spend most of each summer at the Park Live. Elnora always wore an apron over her dresses and kept her white hair tucked in a hair net. She was usually content to sit quietly and crochet while the kitchen bustled around her. Joseph, whom Marie affectionately called Papa, wore striped bib overalls over a plaid shirt with the yellow drawstring of a Bull Durham tobacco sack sticking out of his pocket. The small man barely bent his legs when he walked, causing him to have a little hop when he hurried along. He combed his thin hair straight back from his toothless face and fascinated the kids both by touching his chin to his nose, and by having no trouble when he crunched on an apple. Joseph had a drinking problem, and still depended on Bill for many things, but he was extremely kind and tried very hard to help out around the ranch. He often did the hay mowing with Bill's little gray Ford tractor and helped Marie, whom he dearly loved, with the chores.

Brown's Park was steadily growing in popularity with the sportsmen. The river bottoms, ponds, and ranch fields were

268

havens for ducks, geese, and deer and they enticed the red-clad hunters to bring their jeeps, campers, and rifles to the valley. Bill Allen was a very successful guide to deer hunters from all over the United States. Marie always looked forward to that special time. For two or three weeks each fall, she left the kids in Rock Springs in school and stayed at the ranch to cook for Bill and the hunters. Every evening, the men ate heaps of Marie's cooking and laughed as they swapped stories about their day. They inevitably left with a truck load of big-antlered deer.

Most of the duck and goose hunters who descended on the valley were friendly people and respectful of where they were allowed to hunt and stayed away from closed areas. However, there were those who did not understand such courtesies. It was these who left gates open, cut fences where there were no gates, pitched garbage to the wind, and ignored the wishes of the owners of the land. One fall, four such men made the mistake of ignoring Marie Allen.

The sun wasn't very far above the O-Wi-U-Kuts one morning when a jeep drove in the yard at the Park Live. Marie had just finished drying the breakfast dishes and Joseph had gone to the corral to milk the cow. Just the two of them were home. Marie walked up the pathway to meet the four men who climbed out of the jeep. They smiled and nodded.

One of the men pointed his finger toward the lower pastures and said, "How do we go about getting down to that big bunch of geese that we just saw flock in there?"

"Sorry fellas," Marie shook her head, "but we have lots of cattle and a few head of sheep and horses in those fields and we don't allow any shooting there. Our own boys don't even hunt there."

Marie gave directions to the men where they were welcome to hunt, but it was no where near the lower fields. The men thanked her, climbed back into their jeep, drove across Crouse Creek, and disappeared around the bend of the rocky hill.

A few moments later, Joseph hurried into the kitchen carrying the nearly full milk bucket. "What's that outfit parked down around the corner for, Marie?"

"What!"

"Well, as I came up from the corral, I saw a jeep pull around the corner out of sight of the house and stop. You didn't tell 'em they could hunt over there, did ya?"

Joseph's eyes popped open and he ran three steps backward when he saw Marie grab a rifle from the gun cabinet.

"Oh m'gosh, Marie, what're you doing? You're not going to ... oh Marie!"

"Don't worry, Papa, I'm just going to take care of those

269

yahoos," Marie said.

The little man's face was the color of buttermilk as he hopped on one foot and then the other. Marie hurried out the screen door, loading the 30.06 as she went. She calmly walked to the fence, rested the rifle against a post and took aim. In the distance, the four trespassers were blatantly walking across the sloping pasture on their way to the lower field, their shotguns over their shoulders.

"Ka-boom!" Marie's rifle exploded.

The four men stopped laughing and talking. They turned toward the house and stared at the woman who was looking down her rifle sights at them. The bottom of her green print apron gently rippled in the breeze.

"Ka-boom!" the rifle repeated and the would-be hunters dove into the grass.

By then Joseph was laughing so hard he had to lean against a tree. He saw that Marie had aimed the rifle a perfectly safe distance away from the men, but they sure didn't know that.

Marie never moved, except to follow the rustling grass with the rifle. The hunters crawled, bellies scraping the ground, until they reached their jeep. Seconds later, with the rubber tires throwing dirt and pebbles behind them, the jeep took off down the road.

The next fall when hunting season opened once again, one of Bill's hired men was bringing some cows home from the river bottoms near the swinging bridge. A jeep drove up beside the horsebacker and a man asked, "Where would you say would be the best place to hunt some geese around here?"

The cowboy shrugged his shoulders and said, "Well, there's a lot of geese at the ranch up the road here a ways."

The driver of the jeep reared back in the seat and said, "Ohhhh no. We're not going near that place. When that woman says no, she means NO!"

Marie had definitely made her point.

Through the years, Bill's Uncle Charlie Green's red hair had turned a rusty white. He spent a lot of time at the Park Live and still attempted to do a little prospecting. He was convinced that an old remedy using charcoal water kept him healthy. He made the remedy by soaking burnt cinders of sagebrush in a jar of water. Then he strained the liquid off and drank it. Bill wrinkled his nose and wondered how that could possibly be good for anybody.

One day, Uncle Charlie startled Bill when he jumped to his feet and hobbled out of the house at a gallop. Outside, some of the boys had nailed a target to a log on the side of Bill's large storage building and had started target practicing with their .22 rifles.

"Stop it, you damn kids, you're gonna hit my still!" Uncle Charlie screamed.

Bill nearly fainted. He had no idea that his uncle had been brewing moonshine in the corner of his storage building!

Another prospector-bachelor who was great friends with Brown's Park and with the Allens was Murty "Murt" Taylor. Murt was born in 1888 and spent most of his youth around Riverton, Wyoming. He was a heavy-boned man, but because part of his stomach had been removed, he had a hard time digesting food and was quite thin. Every morning when he shaved with a battery operated razor, he shaved his head as well. When he laughed, he threw his head back and opened his large toothless mouth wide. Then he'd say a few cusswords and throw his head back and laugh some more. Murt always had a little dog that he kept for company. He was a very early riser and liked to take a stroll with his dog, Taffy, to the outhouse and around the barnyard during the fresh dawn. He enjoyed his tailor-made Camel cigarettes and stuffed one halfway into his mouth before he lit it.

When Murt was not staying at the Park Live, he was at his camp in the foothills of Diamond Mountain, usually somewhere near Kendall Spring, where the old stage stop had once stood. For many years, he searched those foothills each summer for a gold mine that he swore he had found before an illness had nearly killed him and kept him away from Brown's Park for several years. Bill and Marie always suspected that Murt's mine had never truly existed, but had been created in his mind when he was so sick. However, they knew that the mine gave the old fellow a purpose in life. They always loaned him a gentle horse to keep at camp and let one or all three of the younger kids, who were very fond of Murt, go help him in his search now and then. When Murt was alone, and too many days went by without him showing up at the ranch, someone would drive the bumpy road over the top of Swallow Canyon to check on him. Each fall he left Brown's Park to spend the winter in Riverton "trying to get it all figured out." As soon as the roads dried out in the spring, he returned in his little jeep and homemade camper and began his search again.

Murt and Joseph were pretty good friends, and the biggest thing they had in common was teasing Nonie, now a teenager, about her boyfriends. Nonie was not shy and would go toe to toe with them and playfully argue and tease them right back.

Marie saw a lot of herself in Nonie. The girl was tall for her age, energetic, and could "buck" hay bales right alongside of the men. She always tanned copper from the sun and had thick coffee-brown hair and greenish tan eyes. She could run the kitchen if that's where she was needed, but she enjoyed the

271

Nonie Allen and Chocko

Nonie Allen in front of double-walled ice house

ranch work best. When she worked cattle, she rode with her Aunt Bessie's saddle on a tall, chocolate-colored gelding. Chocko was high-strung and always reared and lunged two or three times when she first climbed on him. Nonie was unafraid, and rather enjoyed the big gelding's enthusiasm.

The three older kids had long since left home and Bill and Marie relied on Nonie, Bob, and Diana in the hay field and on horseback. In 1958 Bill hired Clyde Thompson, a blue-eyed, blonde young man from Vernal. Clyde was extremely good

272

natured. He worked hard, but he enjoyed riding his high-stepping horse, Brownie, for the fun of it, too. He soon became such a part of the family that everyone forgot that he hadn't been born into it. When he married Leslie Allen's ex-wife, Velma, Marie could not have been more pleased. She loved them both very much.

In the early sixties, when electricity surged through the new power lines in Brown's Park, Marie and her son, Bob, were the first ones in the valley to actually see the lights come on. Electricity in Brown's Park brought swift changes to the valley. About that same time, Bill piped water from the spring at the mouth of Crouse Canyon down to the house.

Time flew by. Marie was nearing the end of her task of getting her children through high school. She longed for that day so she could stay year around with Bill at the Park Live. For several years Marie had worried about Brown's Park. A proposed project called the Echo Park Dam had nearly become a reality. If the dam had been built, the Green River would have flooded and filled Brown's Park halfway up her mountains. That threat faded when plans to build Flaming Gorge Dam were settled on. But in the early sixties, representatives of the Federal Fish and Wildlife began showing up at the ranch proposing a new threat.

The government wanted to own the Park Live. At first Bill adamantly refused its request that he sell the ranch. Then Marie received word that her brother Jesse Taylor had sold his place to the government and was leaving Brown's Park. When the representatives returned to the Park Live, they used the words "eminent domain" in their persuasive pitch.

"We're going to have this place, Mr. Allen. If we have to take you to court, we'll still get the ranch, but you may not see a penny out of it for over two years. We don't intend to have live-stock back on this range, but it'll be in the contract that you will have first chance to get the permits back if we ever do."

In January, 1964, Nina Taylor died a quiet, painless death in the Rock Springs hospital. Within a year, the papers were signed and the Brown's Park Livestock Ranch belonged to the Federal Fish and Wildlife who turned it over to the Utah Fish and Game. The grazing permits were turned over to the Bureau of Land Management.

Marie flinched when men arrived and began nailing signs to the buildings, declaring them state property. There was nothing she could do but continue packing things up. Bill, Marie, and their teenagers, Bob and Diana (Nonie had married a fine young man from La Barge named Carmen David) would soon be moving into a new trailer home on forty acres on Bake Oven Flat that Bill had insisted on keeping out of the sale.

273

One afternoon, when time at the Park Live was growing short, Marie put on her familiar gold-colored cowboy hat and she and Diana walked halfway up the side of the nearby rocky hill. They stood there for a long time, silently and sadly memorizing the look of every building, bush, and tree. Marie took several pictures, then the two turned to hug each other. They tearfully made their way down the steep hill, slowly following the road back across the creek, breathing deeply of the cool, fresh air. They walked up the little hill and passed the shop where Bill had so often repaired the tractors and did the welding. They walked past the metal granary and the big log storage building. They walked by the house and followed the path to the corral. The barnyard seemed lonely without the chickens, turkeys, guineas, and peacocks. When they reached the corral fence, Marie climbed halfway up the grayish white poles. She gazed across the corrals where Charlie Crouse, Albert Williams, Butch Cassidy, Ford DeJournette, her own family, and so many others had made plans and worked stock. A tear soaked into the weathered wood as Marie slowly took off her hat and hung it on the top of a post. Arm in arm, mother and daughter walked away.

Marie's footsteps echoed in the emptiness when she walked across the kitchen floor of the old log house. She stopped at the door and turned for a final look. She had cried a lot in the last year. She would cry some more today.[3]

Chapter XXIX

CHANGES

Whether they were right for her or not, Brown's Park had no way of protesting the plans of the men of the Fish and Wildlife, the Bureau of Land Management, or any other government agency. She remained silent when the BLM, with the cooperation of the Utah State Division of Fish and Game, hooked massive chains between two Caterpillars in preparation to "rail" the cedars of a large area along Diamond Mountain. (The plan was to improve the wildlife habitat by encouraging more grass to grow.) But when the metal belts began to clank and pull the tractors forward, they, nor the noisy engines, could completely drown out her moans. Old gnarled cedars and their babies were caught by the chain and ripped and torn from the ground. Dust clouds boiled into the air. Rocks and boulders rolled and tumbled along with the trees and brush. Sadly, all the remnants of long ago Indian encampments were crumbled and smashed. When the railing was completed, there was nothing familiar remaining about the ancient campgrounds. A close look revealed grotesque heaps of broken slab rocks and boulders and pile after pile of cedars - which were declared "off limits" to the locals to be gathered for firewood or any other purpose. The distant view revealed a tremendous scar left on the face of the valley.

As was the common practice with the places the government was rapidly accumulating in the valley, the historical significance of the old Brown's Park Livestock Ranch was not considered. The old log house and outbuildings at the Park Live were ripped apart and torn down; the corrals were bulldozed and burned. For three years Crouse Creek was allowed to run free, washing where it pleased and ending up in the river. At the same time, the fields, most of the trees around the home site, and several of the huge apple trees of the old orchard died of thirst.

Marie Allen shook her head at the ugliness but had no idea how to stop it. She went ahead trying to make a home next to the river on Bake Oven Flat. It took a lot of work and time, but the greasewood-covered red alkali clay eventually gave in to plowing, tilling, grubbing, and fertilizing. Finally, apple, apricot, peach, and cherry trees, rhubarb, raspberries, and lilacs began to grow. The garden leafed out and bore plentiful vegetables. A new hay field soon spread up river and was sprinkled with cattle in the winter. The cottonwoods, which had shaded the meeting of the Powell expedition with the Texas cattlemen in 1871, now

275

shaded Bill and Marie's white mobile home. As Marie looked down river a short way, she could clearly see the cottonwoods where her folks had first parked their wagon at Bridgeport. There was nothing left of Bridgeport now, except for the ruins of Charlie Crouse's cellar. Marie discovered that the Doctor Parsons' smelter, which had stood nearby, was about gone, too.

Bill and Marie traveled some, looking for a ranch to replace the Park Live. They leased the Patjanella Ranch east of Brown's Park and later bought the Toothacher Ranch near Encampment, Wyoming but only kept it for a few years and never did live there. When the BLM began allowing herds of outside cattle on Bill's old range in the Park, Bill was shocked. It had been in the contract that he would have first right to any grazing permits issued on the land. However, the BLM claimed that since the contract was with the Fish and Wildlife and not them, they were not bound by what it said. Bill fought that notion in court. (The legal battle took many years, but Bill finally regained his permits in the spring of 1975.)

In 1972 Bill and Marie purchased the Red Creek Ranch. Marie never had been able to bear living away from her valley, and because of her youngest son, Bob, who had married pretty Patty Morgan, she never had to. Bill and Marie counted on Bob to take over more and more of the ranching responsibilities.

Things changed rapidly for Brown's Park. Ninety-seven percent of the valley came to be government owned: U.S. Fish and Wildlife Service - 49%; Bureau of Land Management - 30%; State of Utah - 10%; National Park Service - 8%. In Colorado, all the river bottoms were included in the Brown's Park National Wildlife Refuge except for the area around the mouth of Lodore, which was included in the Dinosaur National Monument, under the control of the National Park Service.[1]

The river poured out of Flaming Gorge Dam cold and clear all year long and never froze over in the winter. All the fish, including the large whitefish, had been poisoned in Brown's Park and replaced with trout. Telephones rang in houses and offices throughout the valley and a paved road left a licorice strip through the Colorado portion. Men and women followed directives to create what they considered to be desirable habitats for waterfowl and other wildlife. Campgrounds and boat landings were established and encouraged visits from rafters as well as trout fishermen and campers. The food around the campgrounds, along with the disappearance of mountain lions and bobcats, encouraged an increase in skunks, weasels, and other small predators. Noxious weeds got a toehold in former hay fields and began to multiply and spread.

Duward and Esther Campbell had years before traded Bill and Marie some land on Douglas Mountain for a few acres at

Parsons cabin taken in 1953

Minnie Crouse Rasmussen taken August, 1970 at Allen Place on Bake Oven Flat

the Jarvie place, and they still lived there. Steve Radosevich retired from the Fish and Game and stayed at his ranch on Willow Creek, which was the only ranch left intact in the Utah end of the Park.

Tom Blevins kept his place as did the Raftopoulos family at Pablo Springs, and the Simpsons kept their little spot in Bull Canyon. The man whom Nina Taylor had chosen to own the C.M. Taylor Ranch, Harold Calder, sold the home site to the

Fish and Game, subdivided the large sagebrush bench below the Joe Tolliver Draw, and established the town site of Taylor Flats. When Marie heard that the Parsons cabin, along with the rest of the Taylor buildings, was to be piled and burned, she became desperate to halt the destruction.

Marie had been busy for a long time gathering notes on the history of Brown's Park; there was so much that she wanted to preserve. She had spent many hours getting information from her brother Jesse and had enjoyed numerous visits with former residents and their offspring. She became involved with the Daggett County Historical Society and the National Association for Outlaw and Lawman History where she met and became friends with Daggett County Historian and president of the National Association, Kerry Ross Boren. In him she found an ally. Together they compiled a history of the Parsons cabin, and on January 12, 1972, presented it to the Utah State Historical Society in Salt Lake City. The next morning, Marie was told that the cabin would be put on the state register and saved from destruction.

Marie walked along the rocky ridge above the ranch where she was raised. In a few days, all but the Parsons cabin and the springhouse would be gone. She lowered her head and squeezed her eyes shut. Then she looked up, tightened her lips together, and shook her head. Oh, but it had been a wonderful place, and it had given her a splendid start in life. She was proud of that. She wiped her eyes and stood up straight, knowing that when she walked away, all those beautiful memories would go with her.

In April, 1974, Marie was thrilled to watch the frame of the dream house Bill was building for her on Bake Oven Flat take form. She and Bill were very happy. It was just the two of them home in the Park now, but their children visited frequently. Each spring for the last few years, as soon as the semester ended at the University of Wyoming, Diana and her husband, Mike Kouris, hurried home to Brown's Park where they spent the summer working alongside and enjoying being with Diana's parents.

Mike Kouris was slender and curly-haired and Bob Allen's best friend. Marie had taken Mike, who was on his own, "under her wing" in Rock Springs during his junior year in high school. She became a major influence in his life. In turn, because of his considerate and warmhearted nature, he held a special place in Marie's heart.

Bill and Marie were friendly with all their new neighbors and liked the young families who had been transferred to work at the refuges in Brown's Park. They became especially close friends with Neil and Merlene Folks who lived at the Brown's

Park Waterfowl Management headquarters at the old Park Live, as well as Glade and Sharon Ross from the Gates of Lodore.

Marie's work preserving the history of Brown's Park had begun in earnest. She searched through the files of newspaper offices, received information from museums and libraries, and was happy to conduct some historical treks through the Park. She corresponded with and encouraged people like Minnie Crouse Rasmussen and Butch Cassidy's sister, Lula Parker Betenson, to visit her in Brown's Park. On February 24, 1975, she got Lodore Hall placed on the National Register of Historic Places. In the meantime, Kerry Ross Boren was busy finalizing plans with actor Robert Redford and National Geographic Magazine for Marie and Bill to host Redford and his party during their stay in Brown's Park, as Redford rode the Outlaw Trail.

Marie continued to gather history. The first lines of the book she hoped to write about Brown's Park began to form in her mind; and the museum she planned to have in the old Bridgeport school buildings were nearing reality. She was also busy being a ranch wife. She joyfully found herself in the saddle quite a bit since they bought Red Creek, even though she had not been feeling well for quite a while.

Clyde Thompson was now living in Vernal with Velma and their children. Whenever they could get away, they drove over the mountain to lend a hand to the Allens. One morning, Marie and Clyde were helping Bob gather the cattle in the big pasture at Red Creek. They had the herd trailing toward the gate when Marie saw Clyde look over his shoulder and heard him say, "There's a coyote!"

Before Clyde got turned back around in his saddle, both Bob and Marie had whirled their horses around and were on a dead run after the coyote.

Marie leaned forward and gave her horse his head. Her eyes grew moist from the wind in her face and she laughed. No longer was she a lady in her late fifties trying to ignore the nagging discomfort so often present in her right side. No, she was once again sixteen, dashing across the countryside on her big black gelding, Speed, with the ability to rope that coyote if she wanted. She let out a "whoop" as her horse cleared a ditch and flew down the slope and across the pasture.

When the coyote ducked under the pasture fence and disappeared into the sagebrush, Marie and Bob pulled their horses up. Marie, out of breath, was grinning wide.

"Guess we showed that dirty bugger that he'd better stay outta here!" she panted.

Bob nodded his head and laughed and they rode back toward Clyde on a trot.[2]

Bob Allen

The last time Marie ever rode horseback, she rode with Bob. Since their coyote chase together, she had been through gall bladder surgery and was told that she would soon be feeling better than she had in several years. She had felt better for a short while, but now, seemed to be losing ground.

It wasn't going to be a hard day of riding, Bob told his mom. "If you feel up to it, we'll just take this little bunch over to Meadow Gulch."

Marie climbed on the buckskin quarterhorse named Joker. She told Bob she liked the gelding best because, "He always stands still 'till I get on."

Bob was very much like his mother. He had her blue eyes, dark hair, and natural ability on a horse and with cattle. He had an engaging personality and was quite tall, reaching a height of six feet. When on the back of a horse, dressed in his hat and tan chaps, he was extremely handsome. He was beginning to remind Marie of her dad; she knew the Red Creek Ranch was going to be in good hands.

Marie's horse was following slowly behind the cattle when he unexpectedly shied. Marie was jerked sideways and the saddle horn caught her in the side of the abdomen. It hurt her worse than she said. It never stopped hurting again.

In the very early morning on April 7, 1975, Marie was

wheeled down the Rock Springs hospital corridor on her way to exploratory surgery. At the Red Creek Ranch, and with his mother strongly on his mind, Bob walked down the hill toward the corral to check on a cow who was about to have a calf. During the next few hours, the cow struggled to give her baby life. Things went wrong with the birth though, and Bob worked over the suffering cow until the sweat ran down his cheeks. All the while, he felt very uneasy on this soft, spring morning. He looked up and unexpectedly saw Mike's car making its way down the Hoy dugway. His innards tightened; still he knelt over the cow and worked. The young cowboy barely glanced up when he heard the squeak of the corral gate as Mike slowly opened it. Mike stood silently nearby as Bob made the last pull on the calf and the tiny heifer finally slid into the world. Bob got to his feet and looked at his friend, his eyes red-rimmed and fearful.

Mike's voice quivered softly. "Your mom has cancer and only about four to eight months to live." The two stood together and cried.3

In the coming months Marie fought her toughest battle. With gentle strength, she put up an incredible fight against a spreading pancreatic tumor.

During the month of October, 1975, Bill arranged for Marie to fly home to her pretty new house in Brown's Park from the University of Utah Medical Center in Salt Lake City. She made the trip in an air ambulance so that she could take part in the event when Robert Redford and his party were there. Although very thin and weak, Marie gracefully invited Redford to sit at her bedside for a visit.

Arrangements for Marie to fly home were made again in November so that she could spend Thanksgiving with her family. Then on December 11 in Salt Lake City, with Bill holding her hand, Marie passed away. Brown's Park had lost another dear friend.

Marie Taylor Allen joined the list of those now gone who had loved Brown's Park with a passion, and who had entrusted their dreams and their lives to the valley. Their voices and their laughter still blend with the soft flutterings of the cottonwood leaves and their sighs whisper in the boughs of the cedars and pines. Every word that they spoke and every track that they made remain somewhere within her mountains.

The valley can still hear the clanking of the mountain men's beaver traps and the laughter of Kit Carson and Uncle Jack Robinson during a rum-soaked rendezvous at Fort Davey Crockett. A whiff of cedar smoke curling skyward carries with it the image of a thousand busy tepees on the nearby river bottom.

When dust rises from behind a knoll, the valley is reminded of a herd of longhorns and its drovers moving out of the valley, heading for California and the hungry forty-niners.

When the late autumn fog lies thick along the river, the valley can glimpse a stagecoach come dripping out of the mist. The harness is jingling as the horses pull the coach up the bank from the Indian Crossing river ford near the old rock saloon.

In a sudden downpour, as water washes off the ridges in rivulets, Brown's Park remembers the tears shed when John Jarvie was robbed and murdered, and when little Nancy Taylor, and later her younger sister, Bessie, died of scarlet fever. She remembers many sad days.

But when a jackrabbit darts from behind a bush, she also remembers the hilarity of Wildcat Sam riding Jyperina. She smiles when she sees a birch sapling growing on the creek bank. She remembers a sapling in the hands of Harry Hindle as he stands up in the wagon, lets out with a "ya-hoo!" and bounces away behind his team of wild horses.

Night shadows remind Brown's Park of hired gun Tom Horn and his deeds; of Butch Cassidy and the other outlaws slipping through the pasture gate at the Park Live to catch fresh horses.

Dark silhouettes on a purple velvet skyline are memories of the big gray wolf nuzzling his mate, just before his howls stir the night.

The clap of thunder brings to life Joe Tolliver, Jessie Ewing, Charlie Crouse, and Mexican Joe, packing their knives. The calm that follows the storm is the delicate friendship between Charlie Crouse and Albert Williams, and between Mexican Joe and his companion, Judge Conaway.

The remnants of a rock fireplace bring back the feeling of warmth and caring that the pioneer women, like Alice Davenport, Jennie Jaynes, Mary Crouse, and Pretty Little Nell, brought to the small cabins.

A wild wind brings with it images of Elizabeth Bassett, Queen Ann, and Marie Taylor, riding their horses on a lope, ropes dangling ready in their hands.

When the lowering sun makes blue shadows on the mountains, the image of C.M. Taylor riding Coon behind a herd of steers ripples into sight. He coils his bullwhip around his saddle horn, pushes his hat back, and is once again captivated by the view above him.

All who love Brown's Park today take comfort in knowing that year after year, one season will give way to another and the valley will live on long after they are gone.

As mountain man Rufus B. Sage wrote during a golden autumn in Brown's Hole in 1842, this special valley is where

"spring wedded to summer seems to have chosen this sequestered spot for her fixed habitation, where when dying autumn
woos the sere frost and snow of winter, she may withdraw to her
flower-garnished retreat and smile and bloom forever."

Chapter XXX
EPILOG

Marie Allen was first buried in the Rock Springs cemetery, but was later returned home to Brown's Park, along with her daughters, Billie Dee and Barbara Lee. She rests there on a knoll overlooking the Green River, very near where her folks first stopped their wagon under the cottonwoods at Bridgeport.

Shortly after Marie's death, careless deer hunters burned both the Parsons cabin and the homestead cabin at the head of Galloway to the ground.

Soon after Duward Campbell died, Esther sold the Jarvie place and it came under the management of the Bureau of Land Management. Fortunately, by then, the desire to preserve Brown's Park history, had grown within the BLM. Many caring people have worked hard and the John and Nellie Jarvie home site has been historically restored.

When Jesse Taylor sold his place in Brown's Park, he bought and moved to the Canyon Creek Ranch northeast of there. A few years later, he sold out and retired to Rock Springs. In 1982 he went to visit his son Orvil and his family west of Maybell, Colorado. One evening he said, "You know, now I know how an old horse feels when he's getting ready to die." He passed away quietly in his sleep two nights later, on the twenty-first of October.

The Raftopoulos family still have their place on Pablo Spring, and have spread their holdings considerably. The boys, John and Steve, were both taught the importance of a good education by their parents. In 1975, while John continued in veterinary school, at Colorado State University, Steve graduated from the University of Colorado at Boulder, and returned to run the ranch. George Raftopoulos was ill with Parkinson's disease and unable to manage it by himself.

In 1977 when the coal boom was on in the Craig area, the Raftopoulos family sold their property south of Craig to a mining company. At that time the decision had to be made whether to expand the ranching operation to support more than one family, or to invest the money in other ventures. The decision was made to expand.

In 1978 John graduated from veterinary school and returned to the ranch. Several trips to surrounding western states were made, but it was decided by the Raftopoulos family that "the best place to raise a fat lamb is in western Colorado." It was then that the family purchased the Two-Bar Ranch. It had summer range in the Bear Ears area north of Craig, lambing ground in the area northwest of Craig, and winter range between Craig and Brown's Park in the Sand Wash Basin. The purchase nicely complemented their other holdings.

In the early eighties, the lamb market dropped. That, along with high interest rates, made it necessary for extremely tight money management. It was decided that Raftopoulos Ranches would have to run at near maximum numbers with the lowest possible expenses. Sheep and cattle numbers were increased.

Then came the bitter winter of 1983-84. It started snowing the last of November and by the first of January, there was eight to ten feet of snow in the higher ranges and two to three feet in the desert country. Except in Brown's Park! The Raftopoulos family was able to move several bunches of sheep to the Park and with corn and pellets made it through the winter in pretty good shape. But other sheepmen not only suffered substantial winter losses, they lost three hundred thousand more sheep when an arctic storm bullied its way across the western states shortly after the sheep had been sheared that spring. The depleted herds caused higher sheep prices and better profits for the Raftopoulos's.

The Raftopoulos family discovered during that bad winter that it took thirty to forty pounds of hay a day per head to feed their cattle in the Little Snake River area, while in Brown's Park the cattle flourished on only twenty to twenty-five pounds. Also, the cattle in Brown's Park didn't have to be fed nearly as long. They decided that Brown's Park should be their winter headquarters for the cattle operation, providing suitable surrounding range could be purchased that was close enough so the cattle could be trailed instead of trucked. That summer area was found north of Brown's Park on the Colorado-Wyoming line and was known as the Buckley-Sparks Ranch. Under strong management, Raftopoulos Ranches now has a capacity to run twelve thousand sheep and twenty-one hundred cows.[1]

Undoubtedly appreciated by the many tourists and travelers visiting Brown's Park, Fred--the late Tom Blevins' son--and Joy Blevins started the Brown's Park Store and Garage on the Blevins place. Joy runs the store and Fred works there as a mechanic and runs a few head of cattle as well.

After Marie's death, Bill Allen married Ella Gurr Shiner, whom he had known since childhood. They made their home in Vernal, Utah, where Bill's sister Zora and her husband Lawrence Gurr (Ella's brother) live. Bill lives a quiet life in Vernal, but is still active in the running of the ranch along with his son, Bob. Although in his mid-seventies, it is not unusual for Bill to spend time in the saddle in the spring when the cattle are taken to the summer range and in the fall during gathering and shipping time.

Marie Allen was right when she said that the Red Creek Ranch was going to be in good hands. Bob Allen is a talented cowboy. He headquarters on Bake Oven Flat at the home place in Brown's Park and works steadily at running Allen Livestock, Inc.

THE STATE HISTORICAL SOCIETY OF COLORADO

Colorado State Museum, 200 Fourteenth Avenue, Denver 80203
January 9, .1976

William Allen
Brown's Park, Utah
c/o Greystone, Colorado 81636

Dear Mr. Allen:

I most regretfully learned that your wife had passed away
recently and wanted to personally extend my own condolences
as well as those of the Society to you. Your wife had been
of enormous help to us not so long ago in the matter of
the National Register designation of the school there in
Brown's Park. She sent us some of the finest research information
and photographs that we have gotten from a local historian.
I thought perhaps you might wish to have a copy of the
National Register Form, which legally designates the school, and
which she was so instrumental in producing.

Certainly, we continue to owe to your wife's memory a great
debt for the information and understanding of the Brown's Park
area which she was able to impart to us so vividly. We cannot
but help to feel her loss as a fine historian and as a
tremendous help-mate in our efforts to record the history and
the heritage of our state.

Sincerely,

Cynthia Emrick

Cynthia Emrick
Preservation Assistant
State Historic Preservation Office

STATE OF UTAH
OFFICE OF THE GOVERNOR
SALT LAKE CITY

CALVIN L. RAMPTON
GOVERNOR

January 20, 1976

William Allen
Brown's Park, Utah
c/o Greystone, Colorado 81636

Dear Mr. Allen:

    I am writing to offer my condolences at the passing
away of your wife. Her vigorous efforts to preserve Utah's
heritage through its historical sites will serve as a
lasting monument to her life. The lives of all of the
citizens of Utah can be enriched with a sense of our cultural
heritage because of her diligent efforts.

    It is with a deep sense of sorrow that I pay tribute to
your wife and her contributions to restoring Utah's past.

                              Sincerely,

                              Governor

289

NOTES

CHAPTER I. The Dawning

1. John G. Neihardt, **The Splendid Wayfaring**, p. 191.
2. Ibid., p. 192.
3. Ibid., pp. 192-193.
4. Kit Carson, **Kit Carson's Autobiography**, edited by Milo Milton Quaife, pp. 4-5.
5. Ibid., p. x.
6. Ibid., p. 54.
7. Thomas J. Farnham, **Travels in the Great Western Prairies, the Anahuac and Rocky Mountains, and the Oregon Territory**, p. 57.
8. Frederick A. Wisizenus, **A Journey to the Rocky Mountains in the Year 1839**, p. 129.
9. William T. Hamilton, **My Sixty Years on the Plains: Trapping, Trading, and Indian Fighting**, pp. 84-85.
10. Robert Newell as quoted by Fred R. Gowans, **Rocky Mountain Rendezvous: A History of the Fur Trade Rendezvous 1825-1840**, p. 130.
11. LeRoy R. Hafen, **Mountain Men and Fur Traders of the Far West**, p. 359.

CHAPTER II. The Longhorns and the Cowboys

1. Mari Sandoz, **The Cattlemen**.
2. William H. Forbis, **The Cowboys**, pp. 53-54.
3. Marian Tolmadge and Iris Gilmore, **Six Great Rides**.
4. Information on Mexican Joe compiled from John Rolfe Burroughs, **Where the Old West Stayed Young**; Dick and Vivian Dunham, **Flaming Gorge Country**; Jesse S. Hoy, "The J.S. Hoy Manuscript."
5. Ann Bassett Willis, "Queen Ann" of Brown's Park, in **The Colorado Magazine**, April, 1952, p. 84.
6. John Rolfe Burroughs, **Where the Old West Stayed Young**, p. 3.

CHAPTER III. Mexican Joe

1. T.A. Larson, **History of Wyoming**, p. 112.
2. John Rolfe Burroughs, **Where the Old West Stayed Young**, pp. 18-19.
3. Lola M. Homsher, **South Pass, 1868**, p. 75.

CHAPTER IV. The Expedition of John Wesley Powell

1. Wallace Stegner, **Beyond the Hundredth Meridian**, p. 54.
2. Phil Roberts, Editor, **More Buffalo Bones**, p. 20.
3. Laura Evans and Buzz Belknap, **Dinosaur River Guide**, p. 17.
4. Ibid., p. 21.
5. Ibid., p. 22.
6. Ibid., p. 25.
7. Wallace Stegner, **Beyond the Hundredth Meridian**, p. 62.

8. Ibid., p. 62.
9. Laura Evans and Buzz Belknap, **Dinosaur River Guide**, p. 31.
10. Ibid., p. 33.

CHAPTER V. Maggie's Nipple

1. John Rolfe Burroughs, **Where the Old West Stayed Young**, pp. 10-11.
2. William E. Allen, interview with author.

CHAPTER VI. J.S. Hoy

1. Jesse S. Hoy, "The J.S. Hoy Manuscript."
2. Ibid. This and all subsequent quotations in this chapter from the "J.S. Hoy Manuscript."

CHAPTER VII. The Big Gray

1. Information on wolf behavior compiled from: L. David Mech, **The Wolf: The Ecology and Behavior of an Endangered Species**; Richard Fiennes, **The Order of Wolves**.
2. Jesse S. Hoy, "The J.S. Hoy Manuscript."

CHAPTER VIII. The Scuffles

1. Jesse S. Hoy, "J.S. Hoy Manuscript."
2. Ibid.
3. Ibid.
4. Ibid.
5. Ibid.
6. Ibid.
7. Ibid.
8. Ibid.
9. Ibid.

CHAPTER IX. The Women

1. Information on pioneer women compiled from: Kerry Ross Boren with Marie Allen, "Dr. Parsons' Cabin of Brown's Park, Utah;" Erickson history submitted by Sandy Barton; Burroughs, **Where the Old West Stayed Young**; Dunham, **Flaming Gorge Country**; Grace McClure, **The Bassett Women**; William L. Tennent, **John Jarvie of Brown's Park**; Butch Cassidy, **My Brother**, Lula Parker Betenson as told to Dora Flack.

CHAPTER X. The Families

1. Kerry Ross Boren with Marie Allen, "Dr. Parsons' Cabin of Brown's Park, Utah."
2. Josie Bassett Morris interview with G.E. Untermann, A.R. Mortensen, and E.L. Cooley on September 25, 1959.
3. Ibid.
4. Ann Bassett Willis, "Queen Ann" of Brown's Park, **The Colorado Magazine**, April 1952, p. 88.
5. Ibid. pp. 91-93.
6. Grace McClure, **The Bassett Women**, p. 33.

CHAPTER XI. John Jarvie

1. William L. Tennent, **John Jarvie of Brown's Park.**
2. Minnie Crouse Rasmussen interview with Marie Taylor Allen in August, 1970.
3. Ibid.
4. Description of Jesse Ewing compiled from Jesse Taylor interview with author as told to him by John Jarvie; Burroughs, **Where the Old West Stayed Young**; Hoy, "J.S. Hoy Manuscript."
5. Minnie Crouse Rasmussen interview with Marie Taylor Allen.
6. Marie Taylor Allen written account of story told to her father C.M. Taylor by John Jarvie.
7. Jesse Taylor interview with author.
8. Ibid.
9. Josie Bassett Morris interview with G.E. Untermann, A.R. Mortensen, and E.L. Cooley.
10. Jesse Taylor interview with author.

CHAPTER XII. Charlie Crouse

1. Minnie Crouse Rasmussen interview with Marie Taylor Allen.
2. Stanley Crouse, Jr. interview with author.
3. William Allen interview with author as told to him by Stanley Crouse, Sr.
4. Minnie Crouse Rasmussen interview with Marie Taylor Allen.
5. Burroughs, **Where the Old West Stayed Young**, pp. 33-34.
6. Minnie Crouse Rasmussen interview with Marie Taylor Allen.
7. Ibid.
8. Ibid.
9. William Allen interview with author as told to him by Stanley Crouse, Sr. Shortly before his death, Stanley visited the Bill Allen home in Rock Springs and asked Bill to take him to the Park Live in Brown's Park. Bill did so, and at the kitchen table, Stanley talked openly to Bill about memories of his dad, Charlie Crouse.
10. Ibid.
11. Ibid.
12. Matt Warner as told to Murray E. King, **The Last of the Bandit Riders**, p. 123.
13. Stanley Crouse, Jr. interview with author.
14. **The Denver Post**, November 20, 1977.
15. Larry Pointer, **In Search of Butch Cassidy**.
16. Matt Warner as told to Murray E. King, **The Last of the Bandit Riders**.
17. Josie Bassett Morris interview with G.E. Untermann, A.R. Mortensen, and E.L. Cooley.
18. Larry Pointer, **In Search of Butch Cassidy**.
19. Kerry Ross Boren, **Newsletter of the National Association and Center for Outlaw and Lawman History**, Spring 1975, pp. 8-9.

CHAPTER XIII. The Lynching

1. Grace McClure, **The Bassett Women**, p. 50.
2. Abstracts of the Red Creek Ranch.

3. Dunham, **Flaming Gorge Country,** p. 234.
4. Jesse Taylor interview with author, as told to him by Eb Bassett. The lynching was specifically described as having occurred on the yard entry gate, not the corral gate as has been said.
5. Ibid.
6. Ibid.

CHAPTER XIV. The Conflict

1. William H. Forbis, **The Cowboys,** p. 58.
2. Mari Sandoz, **The Cattlemen,** p. 209.
3. T.A. Larson, **The History of Wyoming;** Mari Sandoz, **The Cattlemen.**
4. Ann Bassett Willis, "Queen Ann" of Brown's Park, in **The Colorado Magazine,** January 1953, p. 60.
5. Grace McClure, **The Bassett Women,** Appendix: Confidentially Told, p. 210.
6. Burroughs, **Where the Old West Stayed Young,** p. 203.
7. Josie Bassett Morris interview with G.E. Untermann, A.R. Mortensen, and E.L. Cooley.
8. Ann Bassett Willis, "Queen Ann" of Brown's Park, **The Colorado Magazine,** January, 1953, p. 62.
9. Hazel Teters Overy interview with author.
10. Ann Bassett Willis, "Queen Ann" of Brown's Park, in **The Colorado Magazine,** January 1953, p. 66-67.

CHAPTER XV. The Gentle and the Rowdy

1. Jesse Taylor interview with author.
2. William Allen interview with author, as told to him by his uncle Charlie Green.
3. Ibid.
4. Minnie Crouse Rasmussen interview with Marie Taylor Allen.
5. William L. Tennent, **John Jarvie of Brown's Park,** p. 78.
6. Ibid, p. 77-78.
7. Jesse Taylor interview with author, as told to him by John Jarvie, Jr.
8. Ibid, p. 89.

CHAPTER XVI. C.M. Taylor

1. Jesse Taylor interview with author. Except where otherwise noted, information for this chapter compiled from Jesse Taylor interview with author.
2. William Allen interview with author as told to him by C.M. Taylor.
3. William Allen interview with author as told to him by Nina Taylor.
4. Francis Taylor interview with author, as told to her by Nina Taylor.

CHAPTER XVII. Heartbreaks and Heartaches

1. Jesse Taylor interview with author. Except where otherwise noted, information for this chapter compiled from Jesse Taylor interview with author.

2. Minnie Crouse Rasmussen interview with Marie Taylor Allen.
3. E.W. "Wilson" Garrison interview with author.
4. William Allen interview with author.
5. Minnie Crouse Rasmussen interview with Marie Taylor Allen.
6. William Allen interview with author.

CHAPTER XVIII.   Unavenged Murder

1. Jesse Taylor interview with author. Except where otherwise noted, information for this chapter compiled from Jesse Taylor interview with author.
2. **The Vernal Express,** July 23, 1909.
3. William L. Tennent, **John Jarvie of Brown's Park,** pp. 88-89.

CHAPTER XIX.   The Flynns

1. Information for this chapter compiled from Jesse Taylor interview with author.

CHAPTER XX.   Ann and Josie

1. Grace McClure, **The Bassett Women.**
2. Jesse Taylor interview with author.
3. Josie Bassett Morris interview with G.E. Untermann, A.R. Mortensen, and E.L. Cooley.
4. Minnie Crouse Rasmussen interview with Marie Taylor Allen.
5. Jesse Taylor interview with author.
6. Ibid.
7. Josie Bassett Morris interview with G.E. Untermann, A.R. Mortensen, and E.L. Cooley.
8. Ann Bassett Willis, "Queen Ann" of Brown's Park, in **The Colorado Magazine**, January, 1953, p. 76.

CHAPTER XXI.   The Lodore School

1. **The Empire Courier,** November 23, 1911.
2. Ibid, May 25, 1912.
3. Jesse Taylor interview with author.
4. Ibid.
5. Marie Taylor Allen, "Lodore Hall," write-up for presentation to have building placed on National Historic Register.
6. Ibid.
7. Ibid.

CHAPTER XXII.   The Taylors

1. Jesse Taylor interview with author.
2. William Allen interview with author. Some time later, the government, wishing to test the flow of the Green River in anticipation of the building of a dam, built a water gauging station down the river a short distance from the Parsons. The little house sat in the rocks overlooking the river and contained instruments that judged the rise and fall of the water. They also built a sturdy trolley with cable lines stretching across the river. The trolley was equipped with pulley wheels used to raise and lower an instrument to judge the speed of the flow of the river. C.M. Taylor was asked to take the readings over a period of time until

the government obtained all the information they required. They then abandoned the little gauge house and left the trolley for C.M. to use as he wished. The trolley was a handy way for people to cross the river for many years.

3. Francis Taylor interview with author, as told to her by Nina Taylor.
4. Jesse Taylor interview with author.
5. Hazel Teters Overy interview with author.
6. Jesse Taylor interview with author.
7. Hazel Teters Overy interview with author.
8. Ibid.
9. Jesse Taylor interview with author.
10. Hazel Teters Overy interview with author.
11. Wilson Garrison interview with author.
12. Jesse Taylor interview with author.
13. Allen Taylor interview with author.
14. Jesse Taylor interview with author.
15. Stanley Crouse, Jr. interview with author.

CHAPTER XXIII. Rattlesnake Jack and Wildcat Sam

1. Jesse Taylor interview with author.

CHAPTER XXIV. Marie Taylor

1. Hazel Teters Overy interview with author.
2. Ibid.
3. Jesse Taylor interview with author.
4. Lucille Fleming interview with author.
5. Wilson Garrison interview with author.
6. Allen Taylor, Jesse Taylor, and William Allen interviews with author.
7. Information from Marybeth Wilson Carr.
8. Allen Taylor interview with author.
9. Bertha Worley Simkin interview with author.
10. Hazel Teters Overy interview with author.
11. Ibid.
12. Except where otherwise noted, stories were compiled from Marie Allen's notes and diaries and from recollections of stories told to the author by her mother, Marie Allen.

CHAPTER XXV. Bill Allen

1. William Allen interview with author and letter from Zora Allen Gurr.

CHAPTER XXVI. Romances and Farewells

1. William Allen interview with author.
2. Ibid.
3. Ibid.
4. From the diary of Marie Taylor.
5. William Allen interview with author.
6. Wilson Garrison interview with author.
7. Bill Allen, Hazel Teters Overy interviews with author.

8. William Allen, Wilson Garrison interviews with author.
9. Ibid.
10. William Allen interview with author.
11. Hazel Teters Overy, William Allen interviews with author and recollection of the account of the tragedy as told to the author by her mother, Marie Allen.

CHAPTER XXVII. Jesse Taylor

1. Except where otherwise noted, information compiled from Jesse Taylor interview with author.
2. Allen Taylor interview with author.
3. Ibid.

CHAPTER XXVIII. Life on the Park Live

1. Nonie David interview with author.
2. Georgia and John Raftopoulos written history of family to author.
3. Except where otherwise noted, information for chapter compiled from William Allen interview with author, and from author's recollections of growing up on the Brown's Park Livestock Ranch.

CHAPTER XXIX. Changes

1. **National Park Service, Draft Wild and Scenic River Study and Draft Environmental Statement, Green and Yampa Wild and Scenic Rivers**, p. 105.
2. Clyde Thompson, Bob Allen interviews with author.
3. Mike Kouris interview with author.

CHAPTER XXX. Epilogue

1. Georgia and John Raftopoulos written history of family to author.

BIBLIOGRAPHY
BOOKS

Betenson, Lula, as told to Dora Flack. **Butch Cassidy, My Brother.** Provo, Brigham Young University Press, 1975.

Burroughs, John Rolfe. **Where the Old West Stayed Young.** New York, Bonanza, 1962.

Carson, Kit. **Kit Carson's Autobiography.** Edited by Milo M. Quaife. Chicago, R.R. Donnelly and Sons, 1935.

Dunham, Dick and Vivian. **Flaming Gorge Country.** Denver, Eastwood Printing and Publishing Company, 1977.

Dunham, Dick and Vivian. **Our Strip of Land: A History of Daggett County, Utah.** Manila, Utah, Daggett County Lions Club, 1947.

Evans, Laura, and Belknap, Buzz. **Flaming Gorge Dinosaur National Monument Dinosaur River Guide**, Boulder City, Nevada, Westwater Books, 1973.

Farnham, Thomas J. **Travels in the Great Western Prairies, the Anahauc and Rocky Mountains, and in the Oregon Territory.** Poughkeepsie, New York, Killey and Lossing Printers, 1841.

Fiennes, Richard. **The Order of Wolves.** Indianapolis, Bobbs-Merrill.

Forbis, William H. **The Cowboys.** Alexandria, Virginia, Time-Life Books, 1973.

Foster-Harris. **The Look of the Old West.** New York, The Viking Press.

Hafen, LeRoy R. Ed. **Mountain Men and Fur Traders of the Far West: Eighteen Biographical Sketches.** Glendale, California, Arthur H. Clark Company, 1965-72, University of Nebraska Press Lincoln and London.

Hansen, Wallace R. **The Geologic Story of the Uinta Mountains, Geological Survey Bulletin 1291.** U.S. Government Printing Office, 1969.

Homsher, Lola M. Ed. **South Pass**, 1868. Lincoln, University of Nebraska Press, 1960.

Hughel, Avvon Chew. **The Chew Bunch in Browns Park.** San Francisco, Scrimshaw Press, 1970.

Larson, T.A. **History of Wyoming.** Lincoln, University of Nebraska Press, 1965.

Look, Al. **Utes' Last Stand.** Denver, The Golden Bell Press, 1972.

Lyman, June, and Denver, Norma. **Ute People, An Historical Study.** Uinta School District and The Western History Center, University of Utah, Salt Lake City, Utah, 1970.

McClure, Grace. **The Bassett Women.** Athens, Ohio, Chicago, London, Swallow Press/Ohio University Press, 1985.

Mech, L. David. **The Wolf: The Ecology and Behavior of an Endangered Species.** Garden City, New York, The Natural History Press.

Neihardt, John G. **The Splendid Wayfaring.** Lincoln and London, University of Nebraska Press, Bison Book, 1970.

Newell, Robert, as quoted by Fred R. Gowans. **Rocky Mountain Rendezvous: A History of the Fur Trade Rendezvous**. Provo, Utah, 1975.

Paine, Lauran. **Tom Horn, Man of the West**. Barre, Massachusetts, Barre Publishing Company, 1963.

Pointer, Larry. **In Search of Butch Cassidy**. Norman, Oklahoma, University of Oklahoma Press, 1977.

Roberts, Phil. Ed. **More Buffalo Bones**, Stories from Wyoming's Past, Wyoming State Archives, Museums and Historical Department, 1982.

Sandoz, Mari. **The Cattlemen**. Lincoln and London, University of Nebraska Press, Bison Book, 1978.

Stegner, Wallace. **Beyond the Hundredth Meridian, John Wesley Powell and the Second Opening of the West**. Boston, Houghton Mifflin Company, The Riverside Press Cambridge, 1954.

Tennent, William L. **John Jarvie of Brown's Park**. Utah State Office Bureau of Land Management, 1981.

Tolmadge, Marian, and Gilmore, Iris. **Six Great Rides**. New York, G.P. Putnam's Sons.

Wislizenus, Frederick A. **A Journey to the Rocky Mountains in the Year 1839**. St. Louis, Missouri, Missouri Historical Society, 1912.

MANUSCRIPTS AND OTHER RELATED MATERIAL

Allen, Marie. Collection of correspondence, handwritten notes, journals, interviews, and diaries.

Allen, Marie. "Lodore Hall," unpublished manuscript.

Barton, Sandy. Written account of history of John and Elizabeth Erickson to author.

Boren, Kerry Ross. "Fort Davey Crockett," unpublished manuscript.

Boren, Kerry Ross, with Allen, Marie. "The Parsons' Cabin of Brown's Park, Utah," unpublished manuscript.

Christensen, Elnora Green. "History of Ephriam Green and Family," unpublished manuscript.

Hoy, Jesse S. "The J.S. Hoy Manuscript," unpublished manuscript.

Morris, Josie Bassett. Transcript of interview with G.E. Untermann, A.R. Mortensen, and E.L. Cooley, 1959.

National Association and Center for Outlaw and Lawman History newsletter, Utah State University, Logan, Utah, Spring 1975.

Raftopoulos, Georgia and John. Written account of family history to author, September 9, 1987.

United States Department of the Interior, Draft Wild and Scenic River Study and Draft Environmental Statement, 1979.

Willis, Ann Bassett. "Queen Ann" of Brown's Park. Published in **The Colorado Magazine,** Denver, Colorado, The State Historical Society, Volume XXIX April, 1952; Volume XXIX January 1952; Volume XXIX October, 1952; Volume XXX January, 1953.

INTERVIEWS WITH AUTHOR

Allen, Bob, Brown's Park, Utah, March, 1982; August, 1987.

Allen, William, Vernal, Utah, June 6, July 13, July 15, October 10, 1981; October, 1982; March 5, 1983; April, 1987.

Crouse, Stanley Jr., Dubois, Wyoming, May 15, 1983.
David, Nonie, Kinnear, Wyoming, August 5, 1987.
Fleming, Lucille, Green River, Wyoming, June 10, 1981.
Garrison, E.W., Rock Springs, Wyoming, July 14, 1981; October 10, 1981.
Kouris, Mike, Kinnear, Wyoming, August, 1987.
Overy, Hazel, Rock Springs, Wyoming, July 15, October 10, 1981.
Simkin, Bertha, Rock Springs, Wyoming, March, 1982.
Taylor, Allen, Riverton, Wyoming, December 14, 1986.
Taylor, Francis, Riverton, Wyoming, October 22, 1982; December 14, 1986.
Taylor, Jesse, Rock Springs, Wyoming, May 26, May 27, October 10, October 11, 1981; March, 1982.
Thompson, Clyde, Vernal, Utah, July 4, 1987.

LETTERS TO AUTHOR

Garrison, E.W., July 3, 1981; August 31, 1981; August 28, 1985.
Gurr, Zora, September 21, 1981.
Overy, Hazel, July 2, 1981; February 10, 1986; March 7, 1987; April 19, 1987; July 8, 1987.
Simkin, Bertha, July 6, 1981; September 1, 1981; October 23, 1981; December, 1986; July 29, 1987.
Taylor, Jesse, August 3, 1981; September 21, 1981; May 10, 1982.

INDEX

303

Beasley, Neil, 200
Beaver Basin, 33, 200
Beaver Creek (Brown's Park), 46, 48, 71,
101, 102, 107, 121, 128, 140, 142,
161, 162, 171, 179, 198, 229, 239,
241, 255, 257, 260, 264
Beaver Creek Canyon, 71
Beaver Creek Lane, 203, 215
Beaver, Utah, 76, 208, 209
Beddole, Danny, photo of, 244
Bender, Billy "Old Man", 77, 85
Bennett, John "Jack," "Judge," 62, 84, 85,
86, 89, 90, 245
Bent, Charles, 5
Bernard, Ann (see Bassett, Ann)
Bernard, Hiram "Hi", 16, 97, 98, 102,
147, 239, 243
Betenson, Lula Parker, 279
Bicknell, Utah, 207
Bill Spack Ranch, 87
Birch Canyon, 229
Birch Creek, 119, 217
Bitter Creek, 20
Bitter Creek, Wyoming, 217, 243
Black Cattle, 9
Black's Fork, 12
Blackfoot, Indian, 3
Blair, Mrs. William, 46, 78, 85, 121
Blair, William, 46, 47, 78, 85, 86
Blairtown, Wyoming, 174, 225, 230
Blevins Ranch, 286
Blevins, Fred, 286
Blevins, Freddie, 259
Blevins, Joy, 286
Blevins, Sheriff Tom, 259
Blevins, Tom, 259, 277, 286
Board Of Livestock Commissioners, 95
Bolivia, South America, 80, 81
Boone Draw, 199
Boone Meadow, 163
Boren, Kerry Ross, 278, 279
Boulder, Colorado, 196
Bountiful, Utah, 257
Bovey and Company, 7
Bowen, Loren, 226
Bower, Gladys, 162
Bradshaw Place, 129
Bradshaw, Bessie, 139
Bradshaw, Elmer, 129, 139, 162
Braggs, Billy, 100, 117, 118
Brands, Brown's Park Area, IV, X
Bridgeport School (see Schools)
Bridgeport, Utah, 80, 103, 105, 108,
120-123, 127, 128, 131, 135, 137, 142,
154, 162, 181, 182, 248, 253, 276, 285
Bridger, Jim, 5
Brigham City, Utah, 258

Bright, William H., 18
Brinegar Ranch, 173
Brown's Hole Home Demonstration Club,
164
Brown's Park Cattleman's Association, 97,
101
Brown's Park Cemetery, 47, 138, 152,
153
Brown's Park Live Stock Ranch (also
known as Brown's Park Livestock Ranch,
Allen Livestock Ranch, Park Live), 70,
74, 77, 79, 87, 88, 103, 121, 124,
135-137, 143, 144, 148, 167, 171, 175,
181, 214, 215, 255-274, 276, 279, 282;
photos—log home, 73; corrals, 263,
267; ponds 263; old and new bridges,
262
Brown's Park National Wildlife Refuge,
276
Brown's Park Store and Garage, 286
Brown's Park Waterfowl Management
Headquarters, 278, 279
Brown, Baptiste, 2, 3
Brown, Bible Back, 3
Brown, Charles, 3
Brown, Clarence, 163
Brown, Henry "Bo'sun", 3
Brown, Old Cut Rocks, 3
Brush Creek, 87
Buckley, Kenneth, 259; photo of, 234
Buckley, Martha Sparks, 259
Buckley-Sparks Ranch, 286
Budelich, Frank, 164
Buffham, Butch, 164
Buffham, Floy, 260
Buffham, Ginger, 164
Buffham, Katie, 164
Buffham, Reg, 260
Bull Canyon (Brown's Park), 46, 200, 258,
277
Bureau of Land Management (BLM), 273,
275, 276, 285; photo of one of first
meetings in area, 234
Bureau of Reclamation, 264
Burke, Melvin, 213
Burton (from Greendale, Utah), 104, 249
Burton, Clare, 260
Burton, Tom, 260

C

Calder, Harold, 257, 277
Callaway, Boone, 200
Callaway, E.K., 200
Callaway, Fannie, 200

305

G

Gadds, Earl, 194
Gadds, Mrs. Earl, 194
Galloway Cabin, 230, 285; photo of, 231
Galloway Draw, 215, 225, 230
Galvaston, Texas, 28
Gap Creek, 47, 69
Gardner, Art, 260
Gardner, T.A., 210, 211
Gardner, Thelma, 211
Gardner, Vondell, 260
Garrett, Bill, 151-154
Garrison, Ann, 231
Garrison, Bessie Taylor (see also Taylor, Bessie), 226, 228, 229, 230, 234, 250, 272, 282; photos of, 223, 224, 227
Garrison, Edith, 198, 217
Garrison, Edna, 198
Garrison, Elsie, 198
Garrison, Laura, 198
Garrison, Lester, 199
Garrison, Melvin, 226, 231, 234, 235, 257; photo of, 227
Garrison, Shirley, 198
Garrison, Wilson, 199, 224, 226, 228-231, 250; photos of, 193, 223, 224, 227, 228
Gates of Lodore, 25, 55, 276, 279
Gault, Tip "The Sagebrush King of Bitter Creek", 20
Geishow, Jack, 125, 126
George Celvington Place, 119, 129
Glines family, 211
Goodman Gulch, 24, 119
Goodman, Elizabeth, 47
Goodman, Frank, 24, 58, 98
Goodnight, Charles, 16
Goodson, Jimmie, 42, 43, 46, 240
Goodson, Mary Jane "Molly", 46
Goslin Mountain, 77
Gottsche, Carrie, 171
Gottsche, W.H., 171, 172, 214, 257
Graham Ranch, 253
Graham, James "Jim", 119, 253
Graham, Pearl Finch, 253
Great Divide, Colorado, 200
Greeley, Colorado, 39
Green River City, Wyoming (later Green River, Wyoming), 20, 21, 51, 54, 55, 56, 64, 66, 69, 151, 153
Green, Charlie, 103, 104, 129, 203, 205, 214, 215, 225, 231, 248, 249, 270, 271
Green, Ephraim, 205
Green, Retta (see Tolliver, Retta Green)
Green, Sidney Thayne, 205
Greenhow, James, 119; photo of, 117

Greenhow, Mrs. James, 129; photo, 117
Greystone, Colorado, 258-260
Grounds, Bill, 240, 241
Gunn, Jack, 33, 42, 57
Guofonti, Martin, 78
Gurr, Lawrence, 286
Gurr, Sheldon, 265; photo of, 267
Gurr, Zora Allen (see also Allen, Zora), 265, 286
Guttierrez, Joe, 260

H

Hahn's Peak, Colo., 56, 59, 90
Haley Livestock and Trading Company, 97
Haley, Ora, 97, 98, 101, 102, 147, 154, 155
Hall, Andrew, 23
Hall, Orsen, 212
Hambleton (shot Jack Rollas), 58, 59
Hamilton City (Miner's Delight), Wyoming, 17
Hamilton, William T., 7
Hanks, Walter, 143
Hanks, Walter Jr., 136
Harper, Charlie, 43
Harrell (Texas Cattleman), 24
Harry Hoy Ranch, 102
Hatch, Ken, 75
Heartman, Florence, 162
Henry's Fork, 4
Herrera, Juan Jose "Mexican Joe", 8, 11, 17-21, 28, 32, 33, 41-43, 46, 52, 55, 282
Herrera, Pablo, 8, 19, 28
Hicks, James (see Horn, Tom)
Hindle, Harry, 58, 59, 78, 107, 108, 129, 282
Hines, Pete, 66
Hog Lake, 46, 119
Hoight (partner of Crouse in steer operation), 79
Hole-in-the-Wall, Wyoming, 86
Homestead Act of 1862, 93, 94
Hood, George, 135, 137-139
Hook, H.M., 31, 64
Hoover, Dan, 159
Horn, Tom (alias James Hicks), 48, 96, 98-101, 282
Howard County, Missouri, 4, 5
Hoy Bottoms, 119, 155
Hoy Dugway, 175, 281
Hoy, Benjamin, 43
Hoy, Jesse S. "J.S.", 29-33, 37-43, 56, 57, 98, 101
Hoy, Julia Blair, 47, 84

"Old Wes" (trapper), 33
Olmey, Charley, 151, 152
Oregon Dragoons, 6
Oregon Trail, 20
Orr, Frank, 52
Outlaw Cabin, 71, 77
Outlaw Trail (Hoot Owl Trail), 77, 80, 279
Overholt, Aaron, 69, 79
Overland Trail, 12, 20, 47, 64
Overy, Bessie Marie, 202, 203
Overy, Hazel Teters (see also Teters, Hazel), 203, 237; photo of, 194
Overy, Jim, 164, 202, 203; photo of, 194
Overy, Sarah, 202

P

Pablo Spring, 52, 55, 258, 277, 285
Paradise, Utah, 45
Pariats (Indian), 22
Park City, Utah, 211
Park Hotel (in Rock Springs, Wyoming), 137
Park Live Ranch (see Brown's Park Live Stock Ranch)
Parker, Ann Gillis, 76
Parker, Maximillian "Maxi", 76
Parker, Robert LeRoy (see Cassidy, Butch)
Parsons Cabin, 51, 77, 125, 167, 168, 255, 278, 285; photo of, 277
Parsons Place, 48, 53, 169, 174, 248
Parsons Smelter, 51, 80, 276
Parsons, Daphne Dunster, 48, 51, 54, 168
Parsons, Dr. John D., 48, 51-54, 62, 168; photo of, 50
Parsons, Helena, 48, 51, 168
Parsons, Loretta Ann "Snapping Annie", 45, 46, 48, 51
Parsons, Warren D., 46, 51
Parsons, Warren P., 45, 46
Patjanella Ranch, Colorado, 276
Patton, Bill, 147
Patty (sheepherder), 135
Peril, W.A., 14
Perry Place, 211
Perusick, Pete, 260
Peterson, Elnora, 260
Peterson, Tom, 260
Phillips, W.T., 81
Pidgeon, William, 85, 88
Pierce, Abel "Shanghai", 93, 94
Pine Butte, 20
Pinedale, Wyoming, 70
Platte River, 5
Pocatello, Idaho, 139
Point Of Rocks, Wyoming, 138
Pope, Sheriff Richard, 153
Popo Agie River, 5

Pot Creek, 53, 103, 104, 141-143, 197
Powder Springs Gang, 77
Powder Springs, Wyoming, 86, 90
Powell Expedition, 21-24, 275
Powell, Major John Wesley, 21-25, 47
Pre-emption Act of 1841, 93
Preece, Sheriff Billy, 87, 88
Prestopitz, Anton, 162
Price, Utah, 207, 208, 258

Q

Quaking Aspen Mountain, 233
Quincy, Illinois, 46

R

Rabbit Ears Pass, 115
Radosevich, Angelia, 230
Radosevich, Arlie Teters (see also Teters, Arlie), 230, 259; photo of, 234
Radosevich, Danica, 230
Radosevich, Emelija, 230
Radosevich, Fanny, 230
Radosevich, Georgann, photo of, 234
Radosevich, George, 230
Radosevich, George Jr., 230
Radosevich, John, 230
Radosevich, Mary, 230
Radosevich, Olga, 230
Radosevich, Steve, 164, 230, 236, 259, 277; photo of, 234
Raftopoulos Ranches, 286
Raftopoulos, George, 259, 277, 285
Raftopoulos, Georgia (see also Simos, Georgia), 259, 277
Raftopoulos, John, 259, 277, 285
Raftopoulos, Steve, 259, 277, 285
Rainbow, Utah, 239
Rangely, Colorado, 112
Rankin, Joe, 54
Rankin, M. Wilson "Willis", 240
Ranney, Charles, 102, 148
Rash, Madison "Matt", 57, 58, 78, 83, 96, 98, 99, 162
Rasmussen Place, 211
Rawlins, Wyoming, 54
Red Canyon, 22, 64
Red Creek, 20, 22, 30, 33
Red Creek Badlands, 172
Red Creek Canyon, 12, 30, 129, 137
Red Creek Livestock Company, 171
Red Creek Ranch, Wyoming, 46, 47, 84, 85, 89, 128, 163, 171-173, 239, 257, 276, 279, 280, 281, 287; photo of bridge where Willie Strang was shot, 87
Red Sash Gang, 77
Redford, Robert, 279, 281

310

311

South Pass, 17, 19, 64
South Pass City, Wyoming, 17, 18, 21, 42
Southam, Ralph, 213
Southern Stage Lines, 66
Spack, Bill, 87
Spanish American War, 96
Spanish Joe's Trail, 12
Sparks, "Little" Charlie, 161, 167
Sparks, "Wash", photo of, 244
Sparks, Charlie, 48, 78, 100, 140, 171,
  198, 199, 239, 241, 243, 245, 257, 259
Sparks, Mrs. Charlie, photo of, 234
Spicer, George, 39, 43
Spicer, Sam, 43
Spitzie Bottom, 119
Spitzie cabin, 171, 200
Spitzie Draw, 119
Spitzie Place, 239
Spokane, Washington, 81
Spring Creek, 127
Spring Creek Gap (see Minnie's Gap), 152
St. Clair, 6
St. George, Utah, 209
Stallard, John "Shorty", 241, 242
Steamboat Springs, Colorado, 258
Stephens, George, 153
Sterling family, 118
Sterling Place (Brown's Park), 118, 119,
  171, 241; photo of store, 241
Sterling, Cyrill, 118
Sterling, George, 118
Sterling, Mrs. George, 118
Sterling, Rex, 118
Sterling, Will Rose, 118; photo of, 145
Stores Mining Camp, Utah 206, 207
Story, John D., 265; photo of, 267
Strang, John, 87, 88, 90
Strang, Willie, 85, 87, 88, 90, 91, 171,
  172
Strickland, Leanore, 78
Sublette, William, 5
Sullivan, Wilber, 162
Summit Springs, 58, 100
Sundance, Wyoming, 79
Swallow Canyon (Brown's Park), 23, 131,
  144, 148, 256, 264
Swan Land and Cattle Company, 28, 94,
  96
Swanson, Peter, 90
Sweden, 48, 78
Sweet, Mike, 28
Sweetwater River, 17
Sweetwater, Wyoming, 171
Swift, Bob, 80

T

Taylor Family, photo of leaving Nebraska,
  116
Taylor Flat, 248, 251
Taylor Flats, Utah, 278
Taylor Ranch (Brown's Park), 176, 178,
  195-198, 215, 226, 229, 250, 255-257,
  277; photo of buffalo on 166; photo of
  peacocks, 178; photo of, 188
Taylor, Allen, 249, 251, 253; photo of,
  252
Taylor, Ben, 142, 195
Taylor, Bessie Ethel (later Garrison, Bessie
  Taylor), 141, 142, 155, 168, 183, 195,
  199, 218, 222, 223; photos of, 185,
  187, 188, 221
Taylor, Charles Melvin "C.M.", 111-127,
  130-132, 135, 136, 141, 142, 144,
  153-155, 163, 167-170, 174-179, 181-
  184, 195, 197, 198, 201, 214, 215,
  218, 222, 225, 226, 229-231, 234-236,
  242, 248, 249, 251, 253, 256, 257,
  282; photos of, 112, 116; with ferry,
  166; 185, 189, 191, 232, 234
Taylor, Claude, 248, 253; photo of, 250
Taylor, Debra Sharp, 162, 183, 239, 240,
  248
Taylor, Eliza, 111
Taylor, Francis Graham, 253
Taylor, Frank, 111
Taylor, George, 111
Taylor, Jesse G., 112-120, 125, 129-132,
  135, 136, 141, 142, 155, 160, 161,
  164, 167-170, 172, 173, 176, 177,
  179-181, 183, 196, 234, 239-253, 273,
  278, 285; photos of, 113, 116, 133,
  185, 188, 221, 246, 247, 248, 249
Taylor, Jesse Jr., 239
Taylor, Margaret, 239
Taylor, Marie (later Allen, Marie),
  183-203, 215, 217-223, 282; photos of,
  185, 187, 188, 193, 219, 220, 221
Taylor, Mary, 248, 253; photo of, 250
Taylor, Mattie Callaway, 162, 164, 200,
  245, 248, 249, 251, 253; photos of,
  246, 247, 249
Taylor, Murty "Murt", 271
Taylor, Nancy, 111, 142, 195-197, 225
Taylor, Nancy May, 112-120, 125,
  129-132,183,230,282; photos of, 116,
  133
Taylor, Nina Floy Cole, 112-121, 125,
  129-132, 135, 141, 142, 154, 163,
  167-170, 183, 186, 195, 201, 203, 215,
  218, 222, 223, 226, 229, 230, 231,

312

234, 235, 248, 256, 257, 273, 277;
photos of, 112, 116, 185, 191, 234, 261
Taylor, Orvil, 249, 285
Taylor, Roy, 249
Taylor, Samuel, 111, 142
Telluride, Colorado, 76
Templeton, James H., 163
Tepee Mountain, 173
Terresa (outlaw), 20
Teters, Amelia Prestopitz, 129, 171-174,
226; photo of, 190
Teters, Arlie (see also Radosevich, Arlie
Teters), 171, 172
Teters, Bob, 171-173, 196, 226, 228, 229,
240, 248
Teters, Charles, 85, 170, 171-174; photo
of 190
Teters, Clarice, 172
Teters, Dorothy, 172; photo of, 190
Teters, Hazel (see also Overy, Hazel
Teters), 171, 172, 174, 195, 199, 202
Teters, Jack, 174
Teters, Nora, 248
Teters, Rose, 171, 202
Teters, Thelma, 174
Teters, Valentine, 171, 172
Thompson and Sinclair Party, 5
Thompson, Armida "Auntie", 48, 78, 83
Thompson, Clyde, 272, 273, 279
Thompson, Longhorn, 48, 78, 99, 101
Thompson, Phillip, 6
Thompson, Velma, 273, 279
Thornburgh, Major, 54
Timber Culture Act of 1873, 93
Tip Gault Gang, 20
Tisdel, Buck, 260
Tisdel, Ethel, 260
Tittsworth Gap, 69
Tittsworth Gap Ranch, Wyoming 47, 69
Tittsworth, Jean Law, 47, 121
Tittsworth, W.G. "Billy", 47, 69, 121;
photo of, 73
Tolliver, Amanderville "Mandy" (see also
Wiggins, Amanderville "Mandy"), 70,
71
Tolliver, Columbus, 70, 71
Tolliver, Dave, 129, 174, 183
Tolliver, Ellie, 241, 242
Tolliver, Florence, 241, 242
Tolliver, J. Frank, 69-71; photo of, 72
Tolliver, John, 242
Tolliver, Joseph, 70, 71, 80, 103-105, 127,
129, 282
Tolliver, Retta Green, 129, 183, 205
Tolliver, Rosie, 145
Tolliver, Sarah, 70, 71; photo of 72
Tolton, Ed, 153

Tom Crowley Gang, 77
Tommy White Bottom, 101
Toothacher Ranch, Wyoming, 276
Tracy, Harry, 86-91
Trevennon, Elmer, 241
Trinidad, Colorado, 3
Two-Bar Ranch (in Brown's Park), 129,
144, 147, 153, 155, 163, 196, 240
Two-Bar Ranch (on Snake River), 97, 98,
101, 102, 147, 153, 154, 240, 245, 285
Two-Circle Bar Ranch, Colorado (Yampa
Livestock), 98

U

Uinta Canyon, 205
Uinta Mountains, range, 1
Union Army, 21, 69
Union Pacific Railroad, 17, 96
United States Cavalry, 54, 115
United States Geological Survey, 25
Utah State Division of Fish and Game,
273, 275-277
Utah State Historical Society, 278
Utes, Indian, 2, 7, 13, 19, 31, 39, 40,
52-54, 124, 170, 184, 186

V

Valley Hotel (in Rock Springs, Wyoming),
174
Van Horne, Colonel, J.J., 96
Vaquero, 10, 11, 16
Vasquez, Louis, 5
Vaughn, Boyd, 88
Vaughn, Chloe, 260
Vaughn, Minford, 260
Vermillion Creek, 17, 97, 118, 142, 143
Vernal (Ashley), Utah, 54, 62, 64, 67, 71,
79, 87, 88, 105, 117, 121, 127, 140,
144, 153, 162, 170, 183, 195, 211,
212, 215, 225, 226, 272, 279, 286
Vernal Express, 87, 89, 137, 139

W

Walker, Boyd, 260
Walker, Wanda, 260
Wall, Bill, 79
Ward, Charlie, photo of, 106
Ward, Elsie, 173
Warner, Matt (see Christensen, Willard E.)
Warner, Rose, 168
Warren, Catherine, 48, 107, 162, 198
Warren, Jim, 48, 162, 198; photo of, 106
Washakie, Chief, 17
Watson, Lee, 257
Weeks, Nels, 212
Wells, Emerson "Nig", 148-154

313

Wells, Heber (Utah Governor), 91
Whalen, Martin, 135
Whalen, Pat, 167, 170
White River, 13
White River Indian Agency, Colorado 40, 53, 54
Whiterocks Agency, Utah, 54
Widdop, James, 43
Wiggins, Louie, 260; photo of, 234
Wiggins, Mandy Tolliver Lombard, 241, 242, 260; photo of, 234
Wild Bunch, 79, 80, 85, 184
Will Wale Saloon (became Jarvie Saloon in Rock Springs, Wyoming), 61
Williams, Albert, 67, 74, 75, 85, 119,120, 124, 143, 171, 182, 214, 274, 282
Williams, Charles, 148
Willis, Ann (see Bassett, Ann)
Willis, Frank, 156, 157
Willow Creek, 42, 43, 52, 54, 77, 128, 129, 229
Willow Creek Lane, 148
Willow Creek Meadow, 148
Willow Creek Ranch, Utah, 47, 119, 120, 148, 153, 171, 200, 230, 231, 239, 245, 259, 277; photo of shipping, 232
Wilson, Archie, 200
Wilson, Ed, 260
Wilson, Florence Belle, 200
Wilson, Gordon, 136, 142, 196
Wilson, Marybeth (see Carr, Marybeth)

Wilson, William C. "Teto", 200
Wind River Basin, Wyoming, 78
Wind River Mountains, 5, 17
Winton, Wyoming, 200
Wislizenus, Dr. F.A., 7
Wolves, 1, 33-38, 172, 175
Workman, David, 4, 5
Worley, Amos, 200
Worley, Bertha 200, 201, 217; photo of, 192
Worley, Della, 200, 258; photo of, 192
Worley, Doug, 200
Worley, Elija "Lige", 199, 200
Worley, James, 200
Worley, Lona, 200
Worley, Lydia, 200
Worley, Pete, 200
Worley, Zula, 200
Worrick, Rick, 259
Wyoming State Prison, 78
Wyoming Stock Growers Association, 94, 95, 96
Wyoming Territorial Legislature 1876, 43

Y

Yampa (Bear) River, 13, 54, 116
Yampatica Ute Reservation, 53
Yarberry, Tom, 147, 154
Young, Brigham, 11, 79, 80
Young, Deputy Marshal LeGrande, 80, 87, 88